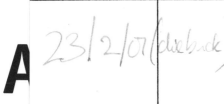

Edited by
Cath Talbot
and
Martin C. Calder

Russell House Publishing

First published in 2006 by:
Russell House Publishing Ltd.
4 St George's House
Uplyme Road
Lyme Regis
Dorset DT7 3LS

Tel: 01297-443948
Fax: 01297-442722
e-mail: help@russellhouse.co.uk
www.russellhouse.co.uk

British Library Cataloguing-in-publication Data:
A catalogue record for this book is available from the British Library.

ISBN: 1-903855-86-1; 978-1-903855-86-7

Typeset by TW Typesetting, Plymouth, Devon
Printed by Antony Rowe, Chippenham
Cover artwork by Guy Rayment, GuyRayment@connections-consultancy.co.uk

Russell House Publishing
is a group of social work, probation, education and
youth and community work practitioners and
academics working in collaboration with a professional
publishing team.
Our aim is to work closely with the field to produce
innovative and valuable materials to help managers,
trainers, practitioners and students.
We are keen to receive feedback on publications and
new ideas for future projects.
For details of our other publications please visit our
website or ask us for a catalogue. Contact details are
on this page.

Contents

Foreword

This timely, practical and absorbing book comes at a critical time in the direction of UK child welfare policy and, the challenge for hard-pressed practitioners of delivering consistent, accountable and evidence-based best practice. This book will help practitioners and managers to understand kinship care challenges and guide them towards evidence-based practice in their work with extended families. The discussions about child protection and family support policies, and of partnership, risk, and assessment models are especially vital at this time.

The UK child welfare policy

The UK child welfare policy context is one of continued search for permanency solutions for those children who can no longer live at home. There will always be doubts about which option is the most appropriate placement option for a child who can no longer live with their parent(s), whether this is adoption, non-relative foster care, relative foster care, residential care, independent living, or kinship care outside the care system supported by the 1989 Children Act S17. The Children Act 1989 (S23) places a duty on local authorities to *first* consider family, friends and 'others' when making the decision about where to place a child. The growth of interest in kinship care in the UK, the USA, and Europe may reflect a lack of appropriate placement alternatives, or it may be indicative of a more positive child and family choice, about sustaining children's identity, and family preservation, or both. It is perhaps worth restating that it is perfectly normal for families to need friendship, support, parenting skills, understanding and money to bring up their children. For those children who, on child welfare grounds, are unable to live with their parents, and live in a kinship care placement, it is especially important that they receive these additional understandings, supports and services.

Kinship care in the UK

Kinship care is at a critical point in its development in the UK because it lacks proper recognition, any ongoing training base on qualifying and post-qualifying courses, or agreed policy base at national and local levels. There is a responsibility on government, so far ignored, to sufficiently acknowledge the inexorable growth in kinship care, especially outside the looked after system, to put the necessary measures and funding in place. To make a sustained impact commensurate with kinship care's usage requires the same level of political energy, commitment, and funding, as emerged for adoption in the UK a few years ago. I hope that we do not have to wait for a tragedy to occur to a child living in kinship care for such a step-change to take place. However I sense that, given the reactive and political basis for much child welfare reform in the UK, and the vested child welfare interests and organisational structures, such a reactive scenario is most likely.

Kinship care policy

At the policy level there continue to be significant child placement and financial pressures on local authorities arising from the high numbers of children looked after each year. In many cases, it seems that social services systems are geared much more towards short-term reactive risk management than resilience-based approaches to working with families. There is a genuine struggle between immediate and short-term child protection measures, and longer-term child protection, prevention, and family support strategies. There is also an argument, except in relation to child protection concerns, that the provision of ongoing kinship care support is beyond the remit of social services.

On a more positive note there are a small but increasing number of local authorities that are fully engaging with kinship care, in some cases promoting family and friends' foster care, in others promoting network support (Children Act 1989 S17) to reduce the numbers being looked after in the first place. Whilst further research is required to examine whether more kinship care placements and family group conferences lead to less children looked after, or whether there are other patterns at work, there are preliminary signs in one or two local authorities that this shift is already occurring.

Kinship care and practice

At the practice level, and to fully engage with children and their extended families and friends requires social care workers to have high skill levels, sufficient time and a supportive organisational vision and support framework. For children living in kinship care arrangements, especially those outside the foster care system, the question is raised 'Who is charged with, and sufficiently resourced to provide, supportive services for these children and their carers?' Cath Talbot and Martin Calder's book tackles this key question in innovative practice-led and evidence-based ways; by examining how local authorities carry out kinship care assessments and the ways they work with other agencies.

About this book

This book takes kinship care practice and developments forward to a new level by illuminating vital research, policy and practice areas previously missing or under-recorded in the literature. Thus the book contains intellectual critiques of existing assessments, as well as exploring work with parents with intellectual disabilities, domestic violence risk assessments, partnership work with families, intergenerational abuse, parental substance misuse, contact issues, and, at the end, a new evidence-based assessment framework for kinship care. The book's knowledgeable contributors make a series of evidenced assessment and legal recommendations. They argue that, 'for kinship care to operate on the same level playing field as other placement options requires investments in research, practice and policy guidance'. There is also recognition that outside local authorities, kinship care is more than a placement option, and is another way to bring up a child within a family.

Cath Talbot and Martin Calder have skilfully put together a knowledgeable group of experienced contributors to produce a thoughtful, coherent, cohesive and groundbreaking book about kinship care that deserves the widest recognition and readership by family placement and frontline social workers, children's guardians, legal advisers and the courts.

Bob Broad
Director, Research and Evaluation,
National Children's Bureau, London

Janet, Stacey and Emma: for reminding me
that what matters most is what happens at home

Martin C. Calder

Acknowledgements

To Janet, Stacey and Emma: all stars in the night sky that motivate me daily

To all the staff at Leigh Library

To Debbie Hulme for her wizardry on the PC
Martin C. Calder

To Nathan and Billy, two of the good guys.

Thanks to my family and friends: you know who you are.

Thanks to Joy Warner, John Ingham, Jane Hopson-Hill, Fran Williams, Chris Boyle, Bob Broad, Jennifer Fleming and Martin Calder.

Special thanks to Harry and Joan Hernon.
Cath Talbot

About the Contributors

The Editors

Cath Talbot is an independent social worker, trainer, lecturer and Director of Connections Social Work Consultancy. She qualified as a social worker in 1983 and works as an expert witness in the family courts. She has a keen practice and academic interest in family assessment work. Cath has published on kinship care (Talbot and Williams, 2003 and Talbot and Kidd, 2004). She is currently undertaking research into children's experiences of kinship care, supervised by Professor Bob Broad.

Martin C. Calder is an independant trainer and consultant in child protection having recently left his Child Protection Operational Manager post with Salford City Council to produce and disseminate evidence-based assessment materials. He is contactable through his website at *www.caldertrainingandconsultancy.co.uk*

The Authors

Calvin Bell is the founder and chief executive of *Ahimsa* (Safer Families) Ltd. and has been involved in the family violence field for over 15 years. In particular, he has extensive clinical experience of working with men, both individually and in groups, who have histories of violent and abusive behaviours. This has included domestic violence offenders on life licence, and sex offenders both in community and prison settings. His practice has also involved supporting both male and female victims of domestic abuse, and in 2003 he set up the regions first telephone help-line for male victims. He has wide experience in carrying out adult family assessments where domestic abuse is a concern, having worked for Cornwall, Devon, Plymouth and Torbay Social Service, among others. He has acted as Expert Witness in Family Law Proceedings since 1996. He is an international consultant and has received numerous commissions to design and deliver training in various aspects of domestic violence from a number of UK and overseas organisations and has also produced many papers on domestic violence.

He has academic as well as clinical responsibilities, apart from being a visiting lecturer and giving numerous presentations to a wide variety of audiences. His qualifications include a Masters Degree in Education, Exeter University, (research into typologies among domestically violent perpetrators) and a Post-graduate Diploma in Community and Youthwork, Exeter University, (special field: domestic violence). He also has a Post-graduate Certificate in Violence in the Home, University of Westminster, (research into domestic violence risk assessment) and a Practitioner Certificate in Cognitive Analytic Therapy from Guy's Hospital. He is currently undertaking PhD research at the Centre for Forensic and Family Psychology at Birmingham University.

Bob Broad is Director of Research and Evaluation at the National Children's Bureau, London. Prior to this he was Professor of Children and Families Research and Director of the Children and Families Research Unit, Faculty of Health and Life Sciences, De Montfort University, Leicester. He was previously a lecturer at the London School of Economics and Political Science. A trained social worker, he was awarded his PhD in 1988 and has undertaken a number of funded research projects about children leaving care, kinship care and youth justice. His publications include *Punishment under Pressure: the Probation Service in the Inner City* (Jessica Kingsley, 1991), *Young People Leaving Care: Life after the Children Act, 1989* (Jessica Kingsley, 1998), *Kinship Care: The Placement Choice for Children and Young People* (Ed) (Russell House, 2001), *Kith and Kin: Kinship Care for Vulnerable Young People* (2001) with Hayes, R. and Rushforth, C. (NCB/JRF), *Improving the Health and Well Being of Young People Leaving Care* (Russell House, 2005) and *Kinship Care: A Good Practice Guide* (working title) with Skinner, A. (BAAF, forthcoming).

Pam Freeman, formerly a social worker, has worked for several universities over a period of 15 years as a full-time researcher on a number of government funded studies in child protection and socio-legal areas of interest. Currently, she is a part-time lecturer in the Department of Social Work at the University of Plymouth, teaching masters social work students. She is also employed in the School of Education, the University of Exeter, where she will be involved in teaching undergraduates in the forthcoming academic year, and continuing her research interest in children and families by currently co-ordinating a team evaluating three local Children's Fund projects addressing social exclusion. Other studies in which she has been involved more recently include assessing attrition rates in child protection and domestic violence, parental perspectives of the statutory system and the use of advocacy in child protection, family support and family group conferencing, and the use of sexual abuse lines.

Pam has on-going links with Bulgaria and their child welfare patterns and has an interest in racial and cultural diversity research. She does a considerable amount of consultancy and has recently completed a report for the Devon Race Equality Council, linked with an EU project, assessing the inclusion of gypsy/traveller children in education at a local level.

During much of her research career, Pam has had close collaboration with the police service, criminal justice professionals, Education and Social Services Departments, in terms of both research and training, and thus has been engaged in a number of local evaluations of service delivery and pilot models. In this respect, and arising out of early research on suspected child abuse (with Hedy Cleaver) Pam has been involved in the research aspects of intergenerational multiple child abuse enquiries since the early 1990s, whilst working at Dartington Social Research Unit. This interest has continued subsequently, advising and training multi-agencies on this particular form of child abuse and neglect.

Her publications include *Parental Perspectives of Suspected Cases of Child Abuse*, 1995 (with H. Cleaver, HMSO, London), *Parental Perspectives of Care Proceedings*, 1998, (with J. Hunt, published by the Stationery Office), *The Use of Advocacy in Child Protection*, June/September, 2001 (with B. Lindley and M. Richards, *Journal of Child and Family Law*) and *The Reform of Child Welfare Service in Bulgaria*, 2003 (with B. Jordan, T. Proykov et al., *Social Work in Europe*, 10: 3).

John Ingham has worked in practitioner and management roles within the statutory, voluntary, and independent sectors of child care social work since qualifying at Exeter University in 1979. He is currently an independent social worker undertaking risk, parenting, fostering and kinship assessments. He had been involved in complex investigations into intergenerational abuse and has an interest in this area. He is also a co-ordinator for family group conferences and is a mediator with the National Family Mediation Service.

Philip Kidd qualified in 1985 and has been a partner in Tozers in Newton Abbot since 1992. Solicitor-Advocate with rights of audience in the higher courts in family matters. He has been a member of the Law Society's Children Panel for 16 years, sits as an Interviewer/Assessor for the Children Panel and is a Member of Resolution (formerly the SFLA) and the Association of Lawyers for Children specialising in representing children in care and adoption proceedings. Phillip has authored articles in *Family Law, Sweet and Maxwell's Family Matters and Practical Research Papers*, is the legal Notes Editor for *Seen and Heard*, been a speaker at various local and national conferences and was short-listed for Legal Aid Lawyer of the Year 2003.

Brynna Kroll is Principal Lecturer in Social Work at the University of Plymouth where she teaches on the Masters course, specialising in practice with children and families. A former probation officer, guardian ad litem and family courts' welfare officer, she has published in the areas of social work with children, children and divorce and the impact of loss, as well as in the area of parental substance misuse and child welfare. She is co-author, with Andy Taylor, of *Parental Substance Misuse and Child Welfare*, and together with him, has just been awarded a grant by the Department of Health for research into interventions for families where parents have drug problems.

Paul Storey Q.C. is a Barrister at 29 Bedford Row Chambers in London. Paul was called to the bar in 1982 and took Silk in 2001 and sits as a Recorder. He specialises in public law children cases and adoption, representing local authorities, children and parents. Paul is a member of FLBA, has lectured to lawyers, Guardians and social workers and has had articles published in *Family Law*. He chaired the NAGALRO National Conference in 1996 and was a speaker at the Local Government Group National Conference in 1998.

Sadie Young is a Consultant Clinical Psychologist and Head of the Child and Special Parenting Service, Devon Partnership NHS Trust, Exeter. She founded the Special Parenting Service in 1988 and has specialised in assessment and support work with parents with intellectual disabilities for the past sixteen years.

Chapter One

Kinship Care: The Research Evidence

Cath Talbot

Introduction

Kinship care has been a significant feature of family and community structures, on an international level and for centuries, but it is only recently emerging as a debate within policy and practice in Britain. Kinship care is interesting and important because it addresses the welfare of growing numbers of vulnerable children and young people. This endorses the need for more social investigation to further an understanding of the features of kinship placements. Relatively little is known about the experiences and views of children themselves, but the existing evidence highlights the importance of a proper consideration of kinship placements when children cannot live with their birth parents. Kinship placements support legal principles and social values and make a significant contribution to scarce local authority resources.

There is emerging evidence that these placements often provide stability and meet the needs of the most challenging of children and young people (Crumbley and Little, 1997; Gleeson and Hairston, 1999; Hegel and Scannapieco, 1999; Greeff, 1999; McRoy, Christian and Thompson, 2000; Broad, 2001; Broad et al., 2001), and that the outcomes for these children are much more positive than those which can be expected for many of the children within 'stranger' placements (Broad, 2001; Broad et al., 2001; Greeff, 1999; Hegar and Scannapieco, 1999; NFCA, 1997). Yet, our systems often fail to support, or even undermine this placement option. Kinship placements are poorly understood at the institutional and at the professional level of practice. As with many other matters in the provision of social welfare, the gap between social research and professional intervention is significant.

The scope of this discussion

This discussion considers the body of literature in respect of kinship care in both Britain and the USA, offering a structure and context in which the emerging evidence can be understood. It suggests a definition. The statistical significance of kinship placements is argued to be of increasing relevance. Contemporary social work practice, however, is struggling to respond with any consistency, and there are discrepancies between the properties of kinship placements and the socio-legal context in which they operate. There are specific phenomena associated with kinship placements, for example, they offer an improved experience of maintaining family relationships (the importance of sibling relationships is specifically addressed in Chapter 9). The discussion challenges the notion of adoption as an uncomplicated panacea and links this to the importance of pertinent, child-focused assessment. It considers the profiles of kinship placements, and suggests that these require a challenge to current policy and practice. It raises the important issue of rehabilitation to birth families, in the context of the contraindications for children to transfer from kinship placements to the home of their birth parents. An international, comparative perspective is offered. The emerging criticism of current policy and procedure is analysed. It concludes that research evidence is positive, but limited, particularly in respect of qualitative research which directly seeks the views of the children and young people themselves.

Defining kinship care

Kinship placements reflect the importance of relationships, as perceived by the children and young people. This may well test the more conventional understandings that adults have in respect of the 'hierachy' of family ties. Waterhouse (2001) found that kinship carers have very diverse relationship ties with the children and more than one in ten had no blood tie with the child in placement. This requires a careful definition of 'kinship' placements, or, as the Department of Health now prefer, 'Family and Friends Care'. This chapter considers kinship care to be:

. . . the placement of a child or young person, with an adult carer, likely, although not exclusively, to have had a significant relationship with the child, prior to the placement. The definition extends the more conventional meaning of kinship as it is not restricted to blood relationships. The paramount consideration is the meaning of the relationship to the child. The carer may be a blood relative, a step relative, or a friend. 'Kinship' reflects the identity of the child, the family and the community. Kinship arrangements may be formal or informal: the legal status of the child does not define a kinship arrangement.

The statistical significance of kinship care

Research estimates that kinship care arrangements now account for between 17 per cent and 30 per cent of all placements for children who cannot live with their birth parents (Broad, 2001; Greeff, 1999). In the USA, where kinship care has been a huge consequence of a significant drug culture, it is estimated that family members provide between 31 per cent and 51 per cent of all placements for children unable to live with their birth parents. This includes between 2.3 and 4.3 million children. In 1960 the total number of children living in kinship arrangements was 2 per cent. This figure has since doubled to 4.3 per cent by 1995 (Hegar and Scannapieco, 1999). In Britain, the Department of Health statistics estimate that relatives provided care for 14.1 per cent of children in need in 1996 and 16.6 per cent in 2000. It is recognised that the number of children in foster care with a relative or friend has increased by 32 per cent over the period 1996 to 2000 (DoH, 2000). During this time, actual numbers have risen from 4,800 to 6,300, and can be compared with a 15 per cent increase in all foster placements over the same period. In the USA, it is estimated that of the 2.3 and 4.3 million children living in kinship arrangements, that 1.5 million of these children are living with their grandparents and that 44 per cent of African-American children who are unable to live with their birth parents now live with their grandparents. In some states, the numbers of kinship placements have surpassed the numbers of 'mainstream' foster placements (Hegar and Scannapieco, 1999). As Broad notes, the percentage of children living in kinship placements, (DoH figures for March 2002) is greater than the total number of children living in children's homes and twice the number of children placed for adoption (Broad, 2004).

The experiences of black children in care have often been ignored. This error should not be repeated, when considering the implications of kinship placements (Ince, 2001). Research findings have recognised that black children and specifically children with African origins are over-represented in kinship placements. Whilst valuing the importance of preserving black family life, Scannapieco (2001) warns about the development of a two-tier, racially segregated system, leaving poorly resourced black families to care for children in unsupported environments. Broad et al. (2001), researching in Britain, raise the same issue, whilst recognising the positive experiences of children of Caribbean, Guyanese and African origin, particularly in respect of maintaining contact with their birth relatives and reinforcing racial identity and feelings of belonging. Scannapieco suggests that the reasons for kinship placements being made have changed over the past century. In the early twentieth century, placements were made because of material advantage, parental death or social values which were rejecting of single parenting. Placements are now most likely to be the effect of parental drug use, crime and custodial sentencing or HIV/AIDS. These are significant statistics, which further endorse the need to develop understanding of this phenomenon.

The socio-legal context

A complex set of factors is shaping children's experiences of kinship placements. Figure 1.1 overleaf is an attempt to make these factors explicit. Most research refers implicitly, or explicitly, to a shifting paradigm (or a set of socio-legal values). Ideology is an expression of institutional and professional power. Hegar has observed that:

. . . as a new paradigm arises, and before an older one is discarded, a professional community finds itself in a period of paradigm conflict, which can last for an extended period of time.

(Hegar, 1999: 225)

This conflict is emerging in professional intervention in families, in care planning and in British courts, as professional values compete and defend their perceptions regarding the best interests of the child. Yet, emerging research evidence either implicitly, or explicitly, challenges the assumptions operating through the

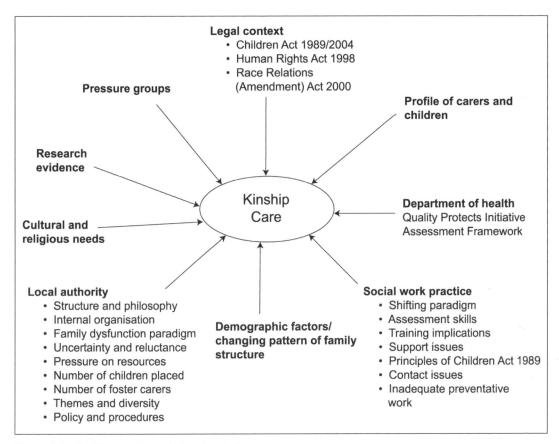

Figure 1.1   Kinship care: the socio-legal context

professional philosophy of 'family dysfunction'. Much of contemporary practice with families lacks the 'evidence based' approach that is now strongly expected. There are suggestions that kinship carers are differently motivated to stranger carers, and that kinship placements offer a qualitatively different experience to children (Tapsfield, 1999). This matter is endorsed by the body of American research, which strongly indicates that non-relative carers attribute their sense of 'responsibility' for the welfare of the child to the 'state', yet relative carers relate this sense of 'responsibility' to the 'family'.

Current legislation provides a crucial context and is one reflection of contemporary values in respect of state intervention in family life. The debate about kinship care is one significant example of the complex and uncertain relationship between the state and the family. In Britain, the Children Act 1989 generally supports the principle that children should live within their birth families, whenever this is possible. It

places a duty to seek the views of the child and to consider the religious, cultural and linguistic background of the child. Kinship placements have much greater potential to provide consistency in meeting these needs and in satisfying these legal requirements. This relationship, however, is rarely made explicit in practice. This links to the reporting of local authorities that, whilst being keen to meet these needs, most struggle to do so in practice. The Human Rights Act 1998 also supports the importance of family relationships and provides further potential for carers to make legal challenges. (Of most likely significance are articles 6, 8, and 14.) The Children Act, however, did not change the legal status of grandparents, and it remains the case that any family member without 'parental responsibility' requires the same permission to intervene in proceedings, as a stranger. Here, legislation reflects social values and power. Family members have been discouraged to apply for the care of relative children by professional assumptions that relatives have to be a *better* prospect than that contained within the local authority care plan. In the past, despite the premises of the Children Act, courts have generally not promoted the stance that children should be placed with family and friends, rather than with strangers. More recently, however, imaginative legal solutions have shifted towards a more sympathetic stance in respect of kinship placements. As a consequence, social work practice is now lagging behind legal developments (Talbot and Kidd, 2004).

The importance of contact between family members

The Children Act 1989 endorses the importance of contact and it is only possible for parents with parental responsibility to be refused contact, via a legal order. Grandparents, however, have no automatic right to contact, being required to seek leave to apply for contact. Kinship placements offer much greater potential for contact to be maintained and this is a very significant issue for children's welfare. This includes contact between parents and children and between siblings. Kinship carers often report that conflict with birth relatives continues into the long term, though there is a good prognosis for contact to be maintained, and conflict between relatives is not generally associated with placement breakdown (Broad, 2001). This suggests that family members are willing and able to maintain important relationships, on behalf of these children, an experience that is often, sadly, lacking in non-relative placements. For example, Waterhouse found that non-relative carers often had a significant level of ambivalence and uncertainty in respect of birth parents and contact with the children placed, and this was especially marked when carers were less experienced. Waterhouse (2001) concludes that the concept of 'partnership' between the foster carer, the social worker, the agency and the birth family was not reflected in practice.

Kinship placements have a significantly greater potential to keep siblings together, but, once again, there is a significant discrepancy between the findings of social research and professional interventions in respect of the value of sibling relationships. In practice, the separation of siblings is common, yet research and legislation argue against it (Elgar and Head, 1999). The

matter of contact is of such importance that it is given specific attention in Chapter 9.

Contemporary assessment

An emerging theme in reviewing the relevant literature has been the format and experiences of the assessment process associated with placement planning. Birth parents, children and carers need support: quality assessment work is an important vehicle to achieve this support. In kinship placements, nobody is neutral (Galloway and Wallace, 2002). This matter is underestimated in current formats for family assessment. Very little attention has been given to the specific issues associated with kinship assessments, and a new framework informed by research findings is urgently required. The Fostering Services Regulations, 2004, requires the same standards for kinship carers as it does for stranger carers, despite evidence in respect of the differences in profiles. This matter can create difficulties for achieving the best placement option for the children, even when parties are agreed about the option of a kinship placement. In the USA, some federal states have formally recognised this difficulty and introduced separate approval processes for kinship placements (Crumbley and Little, 1997). For a critique of contemporary assessment see Chapter 3.

An international and comparative perspective

On an international level, the relationship between political conditions and kinship care arrangements can be seen. Broad (2004) suggests that kinship care is encouraged in political climates where legislation intends there to be a partnership between the state and the family and gives Sweden, Belgium and Germany as examples where the socio-legal framework encourages kinship care. Kinship care has been more widely researched in the USA, but Scannapieco (2001), reviewing the body of North American research, refers to research being in its infancy and contrasts what is known about kinship placements with the much wider body of knowledge in respect of other recent shifts in family structures, particularly the impact of divorce. A recent summary of the breadth of American research has explicitly focused on themes in respect of practice, decision making, legal outcomes, support issues and profiles of children, carers and birth parents (Gleeson and Hairston, 1999). The lack of clarity in respect of policy, practice and procedure, established in Britain by Broad, is a strong theme in this body of American research and is suggestive of the:

> ... *kinship care policy debate (being) largely about distinguishing the* **responsibilities of family and government,** *when children come to the attention of the child welfare system.*
>
> (Gleeson, 1999: 8, my emphasis)

Additionally, the pattern of lesser, inconsistent support, found by Broad (2001) and Broad et al. (2001), is also a feature of the body of American research (Gleeson and Hairston, 1999). In many ways, the experience of kinship care has been rehearsed in North America. The important British ruling by Justice Munby, for example, *R (L and Others) v Manchester City Council; R (R and Another) v Manchester City Council*, (2001) *EWHC Admin 707*, (2002) 1 FLR (43), was established in Illinois in 1979 (Miller v Youakim, 1979, USA Supreme Court).

One general problem, and limitation with American research, however, has been the restricted methodology that has utilised the analysis of administrative data, to the detriment of qualitative research and the capacity to describe and explain. In particular, research with children has been a neglected area. Altshuler (1999) completed a study with children. This was a phenomenological project, designed to describe meanings of the children's experiences in the sample group. The central objective was to establish those specific factors that correlate to the child's 'sense of well-being'. The study's suggestions for further research are interesting, not least the proposal that children's well-being is linked to the circumstances of the birth mother (Altshuler, 1999). The fundamental difficulty with the study, however, is the small sample size, that restricts its capacity to generalise.

The circumstances of birth parents are another neglected area of research, yet these are key to the prospects of rehabilitation for this group of children. There is knowledge emerging that suggests that this group of children are relatively less likely to return to the care of their birth parents, but there is no present understanding of factors shaping this matter. Gleeson and Hairston (1999) researching in North America, found that

the drug and alcohol abuse of birth parents are very significant difficulties, estimating that these factors are present in 80 per cent of kinship placements, whilst only 16 per cent of birth parents had received treatment or support. Drug and alcohol abuse by birth parents may be factors associated with the prognosis for rehabilitation, but this relationship has not yet been tested. They also found a significant over-representation of African-American families involved in kinship care arrangements, that sibling groups were smaller than those placed in 'stranger' arrangements, and that birth parents were more likely to be in prison. In their review of American research, in respect of 'family preservation' and kinship care, McRoy, Christian and Thompson (2000) answer the critics of 'family preservation', but acknowledge that more qualitative investigation is needed. Data has tended to be short-term, lacking comparison and limited to small sample groups.

Placement stability and quality

The outcomes for 'looked after' children are extremely concerning, yet research suggests an improvement for children living in kinship arrangements. The population of 'looked after' children are significantly more likely to be excluded from school, have no formal qualifications, become homeless, be unemployed, go to prison, have mental health problems and have their own children removed from their care (NFCA, 1997). Yet, the children in the study by Broad et al. (2001) reported a sense of permanence, irrespective of their legal status. This finding is important because it contrasts starkly with the experiences of many children who are being 'looked after'. Placement stability in local authority care is a major issue and difficulty for children and young people (Jackson and Thomas, 1999). The harm caused to children should not be underestimated. Stability is multidimensional and affects a young person's experience of the placement, but also of relationships, education, health care, community and personal identity:

> *Attachment theory would predict that a child who has experienced even one extended separation from a primary caregiver is at risk of psychological ill-effects. When this experience is repeated many times the child is placed in a state of chronic insecurity and learns not to form attachments or relationships in order to avoid the pain of losing*

them. New carers then see the child as cold and unrespon-
sive ... These children are at high risk of ending up in
secure accommodation, where the majority of residents
have been through a large number of placements and have
suffered from discontinuity of care resulting in a wide
range of educational and health problems.
(Jackson and Thomas, 1999: 26)

There are factors known to contribute to
instability, and this raises the question of whether
these correlations apply to kinship placements, or
whether there are qualities in kinship placements
which resist these vulnerabilities. Factors
associated with instability include age, with
middle age and older children being the most
vulnerable. Relatively recent placements are the
most unstable. Children joining a family with
birth children and specifically children who are of
similar ages are vulnerable to placement
breakdown. Of great significance is the
association between placement instability and the
separation of siblings. Exclusion of the birth
parents and the behavioural difficulties of the
child are also important factors (Jackson and
Thomas, 1999). The latter two factors were not
contradicted in the kinship research of Broad et
al. (2001).

Consistency in children's reports of feeling safe
and loved is also found in North American
research. Gleeson and Hairston (1999) also
cautiously suggest that there is a lower rate of
child abuse in kinship placements, compared to
non-relative placements. He offers evidence of a
congruent level of behavioural problems in the
two populations of children, but that these
problems are perceived differently, and more
sympathetically by the kinship carers. While the
Department of Health refers to 4 per cent of
'looked after' children having behavioural
difficulties, the study of the sample of children
living in kinship placements by Broad et al. (2001)
estimated that 50 per cent of the young people
had significant behavioural difficulties. In
America, similar research also found that young
people in kinship arrangements showed
significant levels of behavioural difficulty, with
one in five young people expressing a problem
that fell within a clinical range and with one in
three carers describing behaviour which would
be placed within a clinical range. Problematic
behaviour is a more frequent issue with boys
(Starr et al., 1999). In general, however, little is
known about children's behavioural presentation
in kinship placements.

Profiles of the families

Similarly, little is known about the carers
themselves, though the profiles of kinship carers
and non-relative carers appear to be quite
different. Kinship carers tend to be older and
report poorer health. Carers need emotional,
practical and financial support, but there is
considerable discrepancy both within and
between local authorities in respect of policy and
procedure (Broad et al., 2001). Broad et al.'s study
also found both positive and negative aspects of
providing care. Positives included the
preservation of family life and contact, security
for the child and educational and behavioural
achievements. Difficulties were often externally
imposed, linking to the absence of support.
Financial matters were problematic, and some
carers felt they had lost their independence. Some
carers reported ill health, overcrowding and the
challenge of managing the young person's
difficult behaviour (Broad et al., 2001). Support to
carers is a major theme, across the research.
Hunt's (2001) study found that carers with
Residence Orders were usually left without
support, even when cases were 'open' to the local
authority, and this included cases where
Supervision Orders were attached to the
Residence Order. In a study of the delivery of
foster services, Waterhouse (2001) also found that
kinship carers approved as foster carers received
a different level of service from local authorities,
and that, despite need they had less access to
specialist family advice, support and training. In
the USA, research suggests that carers are a
diverse group who also report a high level of
satisfaction as carers, but who are also likely to
pay significant social, economic, physical and
psychological costs (Gleeson and Hairston, 1999).
Again, there is close congruence with the findings
of American and British research. One exception
has been the recent study of foster care by Sykes
et al. (2002) which suggested that kinship carers
expressed less satisfaction than non-relative
carers. This sample, however, was restricted to
those carers who were formally approved as
foster carers, and this is a partial representation of
the population of kinship carers. It does suggest
that kinship carers who are formally approved
may also have distinctive experiences. Given the
lack of support, incoherence of policy and
procedure and the differential treatment of the
two groups, this may well be an anticipated
finding, but the generalisation of the study by

Sykes et al. (2002) must be restricted to the experience of the sample group.

As with the over-representation of black and dual heritage children in the care system, the percentage of children of ethnic minorities in kinship placements are proportionally greater than white children (Broad et al., 2001; Hegar and Scannapieco, 1999). Waterhouse's study included a sample of 11 per cent of this group of children, and was a very ethnically and culturally diverse group. Over the course of the study, the proportion of this group was seen to increase, from 9 per cent in 1995/6 to 17 per cent in 1977/8 (Waterhouse, 2001). Broad et al. (2001) found a similar over-representation, as did the study of a sample of kinship placements by Laws (2001).

Perhaps surprisingly, Waterhouse found that the sample of children in kinship placements during care proceedings were young children. Half (53 per cent) were below the age of five and 24 per cent of children under five, who were not living with a parent were in a kinship placement. This compares with 20 per cent of five to nine year olds and 14 per cent of 10 to 14 year olds. None of the sample aged 15 plus were living in a kinship placement. It may well be that placement planning for the older children is happening outside care proceedings (Waterhouse, 2001). The sample group of children in the study by Scannapieco (1999) had an average age of seven to eight. Of this sample, 68 per cent were living with a sibling. When more than one child lived in the placement, the children were siblings in 95 per cent of cases. A substantial proportion of the children (up to half) were underachieving in school. Many had behavioural problems and this included 35 per cent within a clinical range, but there was also evidence that the age group of four to 15 had fewer behavioural problems than children in mainstream fostering placements. Kinship carers were more likely to see the children in a more positive light, for example, to report the children as being 'good natured'.

Little is known about the views and feelings of the children and young people themselves, but the sense of belonging is captured in the Wandsworth study by Broad, Hayes and Rushforth (2001). This positive experience is contrasted with previous experiences in the care system. This is an important and powerful message:

*Most of the young people had spent time in local authority care and for most **this was a traumatic experience**.*

*They described frequent moves, feelings of rejection, and an increasing sense of isolation ... Almost all those who had experience of local authority care described **how desperate they were to leave residential or foster care ... The young people we interviewed did not want to live with strangers**. Some had experience of family life and thought residential and foster care was a false environment ... For some, the behaviour of adults they had previously lived with – birth parents, foster carers or residential care workers – **made them feel unsafe and vulnerable**.*

(Broad et al., 2001: 17–18, my emphasis)

Policy and procedure

Research in Britain and the USA has a congruent theme in respect of the inconsistency of policy and procedure relating to kinship care (Broad, 2001; Broad et al., 2001; Greeff, 1999; Hegar and Scannapieco, 1999). Scannapieco (1999) found evidence of some more sensitive and informed practice models in the USA, but these are patchy and state policy and practice has continued to vary widely. Greeff et al. (1999) argue that the kinship debate has been forced onto the policy agenda by the crisis in mainstream recruitment, but that social workers lack confidence in fulfilling their roles in assessment, support, networking, negotiating, care planning and managing contact when they are dealing with kinship placements. Broad et al (2001) found widespread inconsistency both within and between local authorities and argue that the case is strong for service delivery of kinship placements being transferred to the voluntary sector and funded by central government. This is the service delivery model in New Zealand, where kinship placements are promoted by law. Laws (2001) also found substantial unmet need. A question emerges about the extent to which kinship placements should be considered differently to mainstream foster placements. In concluding their study of role perceptions of the two groups of carers, Pecora et al. (1999) pose the following assertion:

*Understanding the similarities and differences between kinship care and other forms of foster care should be **an essential part** of any foster care reform or services improvement effort.*
(Pecora, Le Prohn and Natsuti, 1999: 177, my emphasis)

In the USA, greater progress has been made in recognising this and some states have developed legislation and policy to support kinship placements (Hegar and Scannapieco, 1999; Ince, 2001). Strategies should be targeted in respect of comprehensive support to children and their carers, pertinent assessment and reunification efforts (Broad, 2001; Broad et al., 2001; Hegar, 1999; Ince, 2001; Portengen and Bart van der Neut, 1999; Talbot and Kidd, 2004; Waterhouse and Brocklesby, 1999).

Since the introduction of the Children Act 1989, social workers have been more willing to explore kinship placements, but evidence remains that this is inconsistent. The potential in respect of kinship placements are not routinely investigated (Hunt, 2001). Hunt's study of kinship care, child protection and the courts found that the trauma of care proceedings could have been avoided in many cases. Relatives were rarely invited to pre-court case conferences, nor were they being used as short-term protective placements. In the course of care proceedings, kinship care was only considered as a placement option in one of every 20 cases. The study concluded that kinship placements have unique characteristics, which are both strengths and weaknesses, and which require recognition and consistent practice.

Berrick et al. (1999) studied the attitudes of social workers to kinship placements and their findings are of interest. Kinship placements were perceived as requiring more input than non-relative placements in 44 per cent of cases. It was recognised that kinship placements delay prospects for rehabilitation with birth parents and that kinship carers were less likely to be meeting the health and educational needs of the children in their care. Emotional needs, however, are perceived as being well met and the commitment of the carers was recognised. One strongly reported perception related to the dimension of family dynamics, which was seen as the greatest strength of kinship placements, whilst being the greatest challenge to the worker. Conflict between relatives was recognised as commonly including resentment, betrayal and sometimes extreme anger. The realities of complexities and conflict are discussed by Marchand and Meulenbergs (1999) in a context of loyalty in family relationships which 'normalises' this conflict:

> *Loyalty is the key word in contextual thinking about human relationships. The alliance between parents and children can never stop: you can never stop being a mother, a father, a son or a daughter (vertical loyalty).*

> *Loyalty is not a feeling . . . it is a fact, derived from giving birth and being born. Loyalty conflicts are inherent in life itself. In the course of life, horizontal loyalty (for instance the connection between foster child and foster parents) cuts the vertical, existential loyalty. To break, avoid or deny the vertical loyalty will cause serious pain in new relationships with a partner or children. This can cause a lot of conflicts in ordinary foster care situations. On the other hand, in (kinship) care this bonding seems to be an advantage. The gap between foster parents and the home environment is absent, and reintegration with the birth parents can develop naturally with no rupture for the children.*

> (Marchand and Meulenbergs, 1999: 101)

Rehabilitation

It is, perhaps, surprising that kinship placements do not promote rehabilitation home, and the reasons for this characteristic are not yet known. Farmer (2001) has reviewed the body of research concerned with the rehabilitation of children to birth parents. There is a consensus of findings which are interesting and important. For example, there is general evidence that children stay 'in care' through default rather than through explicit decision making. This feature has been related to the demands on professional time. The majority of children (82 per cent) do return home within five years of the initial placement. Three out of five children experience a very short placement and research typically finds that rehabilitation is much more likely to occur if the placement lasts for six weeks or less.

Outcomes for rehabilitation are problematic and there is evidence that as many as 42 per cent of children are neglected or re-abused. This needs to be understood within the context that children still wish to be living at home. The best predictor of rehabilitation is ongoing contact, but this should not be seen as a 'lone' factor. Family members need to work on attachments, but this is skilled work and a rare feature of long-term work. In reality, rehabilitation is usually driven by characteristics in the placement, or pressure from the child and/or the birth parents and a major factor is the family's determination. Farmer identifies three groups of rehabilitated children; 'early returners', 'intermediate returners', (placed for between six months and two years) and 'long term returners' (placed for more than two years). As might be expected, the greatest challenge is posed to the latter group, who may well force significant adjustments to the changes which have occurred in the family during the episode of substitute care. For this reason, Farmer suggests that the rehabilitation plan is viewed as a new placement rather than a return to the same. It has been estimated that rehabilitation is beneficial for 50 per cent of children and detrimental for 20 per cent, while the remaining 30 per cent of children have mixed experiences. Of concern, in respect of the detrimental group, is the finding that the placement level confirmed for up to two years in the experience of 50 per cent of this group. Of specific concern is the finding that 44 per cent of teenage girls became pregnant during the rehabilitation placement at home – this compares with only 3 per cent of the general population.

Rehabilitation can then be a complex and stressful process. Birth parents have to face up to past failures and children need permission to express their hurt feelings and receive reassurance that the placement will not fail. This demands support to ensure that maximum continuity is established. Of particular importance is the inclusive role of the carers, whether foster carers or residential staff. Difficulties in rehabilitation are associated with the ages of the children, parental skills, education and support. Success is more difficult to establish when the period in care has been lengthy and the children are older. Sibling relationships are crucial and prospects improve when siblings are placed together. Success also improves if the preparation for rehabilitation has included a build up of contact and if relatives are supportive. A worrying finding is that large numbers (60 per cent) of children have problematic school attendance when they return home. In reality, one in four young people will move themselves home, but they do also require professional support during this period of transition. Predictors of disruption are single parent status, poverty, limited support and problematic parental skills. Breakdown is also associated with parental drug and alcohol abuse during the period of initial separation (Farmer, 2001).

These findings need to be understood and used to guide the plan for rehabilitation and subsequent support. Children deserve to be supported to live within their birth families, whenever this is possible. Children have very mixed experiences of returning home. Rehabilitation works for every other child, but one in five will have detrimental experiences. Research is available to inform professional intervention and maximise success.

Conclusion: the current body of research and implications for further research

Kinship care is an important phenomenon, of increasing significance, yet so little is known or understood, not least the views, feelings and experiences of the children themselves. A small amount of British research exists and what is available is generally very positive. Given the significance of kinship care in the USA, it is disappointing that the body of American research is also limited, and methodology has been largely restrictive, with relatively little qualitative methodology. Yet, children deserve to have their views and experiences explored, understood and translated. If kinship placements meet children's emotional, physical, cultural and religious needs, provide stability and promote identity, then they must be coherently and consistently promoted as the preferred placement option for all children and young people. Kinship care requires the urgent attention of social investigation.

The views and experiences of children and young people are of great importance and interest, but remain a neglected area in research. In particular, children in middle childhood have received little attention and there is little to inform us about the needs, developments and experiences of primary school-age children (Borland, Laybourne, Hill and Brown, 1998). Children's perceptions of relationships need further investigation: their experiences of attachments, separation and loss are of great importance. Kinship placements have a potential to preserve family relationships by promoting contact. When children are consulted, they report contact as having great importance to them, therefore, the relationship between kinship placements and contact requires investigation. Profiles of children and young people in kinship placements, and of their carers, are beginning to emerge, suggesting particular characteristics, but more evidence is needed to inform practice developments. Research suggests that kinship placements offer stability, yet it is not known how this is achieved. Evidence, rather than speculation, is required. In the context of the general instability for 'looked after' children, this matter merits more attention. Curiously, kinship placements are not associated with rehabilitation to birth parents, yet research cannot yet deal with the reasons for this finding.

The impact of professional values is a further theme which merits attention. These values inform placement decisions, assessment and support. Values are vital contributors to the construction of experiences of kinship placements – they impact on the 'passage' into the placement. Kinship placements, like other aspects of social welfare, raise questions about the relationship between the state and the family, which determines the socio-legal context in which welfare services are delivered. Kinship placements will reflect structural factors, such as the distribution of socio-economic power, but these complex processes have received no explicit attention. Other processes include the impact and experience of race and ethnicity. Ince (2001) draws attention to the continuation of ethnocentrism in child care practice, contrasting developments in the USA with the lack of coherency in major policy changes in Britain. Professional intervention often arises from a value base which does not fit with child-rearing practices in African Caribbean cultures. A good and empowering system for assessment is needed (Ince, 2001; Talbot and Kidd, 2004). These themes should inform the future direction of much needed further research. They are important to the emotional well being of some of the most vulnerable of the population of children in need.

References

Altshuler, S.J. (1999) The Well-Being of Children in Kinship Foster Care. In Cleeson, P. and Hairston, C.F. (Eds.) *Kinship Care: Improving Practice through Research*. Washington: CWLA.

Berrick, J.D., Needell, B. and Barth, R. (1999) Role Perceptions of Kinship and other Foster Parents in Family Foster Care. In Hegar, R.L. and Scannapieco, M. (Eds.) op. cit.

Borland, M., Laybourne, A., Hill, M. and Brown, J. (1998) *Middle Childhood: The Perspectives of Children and Parents*. London: Jessica Kingsley.

Broad, B. (1999) Kinship Care: Enabling and Supporting Child Placements with Relatives and Friends. In *Assessment, Support and Preparation: Implications From Research*. London: BAAF.

Broad, B. (Ed.) (2001) *Kinship Care: The Placement Choice for Children and Young People*. Lyme Regis: Russell House Publishing.

Broad, B., Hayes, R. and Rushforth, C. (2001) *Kith and Kin: Kinship Care for Vulnerable Young People*. London: NCB.

Broad, B. (2004) Kinship Care for Children in the UK: Messages From Research, Lessons for Policy and Practice. *European Journal of Social Work*. 7: 2, 211–27.

Child Welfare League of America (2000) *Standards of Excellence for Kinship Care Services*. Washington: CWLA.

Crumbley, J. and Little, R. (1997) *Relatives Raising Children: An Overview of Kinship Care*. Washington: CWLA.

Department of Health (2002) *Family and Friends Care Discussion Document*. London: DoH.

Department of Health (2002) *Choice Protects Update Bulletin*. London: DoH.

Elgar, M. and Head, A. (1999) An Overview of Siblings. In Mullender, A. (Ed.) op. cit.

Farmer. E. (2001) Children Reunited with their Parents: A Review of Research Findings. In Broad, B. (Ed.) op. cit.

Galloway, H. and Wallace, F. (2002) Managing Contact Arrangements in Black Kinship Care. In Argent, H. *Staying Connected: Managing Contact Arrangements in Adoption*. London: BAAF.

Gleeson, P. and Hairston, C.F. (Eds.) (1999) *Kinship Care: Improving Practice through Research*. Washington: CWLA.

Greeff, R. (Ed.) *Fostering Kinship: An International Perspective on Kinship Foster Care*. Aldershot: Arena.

Greeff, R., Waterhouse, S. and Brocklesby, E. (1999) Kinship Fostering-Research, Policy and Practice in England. In Greeff, R. (Ed.) op. cit.

Hegar, R.L. and Scannapieco, M. (1999) *Kinship Foster Care: Policy, Practice and Research*. New York: Oxford University Press.

Hegar, R.L. (1999) Kinship Foster Care: The New Child Placement Paradigm. In Hegar, R.L. and Scannapieco, M. (Eds.) op. cit.

Hegar, R.L. (1999) The Cultural Roots of Kinship Care. In Hegar, R.L. and Scannapieco, M. (Eds.) op. cit.

Hunt, J. (2001) Kinship Care, Child Protection and the Courts. In Broad, B. (Ed.) op. cit.

Ince, L. (2001) Promoting Kinship Foster Care: Preserving Family Networks for Black Children of African Origins. In Broad, B. (2001) op. cit.

Jackson, S. and Thomas, N. (1999) *On the Move Again? What works in Creating Stability for Looked After Children?* Ilford: Barnado's.

Laws, S. (2001) Looking After Children Within the Extended Family. In Broad, B. (Ed.) op. cit.

Marchand, H. and Meulenbergs, W. (1999)
Working with Family Complexity-Supporting
the Network. In Greeff, R. (Ed.) op. cit.

McRoy, R., Christian, C. and Thompson, E. (2002)
Empirical Support for Family Preservation and
Kinship Care. In Alstein, H. and McRoy, R.
*Does Family Preservation Serve a Child's Best
Interests?* Washington: CWLA.

NFCA (1997) *Foster Care in Crisis: A Call to
Professionalise the Service*. London: NFCA.

Pecora, P., Prohn, N. and Nasuti, J. (1999) Role
Perceptions of Kinship and Other Foster
Parents in Family Foster Care. In Hegar, R.L.
and Scannapieco, L. op. cit.

Pitcher, D. (2001) Assessing Grandparent Carers:
A Framework. In Broad, B. op. cit.

Portengen, R. and Van der Neut, B. (1999)
Assessing Family Strengths: A Family Systems
Approach. In Greeff, R. op. cit.

Scannapieco, M. (1999) Kinship Care in the Public
Welfare System: A Systematic Review of the
Research. In Hegar, R.L. and Scannapieco, M.
(Eds.) *Fostering Kinship: An International
Perspective on Kinship Foster Care*. Oxford:
Oxford University Press.

Scannapieco, M. (1999) Formal Kinship Care
Practice Models. In Hegar, R.L. and
Scannapieco, M. op. cit.

Starr et al. (1999) Behavioural Problems of Teens
in Kinship Care. In Hegar, R.L. and
Scannapieco, M. (Eds.) *Kinship Foster Care:
Policy, Practice and Research*. Oxford: Oxford
University Press.

Sykes, J., Sinclair, I., Gibbs, I. and Wilson, K.
(2002) Kinship and Stranger Foster Carers:
How Do They Compare? *Adoption and
Fostering*. 26: 2.

Talbot, C. and Kidd, P. (2004) Special
Guardianship Orders: Issues in Respect of
Family Assessment. *Journal of Family Law*.
April, 273-81.

Tapsfield, R. (2001) Kinship Care: A Family
Rights Perspective. In Broad, B. (Ed.) op. cit.

Waterhouse, S. (1997) *The Organisation of Fostering
Service: A Study of the Arrangements for Delivery
of Fostering Services by Local Authorities in
England*. London: NFCA.

Waterhouse, S. and Brockelsby, E. (1999)
Placement Choices for Children: Giving More
Priority to Kinship Placements. In Greeff, R.
(Ed.) op. cit.

Waterhouse, S. (2001) Keeping Children in
Kinship Placements Within Court Proceedings.
In Broad, B. op. cit.

Wheal, A. (2001) Family and Friends who are
Carers: A Framework for Success. In Broad, B.
op. cit.

Williams, J. (1999) Kinship Foster Care in New
York State: An African-American Perspective.
In Greeff, R. (Ed.) op. cit.

Worrall, J. (1999) Clear Policy and Good Practice
in Kinship Foster Care. In Greeff, R. (Ed.)
*Fostering Kinship: An International Perspective on
Kinship Foster Care*. Aldershot: Arena.

Chapter Two

Some Advantages and Disadvantages of Kinship Care: A View From Research

Bob Broad

Introduction

This chapter describes the advantages and disadvantages of kinship care as expressed by young people living in kinship care placements as included in a research study (see Broad et al., 2001, for full details of the research project). Reference is also made to the views of those carers and social workers involved in the placement indicating where these are similar to or different from those views held by the young people. Almost without exception the carers spoke passionately in favour of kinship care, and confirmed and mirrored what the young people had said about 'feeling safe' about not being in local authority care and of the family being 'the right place' for a young person to grow. They also considered that being in a kinship care placement helped them develop their personality and a sense of who they are, in other words to understand the young person's sense of identity, as an individual, as a family member, and their racial and cultural connections.

Definition of kinship care

There is very little research published about 'kinship care' in the United Kingdom to draw on, especially research which centres around children's and young people's perspectives. It is also the case that the term 'kinship care', as a relationship concept is potentially complex in that it can describe different types of relationships, each carrying different legal responsibilities, obligations and consequences. It is of especial importance then that a clear definition of the term 'kinship care' is produced, not only as an essential element of this study, but in wider policy terms and recommendations. According to McFadden (1998) writing about kinship care in the USA, kinship care can be described as either an *informal* family arrangement, taking place outside the child welfare system, or a *formal* family arrangement, arranged and approved by

child welfare agencies. This is a useful distinction to introduce the study, concerned with the second of these i.e. *formal kinship care*. Yet it should be noted that the existing literature, (whether relating to the USA or the UK), tends not to make a further distinction within formal kinship care, since the relatives or friends may or may not be approved foster carers. The research study described here mostly concerns formal kinship care placements not subject to a fostering agreement.

In the original study our working definition of a child living in a kinship care placement was:

A child living away from the parental home with a relative or friend and known to the social services department, and who would otherwise be with stranger foster carers, in residential care, independent living, or adopted. The kinship care placement is either initiated by the social services department or via a relative or friend, and involves some sort of assistance or arrangement, including making decisions about legal orders, financial and social work support.

Let me first summarise the original research study from which the material in this chapter is taken.

The research study

The self-standing kinship care research study's findings discussed here (Broad et al., 2001) followed on from two earlier kinship care studies conducted by De Montfort University's Children and Families Research Unit in partnership with the London Borough of Wandsworth Social Services' Department. The entire study arose from concerns from practitioners about the growing use of formal kinship care (in non-foster placements), as well as an ongoing shortage of foster carers for 12-15 year olds. The first of the preceding two local studies had very different emphases to the current study. That first study undertook a mapping exercise of kinship care and obtained *social workers' views* about kinship care in connection with 70 children of all ages notified as being in kinship care. The second local kinship care study had focused on recording the *views of kinship carers* involved in the more established or 'mature' kinship care placements within that authority (Laws and Broad, 2000). A critical research feature of each of those previous studies was both the enormous amount of research time required to establish comprehensive up-to date sample information, and obtain the agreement of a sample of kinship carers, to be interviewed. Young people's views were neither sought not obtained in those studies.

Aims of research study under discussion

The primary aim of this research study was to explore and record the views of young people in formal kinship care, and their carers, about their experiences of kinship care, from their different perspectives. The second aim was to make recommendations about good practice and policy in this area. The research examines the role and contribution of extended families and friends, acting as kinship carers, in supporting young people who are living away from their birth parents and making the transition to adulthood. Given the earlier research study's finding about the relatively high proportion of black children in kinship care, the current study aimed to record the experiences and needs of black and minority ethnic young people in kinship care and their kinship carers, and policy and practice implications.

The research study also set out to understand the views of social workers about kinship care and their involvement, if any, in decision making, assessments, and care plans. It is argued here that the views of social workers are critical in understanding the role, practice and limits of social services involvement in such placements.

The scope and limits of the study

Young people rather than children were required to be in the sample in order to meet the *Joseph Rowntree Foundation* 'young people in transition to adulthood' funding criteria about seeking to understand how young people in need living in kinship care manage their lives. The young people in this study were predominantly in the

14–21 age group. Thus the experiences of this research project's target group will not necessarily be the same of younger children, for example under 10s, living in kinship care. The task of the kinship carers for such a younger group will also be quite different than for caring for teenagers. The latter may want more independence and are more likely to challenge grandparents' wishes and views than younger children. Also and critically, social services legal responsibilities and children and families structures and procedures do not readily apply to over 18 year olds.

The cohort of young people in this study were not only those children placed with relatives at the looked after court proceedings stage (as is the case with Waterhouse's kinship care study [2001]) but, rather, a group that is more widely drawn. In some ways the children and young people in this sample resembles more those in the Hertfordshire kinship care survey (Webster, 2000: 2, 5) which concluded:

> *A wide variety of kinship care placements are made or facilitated under s 8, 17, 20, 31 varying between very short crisis placements to long term . . . all teams facilitated such (S17) arrangements, typically for teenagers in a crisis situation.*

What is being claimed about the young people living in kinship care research study is that through this comprehensive in-depth study of kinship care placements, and children's and carers views, the study has been able to identify a wide range of practice and policy issues with wider application. Additionally and by referring to other known studies, the research team uncovered many of the user, carer and professional, administrative and policy concerns likely to be faced by other local authorities undertaking or wishing to develop kinship care placements.

Research sample and methodology

The following research methods were used in the original kinship care study. Information was gathered about 50 young people, and interviews were conducted with 20 of them:

- Descriptive statistical data about all children and young people aged 14 plus in kinship care using SPSS for Windows software.

- In-depth transcribed interviews with young people in kinship care, using a semi-structured interview schedule.
- In-depth semi-structured interviews with the young person's current or most recent kinship carer.
- Individual interviews and focus groups with social workers.
- Key themes analysis.

Management information

Given the lack of comprehensive data available on local authority databases, a range of descriptive data was sought from various sources. Descriptive data was sought about the children/young people, the kinship carers and the nature of the placement.

This information was obtained from a variety of sources including the social services in need database; social work files; through social work interviews; carers and young people interviews. As anticipated the time required to gather, enter and analyse this data in a clear and consistent way across the entire project was considerable. In this respect the assistance of a professional SPSS consultant was indispensable.

Nevertheless it was not possible to collect all the information required on each young person either because files were incomplete, or there was more than one file across different offices, or cases had been closed because social services no longer had case responsibility. Thus it became the task of the research team to seek out, collect and collate such information as it required.

It was especially difficult to find the contact details of many of these young people, especially in the post 16–17 age group who 'moved around' between friend's accommodation and their carer's home. In some cases, with three young people aged over 18, they lived in other accommodation, including a hostel for homeless young people, bed and breakfast accommodation, and being on remand in custody. Telephone contact proved both advantageous and disadvantageous. Once the research team had obtained the telephone numbers of the carers, if these were known or available, these land line telephone links proved reliable for ongoing contact. Mobile phones, the preferred and costly choice of some of the young people, seem excellent for direct contact, providing the mobile phone was on, is working and is answered by the

young person to whom it belongs and whom the research team is seeking to contact. Where any one of these three conditions were met (often) mobile phone contact became illusory and was more of a blight than a bonus.

Routes into kinship care

Potentially there are two main explanations for the establishment of the kinship care placements described here. These are 'kinship care as the preferred response to a crisis', and 'kinship care as the planned child care choice'. It is the 'crisis' explanation which applies here. The original research study showed that there are a number of different routes into kinship care. These were:

- A final resort for social services after other care options had failed.
- A continuation of relative support originally provided on a short-term basis.
- The first option for social services once the family situation had broken down.
- An option selected by the young people themselves after a crisis at home.

To compound matters further, in some cases these routes were not mutually exclusive. Nevertheless it is the case that it is the 'crisis' origin of the majority of the kinship care placements discussed here which makes their positive outcomes seem all the more remarkable. On the other hand perhaps it was because of lack of suitable placement alternatives combined with these placements being mutually agreed that may go some way to explaining why they were more likely to be viewed so positively.

Advantages of kinship care

Young people's views

There are two connected ways the advantages and disadvantages of kinship care are presented here. First the researchers produced an assessment of the key themes raised in individual interviews with 20 young people. Second the advantages and disadvantages of kinship care are analysed by examining social workers perspectives based on structured one-to-one and group interviews with them.

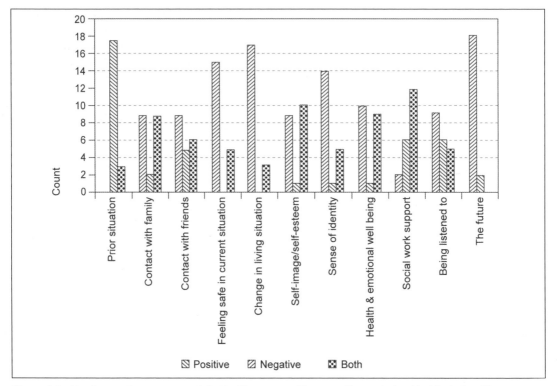

Figure 2.1   Key themes for young people in kinship care: positive, negative and mixed incidents (n = 20) young people)

Key themes

The researchers assessed each young person's situation and judged whether, of 11 key themes identified earlier these were negative, positive or simultaneously negative and positive key themes in terms of their impact on the young person's situation.

Figures 2.1 and 2.2 illustrate the responses to this key themes analysis.

Comment

- Overall the incidence of positive themes is far greater than that of negative themes.

- The most prevalent 'purely' positive factors (excluding 'negative and positive') were: 'the future' (18), 'change in living situation' (17), 'feeling safe in current situation' (15) and 'sense of identity' (14).
- The most prevalent 'purely' negative factors (i.e. excluding 'negative and positive') were: 'prior situation' (17), 'social work support' (6) and 'being listened to' (6).
- The most prevalent simultaneously positive and negative themes occur as follows: 'social work support' (12), 'self-image/self-esteem'(10), 'contact with the family' (9) and 'health and emotional well being' (9).

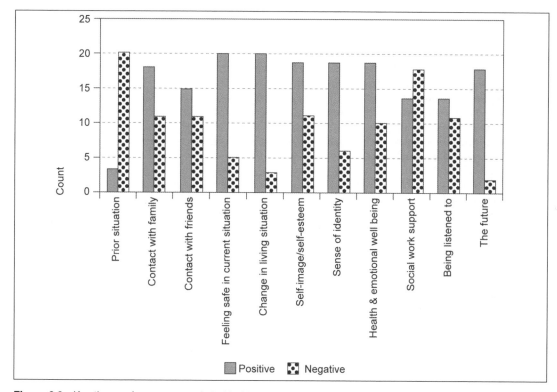

Figure 2.2   Key themes for young people in kinship care: disaggregated positive and negative incidents (n = 20) young people)

Disaggregating the simultaneously positive and negative themes to their individual components produces the key theme analysis shown in Figure 2.2.

Comment

- In all 20 cases, the 'prior situation' is negative, 'feeling safe in current situation' and 'change in living situation' are positive.
- 'Prior situation' and 'social work support' are the only themes where negative associations outweigh positives.

Young people, carers and social workers agreed about the *advantages* of kinship care. These were; feeling safe and settled living with kinship carer, not being in local authority care and having a sense of identify about family and culture. Young people and carers abhor the isolation, constraints, abuse, and lack of respect associated with local authority care. Almost half of the sample had previously been looked after by a local authority. Being brought up by an extended family member, and in many cases still having contact with birth parents and siblings, especially when they live

nearby, contribute to the formulation of the young people's identity.

In respect of racial and cultural issues both black and white young people valued being brought up by their extended family and within their own family culture. Black young people and carers spoke of the importance of family love, being looked after by the whole family, and the importance of other relatives and friends being local. Some young people indicated that they had been the subject of racism either whilst in care or more often at school.

The disadvantages of kinship care centred on 'limits on lifestyle', 'financial hardship' and for the carers 'emotional demands'. So far as social workers were concerns the drawbacks of kinship care relate to an ambiguity by some birth parents and potential carers about kinship care itself, and reservations about a child being brought up in a kinship care placement in respect of the young person's age and age/capacity of the carer. Finally there were major organisational and funding problems which discouraged kinship care.

This key theme analysis highlights three main advantages of kinship care as seen by the young

---

Kinship care key themes

- **Prior situation** including prior placement.
- **Contact with family** including which family members and why.
- **Contact with friends** including new and past friends.
- **Feeling safe in current situation** in respect of safety and free from harm.
- **Changes to living situation** in respect of identifying possible changes to their life by living or in many cases, continuing to live with a kinship carer.
- **School, ambitions, work and leisure** including questions about education, hopes and plans.
- **Self-image/self-esteem** including questions about how they felt about themselves, best achievement to date.
- **Sense of identity** including questions about, race and culture, racism, and religion, the neighbourhood.
- **Feelings about yourself** including questions about, race and culture, racism, and religion.
- **Health and emotional well-being** including general physical and sexual health, and whether there was someone to share any concerns with.
- **Social work support and being listened to** including to what extent have social services supported the placement.
- **The future** in terms of where living, personal plans.

---

people. Interestingly these were shared by all three groups, i.e. the young people, the carers and the social workers:

1. Feeling safe and settled living with kinship carer.
2. Not being in local authority care.
3. Confirming the young person's sense of identity (family/cultural/racial heritage).

Let us now examine the detail of these three main key themes.

Feeling safe and settled living with kinship carer

According to the young people and as with other studies of disadvantaged young people's views of services and needs (for example West, 1995) these young people valued being listened to, being valued, feeling safe, and having their needs and wishes respected. As expected they tended to list these features rather than comment on social services structures or planning, something the social workers did feel they could comment on.

From the basis of living within your own family, or as one young person put it, 'being with people who knew you and you knew them' flowed all the other kinship care 'plus' factors.

It was found that 'feeling safe' was a major theme that ran through all the interviews with

young people. The young people expressed a need to feel that they were in a place where they had significance as a person, and that living with a member of their extended family provided such a sense of belonging. For example:

(Talking about his younger brother) *I feel my brother looks up to me and because he doesn't know everything but he knows a fair bit for a 10 year old, I think he's proud of me, that's how I feel, my Mum always says that we well, that my brother's proud of how I've pulled through things and got better. I know he looks up to me.*

My Gran, she's 100%, she's been our rock and kept the whole family together, if it wasn't for her we would probably all be separated and not grown up with each other and not as close as we are. I wouldn't be the stable person I am today if it wasn't for my Gran.

(Living with Grandma) *I actually like it here, because if I didn't come here I wouldn't have met the people I'd met, I reckon I wouldn't be as advanced as I am now, cause I think staying with my Mum I'd have been kind of held back in certain things. I look at my brother and sister and I think I could have been like that at the age of 10. But I wouldn't have liked to have been like that. I'd rather be the way I am now. It wouldn't have done me a whole lot of good.*

Many of the young people spoke of feeling loved within their families. These were not necessarily birth families but included people the young people were living with and they chose to call their family. For example:

Moving back with my Dad, is one of the things that I am very proud of because through all the time I was in care that's what I wanted to do. My Dad made regular visits to me once a week, took me out, to the cinema, other things and basically everything I wanted to do. I just wanted to live with my Dad. That's what I felt through all of it, so that's one of the things I'm most proud of.

I love to know that I belong to somebody, I'm loved by people and I just, it's good to know that I've got somewhere to come after school that I can call home.

Not being in local authority care

In presenting the advantages of kinship care the question 'advantages in comparison with what?' is also answered and this led many young people to talk about what it was like previously being in care.

Forty-four per cent of the total sample had previously been looked after and a similar proportion of the 20 young people interviewed had also spent time in local authority care. Without exception this had proved to be an unhappy experience. For some young people it had proved traumatic and had increased the sense of isolation and disruption in their lives:

There were too many of us and they (parents) couldn't look after all of us, so, I mean I was out of control – running round the streets at night, setting fire to things, breaking into cars, things like that. I went into a foster home. I kept running away home to Mum and Dad, in the end Mum rang my sister up from the phone box. Since I've been with my sister I've changed a hell of a lot. I've been here about nine years altogether and I mean my sister has done her best and she has put in a lot of effort looking after me, bringing me up from an early age.

I got kicked out and then I was in a children's home. I went back home and was kicked out again, and I was in foster care and then bed and breakfast. The social workers come to a big meeting with my Mum and Dad and they said it would probably be better if I came to live with my Nan for a little while, 'cos I've actually got epilepsy and I can't live on my own until I come off the medication.

Although many of the young people had experienced local authority care, the reasons for this, and the decision making process was often hazy. This is not surprising since many were very young when these decisions were made. There were difficulties experienced in being able to retain the links to the 'normality' of their previous lives. Casework decisions were not obvious to them.

When I was in foster care, I would see my Mum like once a month, at times, then sometimes I wouldn't and we sort of get a lift to school and we'd drive past my house and we weren't allowed to play out, we were shut away from my family and kept inside.

We were like caged in, and we used to drive past and then they would pick us up, and I'd ask if we could get out and see our Mum and 'no you can't see your Mum' and that.

(On being homeless, age 11) *Well the first place I went to was social services in . . . and I told them what had happened but I think as far as they were concerned I had no reason not to stay at home, that's because I chose not to tell them everything. So I didn't want to go into it and they just, I told them I was living on the street basically and I am just staying everywhere, and then they just gave me some money and then they sent a letter back to my Mum's house, but I didn't want her to know that I'd been there, because, I just didn't want her to know.*

I've been in care twice before and I was always moving around the place, I was at my other Granny's then she had a brain haemorrhage, she went to hospital, my Mum looked after me and my sisters for a week then I went into care for another two years and my Dad took us he thought he could cope when he had a flat, I think we were with him for about a year, then we went back into foster care, then Mum came back so he moved out.

I was having arguments with my foster parent, she was an alcoholic and we didn't know that, and she was not giving me the money she was supposed to give me, and she didn't like me standing up for myself, so she kicked me out, that was my last chance, because you can only stay in two, three, no two foster placements.

Confirming sense of identity

Within this 'identity' heading the sub-themes of 'maintaining links with family and friends' and 'valuing racial and cultural heritage' emerged.

Maintaining links with family and friends

This was expressed as being important for many young people. Although they recognised they could not live with their birth family some wanted to maintain the links. It was important to know about their family, if they could not live with them. As we will see later it was also important to carers to help facilitate those links. The following are a selection of quotations from the young people about links and locality:

Yeah my Dad only lives down the road, and my Mum is in Hackney (about 10 miles away), she's always calling us to come there.

My sisters all live near to where my Mum and Dad live so I see them all the time.

(Talking about Mum) I was pigheaded I wouldn't go and see her often and it was still like ... but she would still come to my Nan's and see that I was alright but I wouldn't necessarily go to her house.

I was with my brothers as well, because although the people I was living with before I came to Grandma's like they treated us well, I didn't know them, I just wanted to be with people I knew and they knew me. Being with my brothers made it better, and being with my Gran it made it better as well. I see both my Mum and Dad. My Mum comes round most weekends and my Dad he comes at the weekend as well.

Siblings

Forty-one of the 46 young people in the study indicated they had between one and seven siblings. In giving answers about the advantages of kinship care many of the young people interviewed made reference to the importance of keeping in touch with their brothers or sisters, although surprisingly perhaps 'maintaining contact with siblings' did not emerge as a finding in all cases. Siblings tended to be either still living with the birth parent, living with the young person in kinship care, or looked after. The majority of siblings were living with their birth parents. In those cases this raises the question of why the young person interviewed, and not their brother or sister, was currently living in kinship care. There may be practical issues (i.e. space in the house/rooms available) or other family or even child protection issues. However in discussing family relationships it often emerged that there were regular and ongoing family and sibling separations and in a number of cases a brother or sister was brought up separately for long periods of time, sometimes in another town or even country. Just two young people have spoken of their unhappiness in not being able to make contact with siblings for whom the family links have been lost to them. The interviews with the young people suggest that these may be siblings who have subsequently been adopted. Nevertheless, 'contact with siblings,' as part of family contact, was highly valued by many of the young people as a source of friendship, stability and support in times of trouble. We also know from other research the positive contribution maintaining contact and/or living with siblings usually make to placement stability (Jackson and Thomas, 1997).

Understanding and valuing racial and cultural heritage

Ten young people or 50 per cent of the 20 young people interviewed, the same percentage as for the total sample of 50 young people, were of either African, or Caribbean and Guyanese ethnic origin (using the local authority race record keeping categories). The remaining, 12 (or 54 per cent of those interviewed) were described as English, Welsh, Scots, Irish, or other UK ethnic origin. The semi-structured questions to the young people included questions that explored issues of ethnicity, identity and culture. The young people struggled with a number of these questions. To an extent the young people's reservations about some questions are understandable since they were all young adults who were still coming to terms with who they were as people. Some of the terms, such as 'step-sister' 'half-brother' were rejected and such terms were regarded more as formal distinctions put on them, and not one they made for themselves:

Yes, I have always been OK about who I am, we get all this from each other, my sisters, cousins, Auntie, friends in the street – you know.

I said to my sister a long time ago, I can't remember, I was only about 11 or 12, and I said I think I'm gay and stuff like that and she was going 'are you sure'? and I was saying, yeah. Nowadays 'cos people say I'm confused and I know what I am and I've never told my Mum and Dad 'cos my Mum and Dad come from a background where they sort of don't like people like that – they think it's not normal.

Yeah, I mean the food you eat and the conversation – like they still speak patois and stuff so definitely the Caribbean influence is still there. Socially, you go to school and the majority of people are going to be white, so it doesn't like, I don't know – it balances up and everything.

Cause I'm half black and half white, there's all different shades of black isn't there, there's dark black, light black and there's black people who are my colour. I just see myself as myself.

The research team also asked carers how they assessed the importance of young people maintaining their racial, cultural and religious identities as they grow up, and were in many cases surprised by the strength of feeling these questions provoked. A minority of carers described how important the family ethnic heritage was to the young person. For example:

She loves listening to her great grandmother who talks in brogue. She likes to know her family history.

Another carer described the value of social services paying her grandson's airfare to Jamaica so that he could meet many of his relatives for the first time.

It was easier for researchers and carers to talk about religion than race, and religion seemed less sensitive, and possibly relevant. Just under half the carers spoke of the importance of their faith, and how at one stage they encouraged the young people to participate. Only one young person however remained actively involved in religious practice – the granddaughter of a Baptist who has become a Muslim. Elsewhere, carers accepted, in some cases sadly, that any religious affiliation must be the decision of a young adult.

The black young people did speak of experiencing racism when they were in primary school. This seemed to have been handled more confidently as they have grown older. One young person spoke to us about difficulties in maintaining a relationship with a black friend due to pressure from her family. There did seem to be an issue for some young people about dual culture:

I was raised by my black father, it's the only way I know. I'm black if anyone asks me I'm black. It doesn't make a difference to me, everybody's equal, that's how I see it; I've got a lot of white friends.

There were particular issues about the needs of refugee young people. One young person had been brought to the UK, aged seven, as a refugee. He had been accommodated in this country by an uncle. He had been assaulted in this household and left to live with a 'friend'. This person was hospitalised following a mental breakdown. This led to the young person being homeless at 14 years of age:

So I moved to another guy who was from the same country as me, from ____, who was looking after me, then after I was living there for about two years, a year and a half, then he had a mental breakdown, so he went back to ____ then I was homeless, so I started getting into trouble with the police, and stuff like that.

He has been assaulted in a racist attack on the street and hospitalised. This young person is now living with a friend, but has suffered real hardship. It is hard to understand why his situation was not dealt with by any agency. It raises the question as to whether refugee ch[...] are treated differently.

We asked carers their views on the extent to which social services dealt with issues around their racial, cultural and religious needs. Although several carers did describe experience of prejudice in other areas of their life, for example racist incidents at work, none mentioned any feelings of being treated unfairly due to their race or ethnicity by the social services' department.

Social workers' views

As well as gathering the views of those immediately involved in kinship care, the young people themselves and their carers, to complete the picture we wanted to get the views of the social workers who had day-to-day responsibility for managing kinship care, about the plus factors and disadvantages. We know from other studies that the views of staff who deliver and manage services, and levels of resourcing are crucial factors in service delivery.

All the social workers we spoke with were enthusiastic about kinship care, although some more than others. The reasons they gave confirmed those of young people and the carers:

- The family offered a superior environment in which to bring up young people.
- The recognition that the state care is sometimes a poor substitute for kinship care.

Additional benefits mentioned were that kinship care adds to the range of options available to social workers and families, that in some circumstances it is possible to take more 'risks' with kinship carers, and that kinship care helps birth parents, especially when kinship care is used for respite care.

Let us now turn to the disadvantages of kinship care as perceived by the young people, the carers and the social workers.

Disadvantages of kinship care

As with identifying the positive themes about kinship care, so with its disadvantages, the young people and carers had largely shared views. Because the key theme analysis was not undertaken about carers views (and perhaps it should have been although carers views were not

study) the 'limits on the
...ed other disadvantages
...ere not identified in key
...the key point about the
...of kinship care is that not
only ... ...less stated disadvantages but
that they are of a more extrinsic than intrinsic
nature than the positive factors. The two big
disadvantages then of kinship care to both the
young people and the carers were 'limits on
lifestyle' (young people and carers) and 'financial
hardship' (young people and carers) followed by a
third for carers, 'physical and emotional demands'
(on carers). A further group of disadvantages are
presented under the heading 'child safety,
inter-family conflict, resources and practical issues'.

Limits on lifestyle

Recalling that on average the young people had
been in kinship care placement for an average of
3.8 years, and thus had real experiences to draw
on over time, let us look at what the young
people and carers said, first about limits on
lifestyle. It was found that where the young
people had settled in with their carer and the
arrangement had been longstanding, there was
often a fuller understanding of the sacrifices that
were made by their family or friends. The
younger group were perhaps, naturally, more
preoccupied with possible limitations to their
own freedoms. These quotations by young people
are typical of what they said in interview:

> I'm not going to sit in all day and watch East Enders, I'm
> going to go out with my friends and enjoy myself. I don't
> stay out every night, I stay out about three times a month
> and when I've got money to get a cab I come home, I don't
> want to get on a bus and walk for ever. I stay at my
> friend's house, it's not like he lives at another part of
> London, 10 minutes up the road . . . drinking. I'm always
> saying to my Nan 'teenagers drink'.

> I want to be independent, my Nan won't let me be
> independent. She says 'when are you coming in for your
> dinner, I haven't eaten a thing?' I said in the morning I
> was going out after work, there's no reason why she should
> have to wait for me to come in just so she can eat, she says
> 'I don't want to cook twice', but if my Dad comes in later
> she'll put the oven on twice to cook his dinner, so what's
> the big deal?

> I used to row with my Nan – no one likes my partner cos
> I was 17 when I started going out with him and he was
> 29. They don't like the age gap 'cos he doesn't give me
> money. They don't like things like that.

> I don't do anything apparently, but my Dad's here, she'll
> sit in there with my Dad and there'll be having a chat,
> she'll walk all the way from here to my room to ask me to
> close the kitchen window, and why she doesn't do little
> things like that I don't know.

There was often a link between lifestyle clashes
and the next perceived drawback relating to
finances.

Financial hardship

This was a particularly sensitive issue for young
people living outside family life and were trying
to cope independently. For these young people
the financial pressures were acute. One young
woman looked after her sister for two years on
the money she was getting from her Job Seekers'
Allowance. The two of them were living
independently for under £50 per week.

Some carers also spoke about how siblings in
foster or residential care fared much better
materially than the young people they were
looking after:

> It upset me to see what the girls were getting . . . clothes
> allowance, pocket money, holidays. They went all over the
> world – America you name it, and all through that time
> poor (name of young person) never even got as far as
> Brighton . . . All his clothes were passed down to him from
> his older cousin. But he never said anything when they
> (his sisters) were showing off their new clothes.

The kinship carers spoke at length about the cost
of bringing up a child, the lack of sufficient, or in
most cases, any ongoing, financial support from
the authorities. In one case in the study a child
was taken back to be fostered with non-relatives
after the relative could not cope financially.
Financial tensions fuelled inter or intra family
tensions.

Physical and emotional demands on carers

These quotations are typical of those that were
open about the emotional demands and
responsibilities of looking after a young person:

> It only works if the grandparents are willing. It can take
> too much out of them . . . It's hard, but you adjust. You
> have to have a lot of patience . . . he did need a lot.

> When I first took them in I thought, 'This will be a doddle.
> I've brought up five children on my own'.

He expects me to play football with him at weekends. I do my best, but I get knackered.

A second grandparent described how she has recently been diagnosed with diabetes and her poor health is restricting joint activities with her granddaughter, and a third is losing her eyesight which again is limiting her ability to look after her grandson.

Another grandmother spoke of high blood pressure, resulting in part from the stress of looking after two grandchildren as well as helping her daughter to stay 'in rehab' to deal with her drug problems:

With your own children you can enforce boundaries because you are their mother. They have come from your body. But you can only go so far with them if you are their grandmother. You are not really their parent.

With someone else he may have behaved a bit better. They (young people) are more likely to take grandparents for granted.

Child safety, inter-family conflict, resources and practical issues

The safety of the child
In some families where the child was taken into local authority care this was as a direct result of risk of abuse or actual abuse, and a potential and serious disadvantage of kinship care is that of placing an abused child back into an abusing family. This is why both a full kinship care assessment and risk assessment needs to be made in all cases, prior to any kinship care placement being proposed. Then if a kinship care placement is agreed, that a systematic ongoing support strategy be put in place (see Chapter 10).

Inter-family conflict and resentment
Kinship care is not always the preferred option for carers and birth parents. One social worker explained:

... although they are more willing to become kinship carers, it's not what they would have chosen ... some have very difficult teenagers on their hands, (they) talk about a big impact on their lives, they can't go out ... It's not what they had planned in their lives.

In other cases the feeling amounted to bitterness. The following examples were provided:

I've got grandparents who are looking after three grandchildren and doing so has caused them to become quite resentful towards both their daughter and her husband. They feel lumbered and feel they shouldn't be doing this, their daughter and her husband are just living their own lives. It doesn't seem fair to them.

It's certainly true in shared care and temporary care, that some parents would prefer us (the local authority) to look after children rather than relatives help them.

Some social workers felt that the combination of ageing grandparents and difficult teenagers can be too difficult and wondered whether kinship care works better when younger children are involved, although acknowledged that younger children sooner or later become teenagers.

To many social workers the disadvantages and limits of kinship care were concerned with how difficult and therefore off-putting kinship care was to organise. The lack of a supportive framework is a major disadvantage for social workers, kinship carers and children and young people living in a kinship care placement.

Unsuitable accommodation
Sometimes there is not adequate space to look after an additional relative. A related problem is what happens to any siblings? In one family for example, the oldest of five children was living with a relative. His younger siblings who are in foster care arrangements that are not working out want to join him. The social worker stated 'they are all desperate to be claimed but the kinship carer simply does not have the capacity to look after the whole family'.

Contact issues
The social workers found it difficult and in many cases did not consider it appropriate for them to facilitate suitable contact arrangements with birth parents and other members of the family. For example one child whose parents suffered alcohol problems was placed with an older sister. The parents would turn up whenever they wanted which distressed the child and undermined the caring role of her sister.

Parenting skills
One social worker described how the parents of some of the young people she has met have been so damaged by their upbringing that it is hard to imagine how the grandparents could look after the grandchildren. This however was not a universal view – other social workers argued that

circumstances may well have changed since grandparents raised their first family and that life experience is an important asset to parenting.

Geography

In some cases kinship carers live outside the borough. This means that maintaining contact with the young person can be costly and time consuming. It also seemed much more difficult for social services to arrange outside borough supports for such families.

Organisational issues

Social workers also spoke of major organisational, policy and funding concerns that hindered the development of kinship care. These focused on a lack of resources, and proper planning and financial supports for children and young people living in a kinship care placement.

Concluding comments

In assessing the suitability of kinship care, whether family and friends foster care or a kinship care arrangement outside the 'looked after' system, such as family support (Children Act 1989 S17), risk and resilience issues will need addressing. An assessment of protective and risk factors is essential and, if kinship care is considered the appropriate placement, a comprehensive plan for providing support and services needs to be included in all good practice (Broad and Skinner, forthcoming). The advantages and disadvantages of formal kinship care, as with other placement options, centre on the needs of the particular child, judgements about safety and family relationships, and practical issues. (A model to incorporate the dyad of kinship placements is offered in Chapter 10.) The kinship care research study's findings summarised here clearly indicate that according to the children and young people, often with experience of other placement options, who are living in a kinship care placement, has many more advantages than disadvantages. However this relative 'success' must not be at the expense of the health and well being of the kinship carer. That is the challenge that lies ahead.

References

Broad, B. (Ed.) (2001) *Kinship Care: The Placement Choice for Children and Young People*. Lyme Regis: Russell House Publishing.

Broad, B. (2004) Kinship Care for Children in the UK: Messages From Research, Lessons for Policy and Practice. *European Journal of Social Work*. 7: 2, 211–27.

Broad, B. and Skinner, A. (2006) *Relative Benefits*. London: BAAF.

Hampshire Council (2001) Family and Friends Carers Project. *unpublished report*, Hampshire County Council.

Jackson, S. and Thomas, N. (1997) *On the Move Again? What Works in Creating Stability for Looked After Children*. Barkingside: Barnardo's.

Laws, S. and Broad, B. (2000) *Looking After Children Within the Extended Family: Carers Views*. Leicester: Centre for Social Action, De Montfort University.

McFadden, E.J. (1998) Kinship care in the United States. *Adoption and Fostering*. 22: 3, 7–15.

Waterhouse, S. (2001) Keeping Children in Kinship Placements Within Court Proceedings. In Broad, B. (Ed.) op. cit., 40–6.

Webster, G. (2000) *Use of Kinship Care Placements in Hertfordshire*. Hertfordshire Social Services Department.

West, A. (1995) *You're on Your Own: Young People's Research on Leaving Care*. London: Save the Children.

Chapter Three

Contemporary Assessment: A Critique

Martin C Calder and Cath Talbot

Introduction

This chapter will argue that the current nationally available and mandated assessment structures are inappropriate for application with kinship placements. This contributes to the often problematic contexts in which kinship placements are being considered as placement choices for children and young people. There will be an opening contextualisation of the assessment task and then a critical discussion of the BAAF Form F and the assessment framework (DoH, 2000). This will then uncover the problematic demise of the concept of risk in social work practice and the implications of this for the assessment and support of kinship care considered. A conceptual framework to develop kinship care provision is offered with the aim that it will pave the way for the introduction of a new, sensitive, evidence-based framework for the assessment of kinship placements (see Chapter 10).

The context for current assessment practice

We are experiencing a period of perpetual change in the childcare field, with a continued initiative explosion from central government. Space does not allow for a detailed critique about this although overall there is concern that:

- There is a general inability of the government to make meaningful connections between seemingly disparate initiatives, leaving significant remedial integrative work to be undertaken locally.
- There is little evidence of practice-based materials evolving to support the conceptually-grounded frameworks on offer.
- There is no evidence that any single initiative has been evaluated as a preface to issuing further guidance in the same subject field.
- Allegedly universal materials such as the assessment framework (DoH, 2000) failing to embrace either all the separate disciplines or

even the separate domains that comprise childcare. For example, the assessment framework does not address fostering issues at all whether they are stranger or kinship placements. The well written theoretical material in respect of disabled children and children from ethnic minority groups does not translate into practice tools. Black children continue to be marginalised (Ince, 2001).

There is interestingly no clear model of assessment that unifies all childcare work and this is worrying since the exportation of particular frameworks is inappropriate when applied to varying populations. For example, it is inappropriate to export the assessment framework to assessment practice with foster carers and it is equally inappropriate to export it to kinship placements. It is equally inappropriate to export the BAAF Form F to kinship placements when it was developed for use with stranger foster placement assessments. Indeed, O'Brien (2001) noted that superimposing the assessment model and approach traditionally used with foster parents has and continues to cause problems, as the process by which the relatives becomes connected with the agency, the different demographic profile of the relatives, the fact that the placement is already made, and the family connection between relatives, birth parents and children, are not provided for in the traditional model. The traditional framework was developed to prepare stranger foster parents for a hypothetical child at an imagined future date, which is very different from the characteristics of the relative placement.

Partnership issues

Calder (1995) has pointed to the need to balance partnership and paternalism in any child protection work, rather than swinging the pendulum backwards and forwards between the two. With the emergence of the assessment framework we are likely to witness an operational shift towards paternalistic practice (with the emphasis on getting the job done) away from partnership practice so strongly advocated by government in recent years (DoH, 1995). This is supported in part by the impact of the timescales on professional practice, but it is reinforced through the range of partnership models and the link between the restricted provision of a social work service with an alternative model of assessment. This merits further exploration. There are four possible models of partnership for professionals to choose from:

- **The expert model:** where the professional takes control and makes all the decisions, giving a low priority to parents' views, wishes or feelings, the sharing of information, or the need for negotiation.
- **The transplant (of expertise) model:** where the professional sees the parent as a resource and hands over some skills, but retains control of the decision-making.
- **The consumer model:** where it is assumed that parents have the right to decide and select what they believe to be appropriate, and the decision-making is ultimately in their control.
- **The social network/systems model:** where parents, children and professionals are part of a network of formal and informal development, and social support for the family and the child. They are capable of supplementing existing resources via the facilitation of the social worker who should draw more on the extended family while complying with statutory requirements.

The danger is that workers revert back to the 'expert' model in order to prioritise the timescale above all other considerations. This fits well with the likely choice of assessment style selected by the worker and this is discussed further in Chapter 4.

Models of assessment

The way social problems are understood and defined will vary greatly according to class, culture, religion, ethnicity and geography. Family structures, values, beliefs, attitudes and behaviours are mostly socially constructed and generate different patterns of parenting behaviour that may be apparent to each family member but less so to outside professionals

(Nixon, 2001). Smale et al. (1993) identified three possible models of assessment: the *questioning model*, the *exchange model* and the *procedural model*. The key difference between the models is in how power is used and the impact of this on the service user. Only the exchange model will empower the client to be fully involved as an equal partner in a process of negotiating the nature of 'their problem' and its possible 'solutions' through an appropriate 'tailor-made' response.

The *questioning model* assumes the worker:

- Is expert in people, their problems and in identifying needs.
- Exercises knowledge and skill to form 'their' assessment, identify people's needs.
- Identifies resources required.
- Takes responsibility for making an accurate assessment of need and taking appropriate action.

In this model, the professional gathers information from 'the client' and their carers, forms an assessment of their needs or problems and then works on a solution. The worker's behaviour is dominated by asking questions, listening to and processing the answers, using the information gained to form 'an assessment'. The questions reflect the worker's agenda, not other peoples'. Enshrined in the questions asked will be implicit or explicit criteria or perceptions of the problems that people 'like the client' have, and a view of the resources available to meet them. In this model it is assumed that questions can be answered in a straightforward manner, or that the professional is able to accurately interpret what the client really wants even when they cannot or do not express it. The complexities of communication across cultural and other boundaries, such as race, ethnicity as defined by professionals, gender, class, disability or professional reference group and organisational allegiance, tend to be underestimated or even ignored. An 'accurate professional assessment' may be enough to identify 'need', but it is not enough if goals include increasing the choices of the people involved or maximising people's potential. Additional skills are needed for work with people, that empower them to have as much control over their lives as possible and specifically enables them to exercise choice in how their needs may be met. The worker never has a monopoly of knowledge and can never replace the insight clients bring into their problems and themselves. People are, and always will be the expert on themselves, their situation, their relationships, what they want and need. They also bring a certain degree of control over their own behaviour that professionals will never have and so be able to influence the viability of the present and future relationships that underpin a plan of intervention. One can see that the framework set out in the 'orange book' (DOH, 1988) lends itself to this style of assessment. However, after much research, there was a shift from paternalistic to partnership-based practice, as characterised by the exchange model.

The *exchange model* assumes that people are expert in themselves and that the worker:

- Has expertise in the process of problem solving with others.
- Understands and shares perceptions of problems and their management.
- Gets agreement about who will do what to support whom.
- Takes responsibility for arriving at the optimum resolution of problems within the constraints of available resources and the willingness of the participants to contribute.

In the exchange model, the professional concentrates on an exchange of information between themselves and the client and others. The question and answer pattern of behaviour is avoided. The professional works to engage with the people involved either together or in series and each person's participation is negotiable. The behaviour of the professional is crucial in establishing the respect and the trust of others and will vary over time. Perceptions of the situation, its problems, availability of resources and the need for more, are shared. A definition of the 'problems' and their resolution or management, are arrived at as much through the initiative of the clients (and significant others) as by the professional (such as family group conferences) and is often the product of interaction between them. The worker often negotiates with a range of people to get agreement about who should do what for whom rather than making 'an assessment' and organising a package of care or protection as the latter implies control. In this sense the professional can never be responsible for the whole package. Each participant is responsible for their own contribution, or lack of it.

Typically the professional will not lead the content of the dialogue because they will not know any more, if as much, as the other people about the situation, its problems, or what existing resources could contribute to 'the solution'. The professional follows or tracks what the other people say and communicate. To lead is to assume that the professional knows where to go and often this will go straight to a service-led response.

However, the assessor should be the expert in identifying the relationships between people. This includes understanding how the client's behaviour supports the current situation, and how this may be changed to support a different pattern of relationships so that the problem can be managed differently or even resolved. Professionals need to be able to recognise, understand and intervene in the patterns of relationships that precipitate and perpetuate social problems.

Although the theory underpinning the exchange model is supported by research studies, there are some potential problems with this approach:

- The communication of what people need and want is very complicated and has to include an exploration of, and take into account, the different assumptions of the two or more people involved, the different languages that they use, think and feel in, and the different levels of communication that exist.
- Communication across ethnic, racial, class, gender, professional, or other cultural boundaries needs particular care if preconceived assumptions and prejudices are not going to lead to misunderstandings or worse.
- People have their own ideas, beliefs and knowledge; they are not passive or neutral receivers waiting for messages. In practice, communicators enter into dialogues with people who interpret messages in accordance with their own assumptions and beliefs, which may or may not be the same as the communicators.

The exchange model can be a difficult, complex and time-consuming process for agencies, especially since the client has a greater say in the management of their situation. However, it is clearly much more likely to empower clients and create a framework for their engagement in the assessment and then the problem-solving process. It is also unlikely to allow workers to complete the assessment in the required timescale unless it is their only case. This is an important issue. We have already identified that many social work agencies are establishing thresholds for the provision of services given the mismatch between likely need and available resources. This thus suggests that workers will be manoeuvred from the exchange to the procedural model of assessment.

In the procedural model, the goal of the assessment is to gather information to see if the client 'fits' or meets certain criteria that will make them eligible for services. Those defining the criteria for eligibility, in effect pre-allocating services for generally identified need make the judgement as to what sort of person should get which resources. The worker's task is to identify the specific people who match the appropriate degree of need defined within the categories of service available and to exclude those not eligible. This model represents a variation to the questioning model where the professional is assumed to be the expert in identifying need. In the procedural model, it is assumed that the managers drawing up guidelines for workers have expertise in setting the criteria for resource allocation. To this extent they are experts in how problems should be managed and resources allocated. In this model the worker will complete a referral form and/or an initial assessment with or without the client's involvement. Questions are asked and/or information gathered to answer each of the questions deemed relevant by those setting criteria for resource allocation. The information typically sought attempts to:

- Categorise the 'client'.
- Define the nature of the client's needs in the terms that services are offered, that is whether the client's needs make them eligible for services actually or potentially available.
- Gather information required for agency statistics to aid service planning.

Some of the issues such an approach raises include:

- The client's definitions of their problems or that of others may not be included.
- The client is not empowered by the process and they rarely get choices about the outcome.
- Worker judgement beyond interpreting information and deciding on how to complete

the necessary documentation is not required. They have little room for manoeuvre, acting as agents of their managers.
- The agenda is set by the agency and not the worker or the client.
- Clients may be labelled by workers to ensure they are eligible for a service.

The goal of the procedural model is legitimate when managers are responsible for the allocation of services to meet need within resource constraints placed upon them. It provides a quick, simple, practical and cost-effective approach of identifying clients who are eligible for available resources. If the decision as to who gets what is grounded in professional judgement rather than on the available resources, then workers should use the questioning model. The issue of partnership with children as well as the adults compounds the difficulties of the timescale, as we are also expected to work at their pace and to employ techniques likely to empower them in the process. We also have a professional obstacle to overcome: transforming the worker view that working with children is a problem to be overcome rather than the basis of good practice (Calder and Horwath, 2000).

Most assessment processes are based upon 'expert questioning' or 'procedural' models of assessment. These mainly focus on family pathologies and deficits, or agency criteria of eligibility and rely on professionals or agency determining 'need' and what questions should be asked of others. Far less attention is paid in these models to harnessing family strengths or their own definition of their needs or difficulties. Nixon (2001) noted that any collaborative assessment should take account of all members of the family system and strengths, and the adoption of the exchange model would appear to fit this bill, geared as it is toward greater user participation and attempts to give clients a greater say over their needs. This is a vital component of kinship assessments. For politicians and senior managers this is problematic as it is a more complex task that takes longer and involves more people.

Issues for consideration in assessing kinship placements

Waterhouse (2001) argued that the threshold for assessing kinship placements requires some exploration and amendment. She asked 'how competent does a relative have to be in order to be permitted by the local authority and court to care for a child of the family?' If a parent became unable to care through a fatal accident or illness, a relative in all likelihood would step in to take over responsibility for the child without any need to be assessed as suitable by the state. However, a model of kinship care often prevails in care proceedings where relatives have to prove their ability through assessment to take on the care of the child. This suggests that there is a higher threshold to cross in such circumstances and this may take account of factors such as criminal convictions (such as fraud or handling stolen goods), medical histories or age profiles that make panels respond negatively to such placements. Local authority social services' departments may often be 'split' within the process of care planning. In the event that a relative is approved as a foster carer for the child, the financing, support and training available to such carers is often set at a lower and inferior standard to that of local authority foster carers. This is unfortunate since it is precisely these placements that need the support of the local authority in these identified areas of need. (In Chapter 2, Broad reported on the support matters for kinship carers.)

O'Brien (2001) identified that the assessment of relatives challenges many of the theoretical, professional and organisational bases on which assessments are currently organised. In the process, the agency is confronted with many practical and ethical difficulties. At a practice level, much of the confusion surrounding relative assessments can be traced to the fact that the process is occurring in a context of competing ideologies. The values of partnership and empowerment, on which the self-selection model of assessment is built and which social workers aspire to, are somewhat at variance with practices and values underlying the social control function of child protection practice, which results in a paradoxical situation for both worker and relative. This is compounded further by the protracted nature of the process and the multiple roles and tasks during the assessment stage of relative placements.

The literature suggests that concerns about the welfare of the child in relative care arise in a context where there is:

- A lack of rigorous pre-placement assessment and less monitoring of relative placements.

- Confusion regarding assessment framework to determine suitability of relative homes.
- An implicit agenda among professionals about the relatives inability to protect the child in light of the difficulties of the birth parents (O'Brien, 2001).

It is essential that workers ensure that they avoid problematising a situation which may have many strengths. Indeed, Portengen and van der Neut (1999) have pointed out that social workers can tend to focus on individuals and their problems, whereas family work needs a wider view of a network of relationships. The confusion about what constitutes adequate protection, and what level of support, assessment and supervision is necessary is at the heart of many of the difficulties in relative care, and reflects the fact that a specific model for working with relative care has not yet been developed (O'Brien, 2001).

Family group conferences

Most social workers work with parents and their children, usually the mother, rather than with the wider family. Even when there is an awareness and acknowledgement that the wider family is involved, there is often uncertainty and hesitancy about formalising their involvement. Workers are often anxious about breaching client confidentiality when approaching extended family, although the advent and experiences of the family group conferences has clearly located such reluctance with the professionals rather than with the family. One of the few strengths of the assessment framework is that it encourages workers to consider family and environmental factors when undertaking assessments.

Nixon (2001) pointed out that the growing interest in family group conferences reflects the underlying and continued frustrations over the inability of practitioners and their agencies to work collaboratively or manage the practice tensions between the role of families and the state in relation to children. Research evidence shows that partnership approaches are still conspicuously thin on the ground. Workers find themselves operating with organizational structures and a culture in which service users are routinely marginalised, compounded by practice dictated by eligibility criteria and thresholds approaching child protection, rendering partnership problematic when involved in a social control role with increasingly involuntary clients (Calder, 2003). The family group conference approach conceptually turns the orthodox models of child welfare decision making (built on a culture of professional expertise and control) on their head, by becoming a family meeting to which the professionals are invited.

The two assessment structures: a critique

Good practice is about empowering and engaging families, even in the context of difficulties and conflict. Currently, there are two accepted formats for assessment, used for prospective carers. These are the BAAF Form F, report on prospective substitute carers and the DoH Framework for the Assessment of Children in Need and their Families, the mandatory assessment structure, now inconsistently understood, but widely attempted. Instructions from the Department of Health, Home Office and the Department for Education and Employment (April 2000) state that 'guidance is issued under section 7 of the Local Authority Social Services Act, 1970, which means that it must be followed by the local authority social services unless there are exceptional circumstances that justify a variation' .Yet the framework is weak in respect of its consideration of kinship placements. Kinship carers have a different profile to stranger carers, e.g., they are often older, suffer poorer health, overcrowding and are less affluent. Many are living in poverty. There are often complexities in kinship placements that are less often present in stranger placements. One issue is the management of contact and conflict, which should be made explicit in kinship assessments if the report is to produce realistic and child-focused conclusions. The new Special Guardian provisions will require all prospective carers to be assessed, and within a more demanding and defined timescale.

Both frameworks are systematically applied, irrespective of whether the carer is known to the child. It is our argument that this practice is inappropriate and promotes the risk of excluding many kinship carers, who have the potential to provide the best placement option for the child. Kinship carers often do not share the opportunities, advantages and resources of many of the population of stranger carers. It is crucial

that current research evidence in respect of kinship placements is understood and applied. These placements offer a qualitatively different experience to children. As opposed to the very poor outcomes for many 'looked after' children, kinship placements are often more stable and provide care for many of the children who are deemed 'hard to place'.

The DoH framework for assessment

The DoH Framework for the Assessment of Children in Need and their Families is a triangular, ecological model that directs the assessor to consider three general areas: a profile of the child, the family and parenting capacity, and the wider environment. These areas are broken down into 20 categories that should be addressed in the assessment report. The component of the child's developmental needs, for example, includes health, education, emotional and behavioural development, identity, family and social arrangements, social presentation and self-care skills. The component of family and environmental factors has seven categories that includes 'wider family' but does not offer further encouragement to consider issues in respect of kinship placements. The framework is based on a comprehensive analysis of research evidence and the pack contains 103 references, yet only one title explicitly includes family and friends carers.

The framework is based on ten general principles – that assessment:

- should be child centred
- rooted in child development
- be ecological
- ensure equality of opportunity
- involve children and families
- build on strengths as well as identifying difficulties
- involve inter agency working
- be a process (not a single event)
- parallel the provision of services and
- be grounded in evidence-based knowledge.

These are important principles, to be supported and translated into practice but it is unfortunate that there is no explicit principle that children should live within their families, wherever this is possible, notwithstanding the clear acknowledgement of this by the courts and by virtue of Article 8 of the European Convention.

An additional difficulty is that we are now conducting assessments without a clear concept of risk, because the framework solely operates around the concept of need. 'Risk' and 'need' are not the same, yet attached to every need is a risk, for example, that the need is not being met (Calder and Hackett, 2003). Whilst contemporary research is positive about children's experiences of kinship care, not all kinship placements will be safe. Victoria Climbié tragically died in a kinship placement and we now have a further major critique of poor professional practice and managerial incompetence across child protection agencies (Laming, 2003). The loss of the concept of risk is a significant difficulty in all contemporary assessment work.

Assessment of parenting should have a dual function: to present information which has been analysed in the context of research evidence and pertinent theoretical frameworks. Of at least equal importance, is the concept of the capacity to change behaviour. Again, the framework is limited in this respect and it is necessary to supplement, with a model such as that used by Reder and Lucey (1995). This concept may often take on increased importance when working with prospective kinship carers, who are often in families where there have been significant difficulties. The capacity to change can only be measured over time, when clear and honest feedback has been given in respect of the individual's cognitive and behavioural patterns. The assessor needs to apply the fundamental components of the capacity to change: an examination of the motivation of the individual; an ability and willingness to acknowledge problems, and an ability to see professional intervention as valid and helpful (Reder and Lucey, 1995). Without this component, assessments risk limiting potential for the child, and promote pessimism and the model of 'family dysfunction'.

Many of the scales and questionnaires are helpful assessment tools, though we would question the Eurocentric and class biases, and comment that it is unfortunate that much of the very well written theoretical material in respect of black and disabled children does not translate into practical assessment tools. We are strongly supportive of the framework's principle of child centred practice; though remain concerned that it is poorly understood. It is of such importance that

we have extracted from the text the argument that:

> ... the approach must be child centred. This means that the child is seen and kept in focus throughout the assessment and that account is always taken of the child's perspective ... The significance of seeing and observing the child throughout any assessment cannot be understated.
> (DoH, 2000)

The Form F

The BAAF Form F structure is a generally psychodynamic model, with concepts borrowed from 'systemic' theory. Whilst histories and chronologies are highly valid, important information is often missed when there is a primary focus on the past. Relative assessments must account for recent history and a capacity to change, when relevant. Greeff (2001) would add that families do not ever have one objective truth. Rather, they have a plurality of truths and the pursuit of uni-causal explanation is naïve. Assessments must consider power dynamics, historical change and, crucially, they must accept and value social difference (Clifford, 1999). The assessment should collate evidence in respect of communication patterns. As Worrall (1999) summarises, risk potential is minimised when family connections are strong, when goals and expectations are shared and when the environment is emotionally positive.

In reality, local authority fostering panels are often bureaucratic, inflexible processes that have potential to exclude relatives who offer the best placement choice for the child. These exclusions may relate to difficulties in respect of age, health, past criminal convictions and material resources. Much of this is class bias and is ignorant of the outcomes for children who live in kinship placements. In the USA, some states formally recognise the distinct contribution of families and friends carers and have separate approval systems for relative carers. This assessment process should shift from one of 'approval' to one of 'enabling' (Waterhouse, 2001). In concluding the excellent contribution to the kinship debate, Broad raises questions about the very nature of fostering itself, arguing the case for moving away from the value base, which pursues two adults in a nuclear household (Broad, 2001). The Form F does not challenge that narrow view. A different model of assessment for relative carers is needed quite simply because there are different issues for consideration. We are not assessing a dyad of parent and child, but a triad of child, parent and family. Children, birth parents and relative carers need support. The best chance for achieving support is through pertinent and thorough assessment work. Elsewhere, it has been recognised that there are competing ideologies in social work practice (Broad, 2004; Talbot and Williams, 2003; Tapsfield, 2001). The model of 'control' that is intrinsic to child protection intervention does not sit easily with a model of partnership and empowerment (Calder, 2003). Traditional models of assessment are unhelpful to children and families and they contribute to delay (O'Brien, 2001).

Risk and the current assessment process

In the most recently issued government guidance (DoH, 1999; DoH, 2000) terms such as 'protection', 'abuse' and 'risk' have largely been replaced by 'safeguard', 'promote', 'welfare' and 'need'. Indeed, 'need' is being promulgated as the central organising thesis for future social work policy and practice, with usage of the term 'risk' being eschewed and discouraged (Calder, 2000). This 'new language' may be promoted as being more muted, wider in meaning, less stigmatising, less confrontational and hence more appropriate to a partnership with families approach. They may even argue that the concept of risk is encapsulated within the broad-based concept of need. This change deserves a close analysis.

The government appears to be jettisoning the concept of risk and risk assessment in their latest guidance in favour of a needs-led assessment. This appears to be premised on a partial understanding in government of what a risk assessment is. The DoH assessment guidance of 1988 was built almost entirely on the notions of risk and dangerousness yet these do not appear to have been satisfactorily defined or applied in practice. This may be because it is a term which is often misused in social work because it focuses exclusively on the risk of harm, whereas in any other enterprise a risk equation also includes a chance of benefit resulting (Carson, 1994).

Any risk assessment, should, therefore, be concerned with weighing up the pros and cons of a child's circumstances in order to inform decision-making as to what should happen with

regard to intervention and protection. It involves examining the child and family situation to identify and weigh various risk factors (such as parents, family or other influences that increase the likelihood that a child will be harmed in a certain way) family strengths, family resources, and available agency services. This assessment information can then be used to determine if a child is safe, what agency resources are needed to keep the child safe, and under what circumstances a child should be removed from the family. This understanding of risk is one that is applied on a daily basis in their cases and most definitely in any case being presented to court.

The government appears to be deleting risk for several reasons: in the hope that by deleting risk the association with section 47 child protection investigation will go, and to reinforce this the need to address enquiries pre-investigation is also restated; in the hope that workers will introduce the new concept of assessing and working with client strengths; and in the hope that workers will focus more on 'need'. Unfortunately, this is not convincing when there is repeated backtracking from needs-led assessments to a reminder that the child's safety is the primary objective of professional intervention. Workers will be conscious of the consequences of getting it wrong.

One of the more confusing issues is that at a time in which the government is moving away from notions of risk, there are huge developments in risk assessments emerging in the field of sexual abuse (see Calder, 2000) as well as a move towards risk management in most allied professions. There is also a concern for workers that all their experience of 'risk assessments' in the past is redundant and should no longer be applied to cases. What they need is an up-to-date and accessible framework for assessing risk that they can use to guide their interventions (set out in Calder, 2000).

One of the key issues is where risk as a concept sits within the needs-led framework, particularly when the framework is failing to address child protection issues and many authorities are reintroducing their old documentation to supplement the framework records. This has now officially been looked at by the authors of the record who may consider 'developing some standardised child protection materials to support the integration of child protection procedures with the core assessment process'.

Donnelly (2001) explored the usefulness of the concept of risk as a way of thinking about possible future outcomes as an aid to social work planning. She concluded that rather than seeing the term as a 'hot potato' (difficult to handle and a history of already having 'burnt many fingers') we should see it as part of our everyday life. We should thus see the term as:

> ... an apt and essential feature of our language and its judicious usage, aided by an informed understanding, could enhance rather than undermine partnerships with families ... The framework represents an opportunity lost to define the concept of risk; to explain its chequered history; and to begin to educate social workers on its potential benefits and current limitations. Such an understanding becomes particularly salient when seeking to translate assessment conclusions into future hypotheses and casework plans: risk prediction is fundamental to needs-based planning (p14)

> ... it is difficult to identify how the framework or its materials can assist with risk prediction in seeking to determine whether a child is safe; how to deal with conflicting needs (e.g. siblings of different ages whose needs for permanency and contact may be very different); and in the translation of assessment conclusions into final plans (p19)

> ... In failing to engage with the concept of risk, the framework has failed to provide social workers with significant technical information with which to inform their assessments (p20).

By failing to address the concept of risk, the framework has failed to 'grasp the nettle' and so begin the process of re-definition, education and debate. Social workers and their managers will continue to engage with risk but in the context of official guidance that has nothing specific to say on the subject. The consequences are likely to be a combination of 'best efforts' and 'untutored responses'. The framework misses the opportunity explicitly to advise on current understandings and the result is a perpetuation of a situation in which risk remains poorly understood and lacking in robust evidence. This has, and will continue to have significant consequences for children and their families.

Towards a conceptual framework for kinship assessment

Calder (1999) developed a useful conceptual model to guide local responses to national problems not attended to satisfactorily by central government (see Figure 3.1 overleaf). This can be used as an organizing framework for where the current state of play is in relation to kinship care in the UK.

Aims and purpose

There has to be a local explicit agreement and a shared understanding between workers and agencies about the aims and purpose of work in the kinship care field. If individuals and agencies are working with different aims, they will interpret their roles and responsibilities in different ways.

No one department on its own can address the full range of problems currently apparent in the kinship care field. There has therefore to be an initial recognition of the need to collaborate, a belief that it cannot be tackled by departments or individuals operating alone, and a perception that the benefits far outweigh the costs of so doing. There must be detailed consensus between individuals and departments on what constitutes kinship care. (This is debated further below.)

There is certainly a change required in the attitude of professionals if they are to view kinship care as the primary placement route rather than second best as currently exists. Research in the USA and UK indicate that kinship placements are very enduring and have a high level of stability and satisfaction. Indeed, they are often more stable placements than those made with traditional foster carers (see Chapter 2). However, such placements are often less effectively monitored and supported than traditional foster care despite their complexity often requiring additional supports (Waterhouse, 2001).

It is worth articulating the advantages of kinship placement as it informs any aims and purposes by local authorities:

- The child is spared the trauma of separation. Adoptions may be fraught with difficulties and should certainly not be seen as a general panacea for children in need.
- It is easier for the child to explain that they are now living with family than unrelated carers.
- They are much more likely to be placed with siblings and to have contact with their parents.
- The people and the way of life in the kinship placement are familiar and probably consistent with their previous experience.

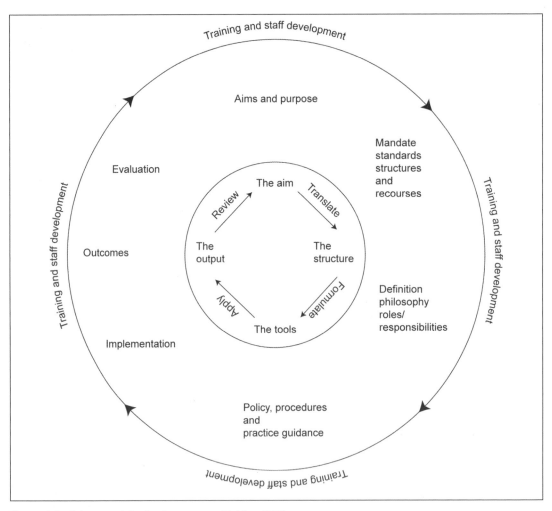

Figure 3.1   A framework for local responses (Calder, 1999)

- Children's needs are better served by kinship rather than stranger care and this is often driven by an investment in the child's future.
- Kinship placements frequently better reflect the child's cultural background and this is linked to identity and self-esteem. Identity is promoted also through a sense of family knowledge and history.
- Kinship placements strengthen families and promote family responsibility. The family acts with collective responsibility for the child. Plans from the family are often more detailed and imaginative than those put forward by professionals, often due to the reality that they are drawing from a wider base of information about their family.

Tapsfield (2001) identified three issues that have prevented social services committing to kinship care despite the research supporting it as a viable and important option:

- They are fearful of being overwhelmed by demand if they were to advertise support services for kinship carers.
- They are fearful of losing professional control and the added complications of involving the wider family. Relatives who are foster carers can be seen as a threat by social workers as they know more about the children and may not be as compliant as non-relative carers. The loyalty of the kinship carer is more likely to be with the child than the agency.

• There is an assumption about parents who fail and this suggests that weakness-orientated approaches implicate the wider family also, ruling them out of consideration.

Broad et al. (2001) identified the following views from young people and carers' about kinship care (see opposite):

support rather than questioning. Waterhouse (2001) suggests that we need to move from an 'approving' to 'enabling' basis with such relatives.

The Department of Health shows an interest in kinship care and recognises the importance of family and friends assessments. It makes reference to a requirement to approach

Young people's views	Kinship carers' views
• Feeling loved, valued and cared for. • Belonging and feeling settled. • Wanting to be with people they know. • Sustaining a sense of who they are (identity) through maintaining contact with family, friends and siblings. • Feeling safe from harm or threatening behaviour of adults. • Being rescued from or not being sent into stranger local authority foster care. • Being listened to.	• Their love for the young person and love and desire to support the birth parents. • The family is the best place to raise young people. • To avoid local authority care. • To support a sense of belonging, and racial and cultural heritage.

Mandate, standards, structures and resources

In order to effectively respond, there needs to be a clear mandate. This is especially so given the climate where social services are introducing explicit thresholds for the provision of a social work service that is often at a child protection level and which demands other agencies construct referrals that cross the defined threshold (see Calder, 2003 for a detailed discussion on this point). The threshold for assessment in kinship care cases is relevant here. An important question to be asked is 'how competent does a relative have to be in order to be permitted by the local authority and court to care for a child?' If a parent became unable to care for a child through illness or accident, a relative in all likelihood would step in to take over responsibility for the child without any need to be assessed as suitable by the state. This is not the case in legal proceedings where the best interests of the child must be considered and often this involves intrusive assessments that often require the carers cross a higher threshold for approval than stranger carers. This may revolve around issues such as a criminal record such as handling stolen goods or around age or health profiles which can result in negative spins on the placement being cast. It could be argued that such placements are most in need of agency

assessment differently because attachments may already be strong and supportive and these kinship relationships need to be balanced with other issues. The Department of Health discussion paper: *Family and Friends Care*, November, 2002, make direct reference to the research of Broad (2001) and Broad et al. (2001) and states that care planning for the child must consider ways of retaining the positive involvement of the extended family: it must support attachments and emotional stability. The paper accepts that children in family and friends placements express an emotional permanence and that carers are passionate about their roles.

Considerable uncertainty exists in local authorities about the proper role in supporting and promoting kinship care. There are individuals and departments who see kinship care as the responsibility of families who think that there is an expectation on relatives to step in and look after children whose own parents are unable to do this. They think families should take on these responsibilities without seeking any help from the state. Others see kinship care as the responsibility of the state and as an alternative to residential or foster care. They think relatives should receive adequate financial and other support to care for children who might otherwise be looked after in stranger foster care or residential care. These different views lead to different services to families being offered. These can best be seen by considering the very different approaches local authorities have to relatives as foster carers, the varied policies around residence orders allowances, the absence of information about support for relatives and the lack of policies about how the wider family is involved in decision making (Broad, 2001; Tapsfield, 2001).

Once a common aim and purpose has been agreed among senior managers, this needs to be enshrined in some local mandate to ensure that each department cannot deny their roles and responsibilities. There is a need to develop a sense of shared meaning, vision, belonging, and inter-dependence. This can be achieved by developmental work which looks at building confidence, understanding and trust in each other's roles, sharing anxieties and feelings, trouble shooting tensions and conflicts early on, and identifying local needs and resources.

Alongside mandate is best value: a government initiative to make public services more accountable and ensure that they provide a high quality service. The current climate of childcare provision and the poor options of stranger foster care and residential care are abundantly evident in the media, literature and inquiry reports.

Standards offer the baseline for quality assurance, audit and inspection, and provide a benchmark against which both agency and professional performance can be measured. They should be constructed with reference to the available resources and thus have to be both realistic and attainable. They should not be seen as a benchmark against which workers constantly fall short. Any standards produced require cross-department support. A failure to provide such standards ignores the emotional aspects of the job and the impact upon the workers. It also leaves managers 'high and dry' when managing the work as there is no agreed baseline from which to work.

Unlike fostering and residential care, kinship care does not have a dedicated organisational structure or focus: this is needed as a matter of priority for it to be a coherent placement option (Broad et al., 2001). Structures would clearly be needed in all of the departments and agencies that have a responsibility for dealing with this area of work. Once an infrastructure is in place, it can be used as the platform from which to construct a corporate framework of response.

Resources are a big issue when we don't have many. It is unfair to ask workers to address kinship care in a more supportive and enlightened way in the absence of the necessary resources. If a relative is approved as a foster carer for the child, the financing, support and training available to such carers is often set at a lower and inferior standard to that of local authority foster carers. Loss of earnings, loss of future plans, plus the extra costs of taking on an additional child need to be taken into account by local authorities in considering how such placements are to be successful. Laws (2001) reported the views of carers when asked what was important to them. The main themes were the need for more financial assistance, and a variety of needs around social support and checks on carers and children (see also Laws and Broad, 2000).

Definition, philosophy, roles and responsibilities and theory: offering a corporate baseline

Definition is important as it sets out clearly the parameters of the issue under consideration. There is no clarity or consensus currently as to what kinship care actually is. The term kinship care may refer to the informal arrangements which take place outside the child welfare system and the jurisdiction of the courts, or the formal arrangements which are arranged or approved by the child welfare agencies or through the courts. There remain a number of definitional problems over what is meant by kinship care. For example, does it refer specifically to extended family or a wider group of non-relative friends of family? Wheal (2001) suggested a starting point as being an acknowledgement of the diversity of the placements – aunts, uncles, parents, neighbours, friends of carer, friends of family, teacher of child, friend of mother, step-father, older sister, but most often, grandparents. Waterhouse (2001) in her research established that a notable feature was the range of different relatives who offered care: 44 per cent were individuals other than a grandparent of the child and more than one in ten had no blood relationship to the child.

Wheal (2001) argued that to enable policies to be defined a series of groupings is needed:

- **Group A – where the state is involved:** containing all children who are the responsibility of a local authority or where the local authority has become involved, regardless of whether the child is the subject of a court order or not. Kinship carers looking after children in this group should be subject to all the same regulations and support as for stranger carers, including similar support for the kinship carers children if required. They should also get the same financial reward as stranger carers.

- **Group B – private intervention:** including a child being cared for as a result of a family crisis, a child rejected by its mother, cases where it is part of a family culture to share the upbringing of the child, private fostering where parents may be studying, working or have returned to their country of origin, or shared/support care provided by the family to assist a parent who is unable to totally care for the child, thus preventing the child being 'looked after'. In order to prevent such groups from entering care, support both short and long term, emotional, practical, financial and technical should be offered to the family or friend carer.
- **Group C – neighbourhood fostering:** comprising those who are recruited within the home location of a specific child and may move on to become stranger carers in the future. This would be most valued in areas where there are consistently high numbers of 'looked after' children.

It is essential that we strive to define the philosophical base for what we do as well as offering a clear definition of the problem being tackled. It is important that the resources and stresses of the child and the different family members are considered and that the available services and the agency expectations are made explicit. The role of a family/professional network meeting is central. In order to maximize the effect of this type of meeting, two principles of the family group conference could be adopted. The first is that the extended family has the ability to make a safe plan for dependent children, unless there are explicit contra-indications, and secondly that the family needs time to take into consideration the information brought by professionals, and to plan in private. Network meetings could provide for inclusive decision-making where the benefits of a range of views will be applied to the protection issue (O'Brien, 2001).

Based on a shared philosophy, each agency next needs to identify its particular roles and responsibilities in relation to this group. The

following represent some of the essential ingredients of a service procedure and philosophy: theory is an essential foundation upon which practice and procedures are built.

Policies, procedures and practice guidance: plugging the gap

It is unfair to ask workers to deal with kinship care if they have not been equipped with the appropriate tools to do so. Policy and practice are both hampered by the ambiguity in defining kinship care.

Horwath and Calder (1999) argued that policies, procedures and practice guidance together provide a useful framework to guide actions and clarify individual roles and responsibilities. They need to reflect the desired standards for practice. They differentiated between the three terms as follows:

- Policies are the principles or recommended course of action based on the mandate and standards agreed by senior managers. They focus on contextualising the task.
- Procedures offer the structural framework for practice based on policies. They focus on the process.
- Practice guidance provides a mechanism for converting the policy and procedures into an operational working tool.

Clearly defined policies, procedures and practice guidance, supported by senior representatives of each agency provide front-line practitioners and managers with a clear remit providing a framework to guide action and clarify individual roles and responsibilities. They should be clear, credible, congruent, resourced and monitored, and reflect local conditions (e.g. formal/informal networks and the local collaborative culture) (see Morrison, 1996).

Inter-agency procedures should always compliment internal agency policies, enabling workers to appreciate not only what is expected of themselves, but of other professionals. Good practice should ensure that the ramifications of changed policies in one agency are clearly planned for and negotiated with the other agencies involved.

Procedures can be a double-edged sword. Firstly, they can help workers by providing a structure for the work, in clarifying professional roles and in resolving any inter-agency difficulties. However, they can constrain practice if they are perceived by workers as an added burden, leading to a rigid and unresponsive service. Many workers tend to utilise procedures as a guide to action so, where none exist, they may hesitate taking any action, fuelled in a belief that the work is of low priority.

We should always remember that procedures are no substitute for good practice and, once constructed, are not inviolate. Procedures should never be regarded as set in stone; rather they represent a distillation of what is believed to be best practice at a given point in time. As the knowledge base expands, so it becomes necessary to re-evaluate established policies and practices in order to ensure that they continue to be relevant and appropriate and make best use of available resources. An over-emphasis on procedure can also mask a lack of exploration about philosophy, values and outcomes. Horwath and Calder (1998) also argued that procedures should be embedded in the real world, with an acknowledgement of the pressures that are being placed on individual agencies and their employees.

Practice guidance is an essential partnership document to policy and procedures, attending to the micro-level detail. In the absence of this document, workers tend to end up working in isolation from each other, and practice develops in a fragmented, ad hoc, and uncoordinated fashion. Good practice can emerge, but cannot be sustained in such an environment.

There is considerable scope for local authorities to be more proactive in the recruitment of relatives to care for children in care proceedings. Agencies should have positive policies and practices to promote such care, by identifying and approaching relatives and others within the child's network regarding support which is available if they take on the care of the child (Waterhouse, 2001). It would be important for the authority to have a clear policy in relation to placement with relatives so that it is not left to the whim of the individual workers involved whilst also clearly setting out that it is the placement of choice that should be seriously explored before other 'stranger' options.

It is unlikely that services for kinship carers will significantly improve unless policies are developed nationally that promote and support kinship care. In developing policies, local authorities must consult with and involve parents, kinship carers and children. Policies to support kinship care need to be seen in the wider context that recognizes and values the contribution the wider family and the community make toward caring for children. Policies that support kinship care must also be placed within the wider context of kinship involvement. It is not sufficient to provide support and financial assistance for kinship carers if relatives are routinely excluded from decision-making about children who are in need of care and protection. Kinship involvement requires that local authority Children Services Plans include statements that recognize and welcome the involvement of relatives when decisions need to be made about children in need of care and protection (Tapsfield, 2001).

Implementation

Whilst careful consideration needs to be given to the choice of workers, it needs to be built on a departmental package of support and procedural guidance. Tapsfield (2001) has noted that considerable uncertainty exists in local authorities about their proper role in supporting and promoting kinship care. There are some workers and departments who see kinship care as the responsibility of families and think that there is an expectation on relatives to step in and look after children whose own parents are unable to do this. Workers do not think they should seek help from the state in such circumstances. At the other end of the continuum are those who see kinship care as the responsibility of the state and as an alternative to residential or stranger foster care. They think that the relatives should receive adequate financial and other support to care for children who might otherwise be looked after in residential or stranger foster care. Such variations are reflected in policies about residence order allowances, the availability of support and the general quality and presence of information for relatives, and the involvement of the wider family in the decision-making process.

Effective supervision needs to look at the triad of feelings, tasks and thinking, and needs to be accompanied by consultation from someone knowledgeable in this area of work. A failure to pair workers together can lead to isolation, stress and secrecy which mirror the dynamics of the abusers themselves, and leads to unsafe decisions and premature burn-out. It is important that the work takes place in an environment which supports the sharing of knowledge and responsibility, whilst also prohibiting scapegoating and secrecy.

Practitioners need to be provided with structured opportunities to reflect on practice, the exercise of professional judgement, feelings and prejudices – either through supervision or consultation – if procedures are not to be used as checklists and families processed through the system without adapting them to the individual circumstances of each case. Senior managers do have a duty to identify ways in which their staff will be provided with opportunities to reflect on and develop their practice. They also need to promote staff care as they remain our most valuable resource.

Outcomes

Outcome measures are important for workers' awareness of the impact of their actions and decisions on others. There needs to be a very clear differentiation between different kinds of outcome: professionals themselves need to develop outcomes so that they have clear expectations about what they are trying to achieve and also about what change has come about. But we also need to explore the introduction of performance indicators, linked to practice standards. This provides a framework enabling the worker to appreciate exactly what is expected, and a measure to determine whether this has been achieved. These should reflect policy and procedures.

One of the main arguments in favour of kinship care is that it minimises the disruption and discontinuity for the child whilst also making it easier to explain to their friends. Most children and young people wish to remain outside local authority care and especially placement with strangers. There is also significant evidence that this type of care is likely to be much more successful than when a child is placed with stranger carers. This is because the child is staying within its own community, have the same friends and health care support, and often attend the same school. Benedict et al. (1996) found that children studied while in kinship care have significantly better levels of functioning compared with those placed in stranger foster care and, once adults, those who enjoyed kinship childhood placements do equally well in terms of

adult functioning as those who have been brought up by stranger carers.

Evaluation: keeping your eye on the ball

There is a need to set out explicit criteria in terms of methods of evaluation so that the goalposts are not moved, and so we begin to get a better feel of what works with children placed in kinship care placements.

Everitt and Hardiker (1996) have noted that:

evaluation involves processes of dialogue and practice and policy change. The structures and processes through which apparently objective facts and subjective experiences are generated and filtered need to be interrogated. Furthermore, the purpose of evaluation is not merely to provide better or more realistic accounts of phenomena, but to place a value on them and to change situations, practice and people's circumstances accordingly.

To enable this to take place, the following should be part of the evaluation:

- Do the aims reflect the purpose of practice in light of national guidance and local policies, e.g. children's service plan?
- Are the standards realistic in terms of mandate and resources?
- Do inter-agency policies complement individual agency policies?
- Is accountability clear?
- What has been achieved in terms of services provided?
- What has been achieved in terms of outcomes?
- What are the opinions of service users regarding policies, procedures and their implementation in practice?

This is a difficult and costly exercise. Gone are the days when a set of procedures could be developed and implemented and the ACPC was able to move on to the next task. Policies, procedures and practice need to be regularly monitored and adjusted to accommodate both local and national changes.

Training and staff development

Training may emphasise the need to follow guidelines and procedures but it is ineffective if professionals do not know how to access them or if training is seen as a vehicle to compensate for any lack of procedures. Training is only effective if it is used as part of a wider strategy to promote and develop practice. This broader strategy should include a framework of policies and procedures, together with resources and support to enable professionals to work within the framework. Training also has a key role to play in the management of change. In a world of fragmenting structures and relationships, training can offer staff a group experience, which is safe and directed at meeting their needs. This can help participants feel a sense of belonging and self-efficacy: both of which are major determinants of successful change and a buffer to burn out. Training is a key for promoting and modeling inter-professional work, desirable inter-professional behaviour and collective responsibility. Effective practice requires a workforce with appropriate knowledge, values (especially around discrimination, perceptions and conflict resolution) and skills. Training is pivotal in developing these areas and in promoting effective working relationships, modeling what is expected in practice. A strategic approach to training is required that focuses not only on practitioners, but senior front-line managers as well: 'Training should help policy makers and practitioners critically evaluate the developing body of knowledge and implement relevant changes. It should contribute to their knowledge of good policy and practice.'

Training is an encompassing structure as it influences every part of the framework. It can become the vehicle whereby senior managers are given an opportunity to consider the aims of intervention using kinship care. Policies and procedures can then follow. Once these are in place, training can help prepare first-line and middle managers to supervise staff involved in this work. These managers need to have knowledge of policy, standards and their role in terms of promoting high quality practice. It is only when these managers have been trained that it is appropriate to train practitioners.

There is acknowledgement that a gap has existed for some time around kinship care. Wheal and Waldman (1997) found no published training materials in England and Wales, although some local authorities were adapting 'choosing to foster' (NFCA, 1994). In response, two sets of training materials were produced (NFCA, 2000a; 2000b) although the low priority of the issue continues to preclude widespread use of the materials produced.

Moving forward

The Department of Health has recognised that kinship placements often involve a lower amount of contact from social workers and this means that the issues of child protection are potentially more difficult to detect (DoH, 2002). There is a tension between the potential for over optimism and a process that is critical of delay. It should be recognised that the confusion about what could constitute adequate protection, and what level of support, assessment and supervision are appropriate arises from the lack of a specific model for kinship assessments (O'Brien, 2001). The authors suggests a model of evolving networks of relative care (ENORC) that features family group conferencing, rapid assessment, explicit care plans and supervision/support. Additionally, we should recognise the very poor, oppressive history in respect of intervention with black families, and act upon the reality that the methods and responses to black families are still not working (Ince, 2001).

Contemporary British research contains implications for the assessment of relative carers. American contributions are more explicit, and the Child Welfare League of America (a parallel organisation to the NSPCC) has produced Standards of Excellence for kinship care services. They state the most desirable place for children to grow up is in their own caring families and that welfare agencies must establish kinship care as an integral part of the community. The CWLA support a comprehensive assessment, to include an analysis of safety issues, relationships and family dynamics, ability to meet the child's developmental needs, ability to work in partnership with professionals, the position of other children within the family, the views of the child and the birth parents, any features of alcohol and substance misuse, health, age and support networks. The latter is a crucial issue in assessing kinship placements. What must be understood is that kinship carers have multiple roles, including that of caregivers, grandparent, aunt or uncle, and parent. These carers do not give up one role when they accept another and the stress from multiple demands may be a very significant feature of the carers' lives (Crumbley and Little, 1997).

There is now a body of British research material that is generally supportive of ongoing contact between family members in post placement arrangements, when this is a safe arrangement. Siblings are often preoccupied with each other and the vast majority of children want to maintain contact arrangements, even when these include difficulties (Macaskill, 2002; McCauley, 1996; Mullender, 1999). Contact issues should be at the centre of kinship assessments and analysis should start with a proper consideration of attachments. As children's views are often different to those of the adults, these should be sought directly, not by proxy and professionals must avoid the imposition of a contact plan that has been poorly assessed. This need is underestimated in existing formats for assessment.

We need a new model of assessment and the new Special Guardianship Order (SGO) will heighten the urgency of this requirement. This assessment format should be rooted in child focused, empowering practice to all families, rejecting of class bias and giving greater prominence to the inherent benefits of kinship placements, whilst incorporating a framework for risk assessment. Children deserve to be supported to live within their birth families whenever this is possible. Their right to respect for their family life is now enshrined in the law.

For family and friends, who offer to care for their relative children, the issue of assessment can present itself as a daunting task indeed. Many potential carers doubt the validity of assessments, often because of the way they are managed. Many experience it as a disempowering and imposing process. Even skilled and experienced assessors often lack the skill and knowledge base required to consider the specific issues, strengths and difficulties associated with kinship placements. Many prospective kinship carers perceive welfare agencies as unsupportive and many are excluded from the care planning process. This is most likely to be the process when professionals operate with a value base of 'family dysfunction'. Broad argues for a new paradigm for practice:

This paradigm is family-centred, emphasising extended family and community involvement in planning and decision making, and acknowledges carers' equity ... In the new paradigm there is a much greater emphasis on the provision of family support at a primary, preventative level through family based interventions. In the traditional paradigm permanency planning is based around support-ing the nuclear family ... in this new paradigm ... there is much more emphasis for work with the child's extended families, friends and communities as prospective sources of support, information and assessment

(Broad, 2004)

This new paradigm should be embraced by practitioners who wish to work in partnership with families. Some families continue to experience professional intervention as cynical and disempowering. Consider the statement of the grandmother, who was poorly assessed and who subsequently and successfully fought to have her three grandchildren transferred from unstable fostering placements into her care:

How dare these agencies tell us that our children's children are not precious and valuable to us, and how dare they decide that we are not important to the children ... all those concerned with the care and placements for children need to be very alarmed about the current practices by social workers and the courts ... grandparents are often custodians of family history who are able to act as advocates in times of difficulty or separation ... we need competent practitioners ... the whole system is currently abusive and needs swift and strong action.

(grandparent interviewed by Cath Talbot, 2003)

References

BAAF (2000) *Form F, Information In Connection With an Application for Approval of Foster Carer(s), Adopters or Other Carers*. London: BAAF.

Benedict, M.I., Zuravin, S. and Stallings, R. (1996) Adult Functioning of Children Who Lived in Kin Versus Non-Relative Family Foster Homes. *Child Welfare*. 75: 529–49.

Broad, B. (Ed.) (2001) *Kinship Care: The Placement Choice for Children and Young People*. Lyme Regis: Russell House Publishing.

Broad, B., Hayes, R. and Rushforth, C. (2001) *Kith and Kin: Kinship Care for Vulnerable Young People*. London: NCB.

Broad, B. (2004) Kinship Care for Children in the UK: Messages From Research, Lessons for Policy and Practice. *European Journal of Social Work*. 7: 2, 211–27.

Calder, M.C. (1995) Child Protection: Balancing Paternalism and Partnership. *British Journal of Social Work*. 25: 6, 749–66.

Calder, M.C. (1999) A Conceptual Framework for Managing Young People Who Sexually Abuse: Towards a Consortium Approach. In Calder, M.C. (Ed.) *Working With Young People Who Sexually Abuse: New Pieces of the Jigsaw Puzzle*. Lyme Regis: Russell House Publishing.

Calder, M.C. (2000) *A Complete Guide to Sexual Abuse Assessments*. Lyme Regis: Russell House Publishing.

Calder, M.C. (2003) The Assessment Framework: A Critique and Reformulation. In Calder, M.C. and Hackett, S. (Eds.) *Assessment in Childcare: Using and Developing Frameworks for Practice.* Lyme Regis: Russell House Publishing.

Calder, M.C. and Hackett, S. (Eds.) (2003) *Assessment in Child Care: Using and Developing Frameworks for Practice.* Lyme Regis: Russell House Publishing.

Calder, M.C. and Horwath, J. (2000) Challenging Passive Partnerships in the Core Group Forum: Towards a More Proactive Approach. *Child and Family Social Work.* 5: 3, 267–77.

Carson, D. (1994) Dangerous People: Through a Broader Concept of 'Risk' and 'Danger' to Better Decisions. *Expert Evidence.* 3: 2, 21–69.

Child Welfare League of America (2000) *Standards of Excellence for Kinship Care Services.* Washington: CWLA.

Clifford, D. (1999) Developing a Research Methodology for Social Work Assessment in Adoption and Fostering. In BAAF *Assessment, Preparation and Support.* London: BAAF.

Crumbley, J. and Little, R. (1997) *Relatives Raising Children: An Overview of Kinship Care.* Washington: CWLA.

DoH (1988) *Protecting Children: A Guide for Social Workers Undertaking a Comprehensive Assessment.* London: HMSO.

DoH (1995) *The Challenge of Partnership.* London: HMSO.

DoH (1999) *Working Together to Safeguard Children: A Guide to Inter-Agency Working Arrangements to Safeguard and Promote the Welfare of Children.* London: The Stationery Office.

DoH (2000) *Framework for the Assessment of Children in Need and their Families.* London: The Stationery Office.

DoH (2002) *Family and Friends Care Discussion Document.* London: DoH.

DoH (2002) *Choice Protects Update* Bulletin, No 1. November, London: DoH.

Donnelly, A. (2001) Recognising Risk and its Importance in Social Care Assessments of Children and Families. Unpublished Project Report. University of Birmingham: School of Public Policy.

Everitt, A. and Hardiker, P. (1996) *Evaluating for Good Practice.* London: Macmillan.

Horwath, J. and Calder, M.C. (1999) The Background and Current Context of Post-registration Practice. In Calder, M.C. and Horwath, J. (Eds.) *Working for Children on the*

Child Protection Register: An Inter-Agency Practice Guide. Aldershot: Arena.

Ince, L. (2001) Promoting Kinship Foster Care: Preserving Family Networks for Black Children of African Origins. In Broad, B. (2001) op. cit.

Laws, S. and Broad, B. (2000) *Looking After Children within the Extended Family: Carers' Views.* Leicester: De Montfort University.

Laws, S. (2001) Looking After Children Within the Extended Family: Carers Views. In Broad, B. (Ed.) op. cit.

Laming Lord (2003) *The Victoria Climbié Enquiry: Report of an Enquiry by Lord Lamming.* London: HMSO.

Macaskill, C. (2002) *Safe Contact: Children in Permanent Placement and Contact with their Birth Relatives.* Lyme Regis: Russell House Publishing.

McCauley, C. (1996) *Children in Long Term Foster Care: Emotional and Social Development.* Aldershot: Avebury.

Morrison, T. (1996) Partnership and Collaboration: Rhetoric and Reality. *Child Abuse and Neglect.* 20: 2, 127–40.

Mullender, A. (1999) *We Are Family: Sibling Relationships in Placement and Beyond.* London: BAAF.

NFCA (1994) *Choosing to Foster: The Challenge to Care.* London: NFCA.

NFCA (2000a) *Family and Friends Carers' Handbook.* London: NFCA.

NFCA (2000b) *Family and Friends Carers: Social Workers' Training Guide.* London: NFCA.

Nixon, P. (2001) Making Kinship Partnerships Work: Examining Family Group Conferences. In Broad, B. (Ed.) op. cit.

O'Brien, V. (2001) Contributions from an Irish Study: Understanding and Managing Relative Care. In Broad, B. (Ed.) (2001) op. cit.

Portegen, R. and van der Neut, B. (1999) Assessing Family Strengths: A Family Systems Approach. In Greef, R. (Ed.) *Fostering Kinship.* Aldershot: Ashgate.

Reder, P. and Lucey, C. (1995) *Assessment of Parenting: Psychological and Psychiatric Contributions.* London: Routledge.

Smale, G. et al. (1993) *Empowerment, Assessment, Care Management and the Skilled Worker.* London: HMSO.

Talbot, C. and Williams, M. (2003) Kinship Care. *Journal of Family Law.* 33: 502–8.

Tapsfield, R. (2001) Kinship Care: A Family Rights Group Perspective. In Broad, B. (Ed.) op. cit.

Waterhouse, S. (2001) Keeping Children in Kinship Placements Within Court Proceedings. In Broad, B. (Ed.) op. cit.

Wheal, A. (2001) Family and Friends Who Are Carers: A Framework for Success. In Broad, B. (Ed.) op. cit.

Wheal, A. and Waldman, J. (1997) *Friends and Family as Carers: Identifying the Training Needs of Carers and Social Workers*. Unpublished. NFCA.

Worrall, J. (1999) Clear Policy and Good Practice in Kinship Foster Care. In Greeff, R. (Ed.) (1999) *Fostering Kinship: An International Perspective on Kinship Foster Care*. Aldershot: Arena.

Chapter Four

Kinship Care: The Legal Position

Philip Kidd and Paul Storey

Introduction

The decision-making process as to whether a child who cannot be cared for by its parents should be placed with a member or members of its wider family, in what is described as a kinship placement, is frequently undertaken in the context of legal proceedings. Statutory intervention by local authorities into the lives of families has, since 1991, required the establishment of a minimum threshold of concern. Only when that threshold has been surpassed is it possible for the court to authorise the local authority's intervention into the lives of the family whose future is before it. This chapter will consider the application of that threshold, within a historical context, offering a view of legislative intention and reality. It sets out current practice and the interpretation of standards for kinship and 'mainstream' foster care, arguing the case for flexibility to secure the best positive placement for the child. It considers the problematic issues of funding for prospective carers and concludes the discussion with suggestions for positive development.

Even if **the threshold referred to above** is passed, however, it is long established law that, to warrant the removal of a child from its natural parent or parents, requires a positive decision on the part of the court that the natural parent is incapable of providing the child with the standard of care that it requires; in other words, there is a presumption in favour of the natural parent. This principle was best expressed in the seminal case of *Re K D (A Minor) (Access: Principles)* [1988] 2 FLR 139 when Lord Templeman said, at p 141 A: 'The best person to bring up a child is the natural parent. It matters not whether the parent is wise or foolish, rich or poor, educated or illiterate, provided the child's moral and physical health are not endangered.' In *Re K (A Minor) (Custody)* [1990] 2 FLR 64 this principle was held to have equal application when those competing for the care of the child were the natural father and the maternal aunt and uncle. In essence, before the child's right to be cared for by its natural parent can be

displaced, there has to be a compelling case for so doing, founded on the child's welfare. As we will examine in this discussion, whilst no such principle exists when the issue is between placing a child with its wider family and in a permanent placement outside the birth family, legal authorities are increasingly recognising the importance of the birth family and have devised, through the resurrection of wardship, a means of overcoming a major obstacle to certain kinship placements.

The history

Extended family members have for many years sought to involve themselves, through the judicial process, in the upbringing of children whose parents have been unable to care for them. This discussion concentrates on the development of the law and procedure following the coming into effect of the Children Act 1989. That Act served to modernise and codify a system in which it had been routinely necessary for an extended family member to have to use the cumbersome mechanism of wardship proceedings in order to secure the care of the child concerned. The introduction of a new order, the residence order, which was capable of being made in favour of any applicant (subject, in the case of a non-parent, to prior permission to apply having been granted) was thought to enhance the profile of extended family members (particularly grandparents) and render it far easier for them to become involved in proceedings in which the state sought the removal of children from their birth families. The reality was, initially, somewhat different.

Kinship intervention into court proceedings

The application

It became apparent, at an early stage, that the courts were not willing to permit family members to intervene in care proceedings (with a view to securing the long term care of the child concerned) unless they were able to satisfy stringent qualifying criteria. Although Parliament had debated the creation of enhanced rights for grandparents, no special provisions were contained in the Act for any prospective kinship carers. Thus, as Butler-Sloss LJ stated (in an application by a grandmother for permission to seek a contact order) '. . . a grandmother is in the group of any person who can apply for a contact order. That person has to apply for leave (all of this under s 10 of the Children Act) and a grandmother, like any other person who is not within the group of people who has an automatic right to apply for contact, is one of those who must apply within the provisions of s 10(9)' (*Re A (Section 8 Order: Grandparent Application)* [1995] 2 FLR 153). (The criteria in s 10 (9) provide that, on an application for leave to apply for a s 8 order the Court must have regard to:

(a) the nature of the proposed application for the section 8 order (see Calder and Talbot, Chapters 1 and 11);
(b) the applicant's connection with the child (see Talbot, Chapter 10);
(c) any risk there might be of that proposed application disrupting the child's life to such an extent that he would be harmed by it; and
(d) where the child is being looked after by a local authority:
(i) the authority's plans for the child's future; and
(ii) the wishes and feelings of the child's parents.)

No emphasis was applied to any particular criterion by statute but experience suggested that ss 10 (9) (c) and (d) (i) were treated by the courts as being of far greater importance than the applicant's connection to the child.

The difficulty faced by relatives in obtaining leave to apply for s 8 orders was puzzling, as the importance of extended family members, particularly grandparents, had been emphasised in various quarters. The duty imposed upon a local authority, by virtue of s 23 (6) (b) Children Act 1989, to seek to place a 'looked after' child with a relative if placement with a parent were contrary to his interests was clear for all to see:

(6) Subject to any regulations made by the Secretary of State for the purposes of this subsection, any local authority looking after a child shall make arrangements to enable him to live with:

(a) a person falling within subsection (4); or
(b) a relative, friend or other person connected with him, unless that would not be reasonably practicable or consistent with his welfare.

This obligation upon local authorities appeared to be reflected, initially, in decisions such as that in *Re U (Application To Free For Adoption)* [1993] 2 FLR 992, in which the Court of Appeal upheld a decision to grant a residence order to grandparents on a local authority's freeing application.

Nevertheless, the courts were soon demanding, for all applications by non-parents, that, in addition to satisfying the criteria in s 10 (9), the applicant should demonstrate 'a case that is reasonably likely to succeed' before permission to apply would be granted (*G v Kirklees Metropolitan Borough Council* [1993] 1 FLR 805). This significant obstacle was raised yet further when, in *Re M (Minors) (Sexual Abuse: Evidence)* [1993] 1 FLR 822, Butler-Sloss LJ, in commenting upon the joinder of grandparents to care proceedings, stated, 'I should not like it to be thought that because the Children Act 1989 and the Family Proceedings Rules 1991, in particular r 4.7, provide for grandparents, among others, to be parties where appropriate, they should in fact intervene unless they have a separate point of view to put forward.' The court was concerned that the grandmother supported the return of the child to her daughter but was only putting herself forward as a carer in the event that her daughter was excluded. The depiction of this as a 'fall-back' position was interesting as, on one analysis, a grandparent is *always* presenting such a position, the law clearly providing, through a long line of authorities, that grandparents can only take on the care of a grandchild if the natural parent has been positively excluded. (See for instance *Re D (Care: Natural Parent Presumption)* [1999] 1 FLR 134.) The decision in *Re M* might also be contrasted with the case of *Re G (Minors Interim Care Order)* [1993] 2 FLR 839 in which Butler-Sloss LJ found that there were no grounds for interfering with a judge's decision to allow *foster carers* to be joined as Respondents to care proceedings! The unsatisfactory position was, therefore, that a prospective kinship carer could expect no special consideration, by virtue of the blood tie, when seeking permission to intervene. Furthermore, the kinship carers had to show that they supported the removal of the child from its parents if they were to avoid being perceived as presenting merely a 'fall-back' position.

Many applications by prospective kinship carers were routinely refused because they failed to meet these stringent qualifying criteria. The impression given to family members and practitioners alike was that, in order to satisfy the court, they had to show themselves to have at least as good a case for caring for a child within their blood family as would a non-family member. It certainly did not seem that either the perceived benefits to a child of remaining within its birth family or the onus upon placing within that family were matters that were given great weight by the courts.

Happily, in recognition of the fact that these criteria set too high a hurdle for applicants, less stringent tests were subsequently approved. The test was initially modified in the case of *Re M (Care: Contact: Grandmother's Application for Leave)* [1995] 2 FLR 86. In dealing with an application by a grandmother for permission to apply for contact pursuant to s 34 Children Act 1989. The Court of Appeal held that if either (a) the application is frivolous, vexatious or an abuse of process or (b) the applicant fails to disclose that there is any eventual real prospect of success, or the prospect is so remote as to make the application unsustainable, the application for leave should be dismissed. It went on to state that, 'The applicant must satisfy the court that there is a serious issue to try and must present a good arguable case. "A good arguable case" has acquired a distinct meaning . . . One should avoid unprofitable inquiry into what precisely these turns of phrase mean. Their sense is well enough known – is there a real issue which the applicant may reasonably ask the court to try and has he (sic) a case which is better than merely arguable yet not necessarily one which is shown to have a better-than-even chance, a fair chance, of success? One should avoid over-analysis of these "tests" and one should approach the matter in the loosest way possible, looking at the matter in the round because only by such imprecision can one reinforce the importance of leaving the exercise of discretion unfettered.'

Practitioners welcomed this useful decision for the manner in which it clearly distinguished between those cases where applications should be rejected out of hand and those that were potentially meritorious. The requirement that the applicant disclose a 'good arguable case' was considered far less onerous than the requirement that they show that they were reasonably likely to succeed in an application to care for the child.

The issue was frequently determined by reference to whether the applicant had overcome the hurdles set out in (a) and (b) above. The application of a less legalistic approach to the test was equally welcome. Nevertheless, whilst acknowledging that grandparents ought to have a special place in a grandchild's affection the court in *Re M* reiterated that 'Parliament has refused to place grandparents in a special category or to accord them special treatment.' However, it was stated that there is a presumption that any contact between a child and its birth family will be beneficial to the child and that, where a local authority wishes contact between a child and its relatives to be curtailed it must file evidence to demonstrate why this presumption does not apply.

The threshold of 'good arguable case' went on to gain approval in subsequent decisions (*Re G (Child Case: Parental Involvement)* [1996] 1 FLR 857, *G v F (Contact and Shared Residence: Applications for Leave)* [1998] 2 FLR 799, and *Re S (Contact: Application by Sibling)* [1998] 2 FLR 897) and remained the test that was routinely applied by courts until 2003.

In *Re W (Contact Application: Procedure)* [2000] 1 FLR 263, Wilson J, repeating an often-cited principle, 'there is no presumption currently written into our jurisprudence that it is in the interests of a grandchild to have contact with a grandparent . . . I anticipate that, when the Human Rights Act 1998 comes into force, it will be argued that a child's right to respect for his or her family life under Art 8 of the Convention requires the absence of such a presumption in the case of a grandparent to be revisited.' The suggestion that the provisions of Human Rights Act 1998 might have some bearing on the manner in which courts deal with applications for permission to intervene has proven prophetic.

The issue was given consideration by the Court of Appeal in *Re J (Leave to Issue Application for Residence Order)* [2003] 1 FLR 114. In that case, a local authority had assessed a grandmother as being unable to provide the care that they believed her granddaughter required and formulated a plan for adoption. The grandmother applied to be joined to the care proceedings. Her application was opposed by the local authority and the guardian and, in turn, refused by the court. In allowing her appeal the Court of Appeal found that where a grandparent sought the court's permission to apply, in care proceedings, for a residence order, that application should not be dismissed on the basis of a summary decision that the prospects of success were slim. Thorpe LJ stated, '. . . it is important that trial judges should recognise the greater appreciation that has developed of the value of what grandparents have to offer . . . Judges should be careful not to dismiss such opportunities without full inquiry. That seems to me to be the minimum essential protection of Articles 6 and 8 rights that [the grandmother] enjoys, given the very sad circumstances of the family.' The test in *Re M* above was not applicable to cases such as this, which were to be determined by reference to the criteria in s 10 (9) Children Act 1989 and in applications under s 10 (9) the applicants enjoy Article 6 rights (to a fair hearing) and, usually, Article 8 rights (to respect for family life).

The removal of the 'good arguable case' test and the emphasis upon the valuable contributions that grandparents can make to the care of their grandchildren were both reinforced in the Court of Appeal decision in *Re H (Children)* [2003] EWCA Civ 369. Once again, a grandmother's application for permission to apply for a residence order had been refused. An adverse assessment had been prepared prior to the court's determination of that application. Regarding the refusal of permission Thorpe LJ expressed the view that the judge, 'faced with an application, which was seen by the Guardian to have perhaps only slender prospects of success . . . misdirected herself in giving that appraisal too much prominence and insufficient prominence to ensuring that the only blood relation who was advancing a case for the child's care should not be dismissed from the process without full participation.' Once again, the court applied the provisions of s 10 (9) and ruled in favour of the grandmother (despite the fact that it was alleged that she had never seen her grandson).

The most recent authority on the issue, *Re W (Care Proceedings: Leave to Apply)* [2005] 2 FLR 468 appears to reinstate the principle established in *Re M (Minors) (Sexual Abuse: Evidence)* (above) that, unless an applicant demonstrates an independent or separate point of view to an existing party to the proceedings, the application to be joined to the proceedings is likely to be refused. This decision of the High Court, does not sit easily with the dicta of the Court of Appeal in the case of *Re P (A Child)* [2002] EWCA Civ 846, 16 May 2002. In that case, the grandmother's application to be joined to care proceedings and

for permission to apply for a residence order had been refused by the trial judge. In allowing her appeal, by reference to the protection that the grandmother was entitled to under the Human Rights Act, Thorpe LJ stated, 'I do not myself see how she could feel that her Article 6 rights had been fully observed if the judge were only to say to her, "Your daughter's case is that you should be the primary carer and you can give evidence in support of your daughter's case" '. He went on to indicate that, the effect of granting her application would be to 'to ensure that she was not only a witness in support of another's case, but a witness in her own cause'. Clearly, the Court of Appeal's reasoning, in determining that the fact that there was an identity of interest between the grandmother and her daughter was not fatal to the grandmother's application, suggests that *Re M (Minors) (Sexual Abuse: Evidence)* should no longer be considered good law in the light of the Human Rights Act. *Re P* was not cited in the case of *Re W* and the Judge did not, therefore, have the opportunity to consider it. In so far as his decision to refuse the application in that case (to the extent that it was founded on the fact that the applicant's own case matched that of another party and that, therefore, she did not bring an independent or separate point of view to the proceedings) conflicts with the decision in *Re P*, the latter is to be preferred. It should be said, however, that *Re W* involved an application for contact that an aunt wished to bring, rather than an application for residence. Furthermore, the aunt's case was felt to correspond with the case of a grandmother, who *had* been joined to the proceedings. It is likely, therefore, that even if there is a tension between the decisions in *Re W* and *Re P*, the former can be distinguished on its facts from applications by prospective kinship carers to be given permission to join in proceedings to advance a case to care for their child relative.

An application to be joined to proceedings, applying the criteria in s 10 (9), clearly engages Article 6 of ECHR. Whether Article 8 is also engaged depends on the nature of the relationship between the applicant and the child. As a consequence, far greater emphasis appears now to be placed on the applicant's connection to the child than was previously the case. A close blood tie, particularly where that is supported by a history of close contact and/or an emotional attachment, will almost certainly mean that Article 8 is engaged and, in turn, is likely to be virtually determinative of an application by a prospective kinship carer for permission to seek a residence order.

It is clear that grandparents in particular and other family members in general have, as a consequence of the coming into force of the Human Rights Act 1998 a significantly greater prospect of being joined to care proceedings with a view to applying for a residence order in respect of the child concerned. It is implicit in the requirement that a 'full enquiry' involving 'full participation' should take place and that the grandparent or other family member be granted the necessary permission to do so. Full participation should, by definition it is suggested, include participation in the legal process. As we will now discuss, full participation in the legal process demands more than simply the opportunity to appear in court with representation.

The process

Once a relative of a child becomes a party to legal proceedings Article 6 is engaged. It is likely that the relative will also have Article 8 rights. Although it might be assumed that a family relative would automatically attract the right to respect for family life, this is not always the case. Whilst it was stated in the ECHR case of *L v Finland* [2000] 2 FLR 118 that '. . . the mutual enjoyment by parent and child, as well as by grandparent and child, of each other's company constitutes a fundamental element of family life, and domestic measures hindering such enjoyment amount to an interference with the right protected by Art 8 of the Convention' the later case of *Lebbink v The Netherlands (Application No 45582/99)* [2004] 2 FLR 463 stated, 'The court does not agree . . . that a mere biological kinship, without any further legal or factual elements indicating the existence of a close personal relationship, should be regarded as sufficient to attract the protection of Art 8.' Each case will fall to be determined on its own facts. What is clearly the case is that the closer the factual (or actual) relationship between the relative and the child the more likely it will be that Article 8 is engaged. The fact that an application for permission to apply for a residence order is granted may, of itself, be sufficient to indicate that the relationship is sufficiently close to carry Article 8 rights with it. The relevance, in the context of involvement in

care proceedings, of whether Article 8 rig... engaged is in relation to the extent of the participation that is afforded to the relative. In *Re M (Care: Challenging Decisions By Local Authority)* [2001] 2 FLR 1300 it was held that certain procedural rights exist under Article 8 which entitle those who benefit from its provisions to involvement in the decision making process to a degree sufficient to provide them with the proper protection of their interests. Any decision that is reached through a process that does not afford such an involvement and is likely to be quashed. This decision was reinforced and fortified in *Re L (Care: Assessment: Fair Trial)* [2002] 2 FLR 730 in which it was held that the right to a fair hearing was not confined to the purely judicial part of the proceedings. Unfairness at any stage of the litigation process might involve breaches not only of the Article 8 right to respect for family and personal life, but also of Article 6. This was of crucial importance because whereas rights under Article 8 were inherently qualified, a litigant's right to a fair trial under Article 6 was absolute, and could not be qualified by reference to, or balanced against any rights under Article 8.

In areas such as attendance at important meetings, disclosure of relevant documentation, legal representation and many more, a relative who has been granted permission to seek a residence order will be afforded the full protections of Article 6, supplemented, in most cases by those of Article 8.

The assessment

The key to any successful intervention in legal proceedings concerning the care of a child is that a fair and effective assessment process is undertaken. For reasons that will be considered later, the assessment of kinship carers has been a complex process, frequently failing to differentiate between the standard of care demanded from a family member and that expected from a local authority foster carer or adopter (see Calder and Talbot in Chapter 1). It should be remembered that the 'natural parent presumption' referred to above does not have a corollary for any other family members, notwithstanding the provisions of s 23 (6) (b) Children Act 1989. The relative seeking to care for the child concerned does, as we have already examined, have the benefit of the protections of Article 6 and Article 8. They also benefit from the same 'rights' to apply for assessments as do the parents. This ability should not be underestimated, particularly when consideration is given to the provisions of s 38 (6) Children Act 1989 and the case law that has flowed from it. It is frequently a criticism of wider family members that they have not experienced first-hand parenting of the child in question. This criticism can be countered by an application, pursuant to s 38 (6), for a direction that there be an assessment of the child *whilst placed in the care of the prospective kinship carer*. If the 'broad and purposive' construction of s 38 (6) that the landmark decision in *Re C (Interim Care Order: Residential Assessment)* [1997] 1 FLR 1 advocated is applied to such an application, there would appear no real obstacle to a direction being made that the residential assessment may take place in the home of the kinship carers. Such a flexible approach has been endorsed by various authorities subsequent to *Re C*. This would clearly be a significant aid to a relative's case. Such a strategy is relatively rarely used and those representing grandparents should be alert to the distinct advantages associated with having the actual care of a child whilst an assessment is being undertaken. It should be added that the placement complexities identified later in this discussion would not apply as, according to *Re C*, the fact that a child is residing with someone pursuant to an s 38 (6) direction does not constitute a 'placement' which would demand compliance with the requisite placement regulations.

If a fair and effective assessment of the prospective kinship carers is to be undertaken it is vital that they are involved in the proceedings as early as possible. It is all too frequently the case that kinship carers are joined to the proceedings at a very late stage. A shortage of experts and the time that a meaningful assessment customarily takes (particularly if it has a residential component) often militate against the family members. It is often the case that, by the time the family members become directly involved in the proceedings the case has been listed for a final hearing. Relying upon the *Protocol for Judicial Case Management in Public Law Children Act Cases* [2003] 2 FLR 719, which requires the completion of the proceedings within a 40 week time-frame, Courts tend to refuse to direct any assessment that cannot be undertaken within the existing timetable. This means that either there is no independent assessment at all

(and therefore, the assessment undertaken by the local authority, if any and the rudimentary assessment of the Children's Guardian is the only material before the court) or the assessment that is undertaken is abbreviated and, naturally, carries less weight. Those representing wider family members should be alert to the protection, referred to above, of Article 6. Read in conjunction with the dicta of Thorpe LJ regarding the significant benefits that grandparents (for instance) can give to a child, a strong case can be made out that the absence of an effective and *independent* assessment is likely to result in a violation of the right to a fair hearing. As mentioned above, this is an absolute right and is not to be qualified by any Article 8 rights that other parties to the proceedings (including the child) might assert. Furthermore, so far as the impact of the Protocol is concerned, reference can and should be made to the decision in *Re G (Protocol For Judicial Case Management In Public Law Children Act Cases: Application To Become Party In Family Proceedings)* [2004] 1 FLR 1119. In that case, a child was placed with her maternal grandparents. The local authority instituted care proceedings in the local Family Proceedings Court and applied for an interim care order with a view to removing the child from the grandparents. A transfer to the care centre was also sought. The guardian supported the removal of the child from its grandparents whilst the mother did not oppose it. The grandparents wished to oppose this course and asked to be joined to the proceedings in order to contest the interim care order. The Family Proceedings Court refused their application, relying on paragraph [2.5] of the Protocol, which states that where a decision is made to transfer to the care centre, the Family Proceedings Court shall 'Except as to disclosure of documents, *make only those case management directions upon transfer* as are agreed with the care centre as set out in the CCP (care centre plan) and the FPCP (family proceedings court plan)'. Under those plans the decision as to party status was not one provided for the family proceedings court to take. Hedley J dealt squarely with the Human Rights implications of rigid adherence to the Protocol in this manner. He found the refusal to allow them to oppose the interim care application to be unfair. Of the Protocol's status he said, 'Clearly it must be read subject both to the Children Act 1989 and the statutory rules. The key, in my view, is to be found in the Practice Direction that accompanies and authorises the Protocol (*Practice Direction (Care Cases: Judicial Case Management)* (29 July 2003) [2003] 1 WLR 2209, [2003] 2 FLR 798). Paragraph [2.1] says 'The purpose of the . . . Protocol is to ensure . . . (a) that care cases are dealt with in accordance with the overriding objective . . .' and then in para [3.1] it continues 'The overriding objective is to enable the court to deal with every care case: (a) justly, expeditiously, fairly and with the minimum of delay . . . (c) . . . in ways that are proportionate . . . (ii) to the nature and extent of the intervention proposed in the private and family life of the children and adults involved'. He went on to consider the manner in which the interest of fairness and justice might demand a departure from the terms of the Protocol, saying, 'In my judgment every court, in approaching the application of the Protocol, must keep clearly in mind not only the terms of the Protocol itself but also its purpose as explained in the Practice Direction and Principles of Application (*Annex to the Practice Direction: Principles of Application* [2003] 2 FLR 802) therein. If the pursuit of that purpose requires departure from the terms of the Protocol, then that must be done with proper reasons being given for such departure.' Clearly, in the context of a relative's pursuit of an effective assessment, if the objection to such an assessment is founded solely on the provisions of the Protocol, the relative will have a powerful argument for departure from those provisions (including the requirement that the proceedings are concluded within a 40 week period) founded on the right to a fair hearing and the decision in *Re G*.

Thus, prospective kinship carers appear now to possess, by reason principally of Article 6 and Article 8, a real and enforceable right to participate effectively in proceedings for the care of children within their families. There remains, however, one critical anomaly, resolution of which may be required to remedy what has already been identified as a potential Human Rights Act violation.

Local authority approval of kinship carers

There are many cases in which an assessment of kinship carers reaches the conclusion that the best interests of the child in question will be served by being placed within the family but the local authority still requires the making of a final care order as a means of exercising a greater degree of control over the placement than would be afforded under a supervision order.

This is a further area in which no distinction is made between family members (other than parents) and local authority foster carers. For the child to be placed with its relatives under a care order it is necessary for the local authority to comply with the terms of the Fostering Services Regulations 2002. Any person with whom a 'looked after' child is placed must have been approved as a foster carer under Regulation 28 (2), which requires that:

(a) that the Local Authority has completed its assessment of that person's suitability to be a foster parent in accordance with regulation 27 (2) and Schedule 3; and
(b) the Fostering Panel has considered the application for approval as a foster parent.

Furthermore, regulation 34 (1) provides that a child may only be placed with a foster parent where that person has been approved by the local authority or another local authority. (Provisions do exist to permit 'emergency' placements for 24 hours and 'immediate' placements for up to six weeks.)

These regulations have various adverse consequences. The first is in relation to assessment. Regardless of whatever independent assessment is undertaken within the course of care proceedings the local authority is required to complete its own assessment if the placement of a 'looked after' child with a member of the wider family is to be approved. This assessment invariably takes the same form as an assessment of prospective local authority foster carers, not surprisingly as the same regulations apply. It is the view of the authors that this is a flawed and potentially unfair approach. It presupposes that family members are on a level playing field with local authority foster carers when it comes to assessing the appropriateness of placing a child in their care. It sets too high a standard, a standard of perfection, for prospective carers who have the distinct advantage over a local authority foster carer of having a family or friend connection to the child whom they wish to care for. An obvious potential consequence is that the local authority's assessment is likely to be adverse to the prospective kinship carers. Of course, this can be redressed by an alternative assessment. Unless, however, the local authority is prepared to either review its own negative assessment in the light of a positive assessment from an alternative source, with a view to securing the approval of the carers as foster carers, or abandon its desire to obtain a final care order the second adverse consequence of the regulations will come into play.

The position of a court that wishes to make a care order on the basis of a plan that a child is placed within its wider family was substantially complicated by the coming into force of the Fostering Services Regulations 2002. Although under their predecessor, the Foster Placement (Children) Regulations 1991, members of the wider family were similarly treated as foster carers, these regulations contained a provision which permitted the court to effectively disapply them to a prospective placement, by stating:

Where a care order is in force the application of these Regulations is subject to any directions given by a court (whether before, on or after these Regulations come into force).

It was frequently the case that the courts would be invited to direct that the regulations did not apply in so far as they required the kinship carers to be approved as local authority foster carers. The absence of a corresponding disapplication provision in the Fostering Services Regulations very rapidly came to the attention of the courts. In *M & J (Wardship: Supervision and Residence Orders)* [2003] 2 FLR 541, the court was asked to make a residence order coupled with a supervision order in respect of a child who was placed with his maternal grandmother. Although a care order may well have been more appropriate, the local authority indicated that such an order would mean that is was obliged to carry out an assessment of the grandmother under the Fostering Services Regulations and that a possible consequence was the mandatory removal of the child from her care in the event that she was not approved as a foster carer. In the circumstances, the court made residence, supervision and wardship orders to deal with the unusual situation it faced. Unfortunately, the situation was not as unusual as it might have appeared and the court soon had the opportunity to consider this type of situation again. In *Re W And X (Wardship: Relatives Rejected As Foster Carers)* [2004] 1 FLR 415 the court was concerned with applications for care orders in respect of four children. The plan for the youngest child was to be placed outside the natural family. For the three older children the local authority's wish was to place them with their maternal

grandparents under the aegis of a care order. However, the local authority had already rejected the grandparents as foster carers and, accordingly, the making of a care order would thwart the plan as it would immediately require the removal of the children from the maternal grandparents. Hedley J addressed the root of the problem and in doing so identified the anomaly referred to above when he said, 'Since the local authority had rejected Mr and Mrs S as foster parents, no such situation was possible under a care order; were one made, the local authority would immediately be obliged to remove the children. This was said to be the inevitable consequence of s 23 of the Children Act 1989 and the Fostering Services Regulations 2002. If right, this leads to the odd result that it is only if the kinship carers are good enough to be accepted as foster parents that a care order can be made in circumstances such as these. Apart from the fact that if kinship care were that good, a care order would be correspondingly less necessary, it raises a further point. Trained and approved foster parents belong no doubt in the upper reaches of parenting skills; local authorities take compulsory powers in a tiny minority of families. In between lies a vast range of parenting skills into which, no doubt, a very large number of potential kinship carers will fall.' He went on to express concern that no disapplication provision was available and questioned the legality of the regulations, in the way in which they thwarted the court's ability to apply s 1 Children Act 1989, although he expressed no clear view about this. As in *Re M & J* above, the court resolved the matter by making the children wards of court, granting a residence order to the grandparents and making a supervision order to the local authority. Thus, the court was able to ensure that the children would be able to continue to live with their grandparents and that the local authority could continue its statutory involvement with the family. The wardship was designed to impose a greater degree of control than might otherwise have been able. What the cocktail of order did not provide, however, was for the local authority to hold parental responsibility as this is prohibited by virtue of s 100 (2) Children Act 1989.

Whilst, clearly, a return to the use of wardship, may be seen as a retrograde step, the decisions in *Re M & J* and *Re W & X* mark the willingness of the courts to resolve technical or regulatory obstacles to kinship placements where such placements are perceived to meet the welfare requirements of the child concerned. In identifying the 'vast' range of parenting skills lying between those of trained foster carers and those of parents which require the use of compulsory powers Hedley J demonstrates precisely the problems facing prospective kinship carers in persuading local authorities to approve them as foster carers.

In an earlier decision, in *Re P (A Child)* [2002] EWCA Civ 846, 16 May 2002, Thorpe LJ, in allowing a grandmother's appeal against a refusal of leave to be joined to care proceedings and to apply for a residence order, Thorpe LJ stated, '. . . the outcome of a fixture to determine whether a close family member can be trusted to provide *good enough parenting to avert the obvious second best of placement out of the family* must depend upon the judge's opportunity to make a direct assessment of the candidate for care through the process of trial, and, most particularly the exposure in the witness box' (our italics). In addition to the obvious support that *Re P* provides for the joining of extended family members to care proceedings, the dicta above, to the effect that the Court of Appeal considers placement outside the family obviously second best and that the family need only provide 'good enough' care, not the 'super' care expected of them from some authorities, gives a clear indication of the standards that are to be expected of kinship carers. Clearly, because the presumption is that kinship care is 'obviously' preferable to care outside the family, the court is saying that the kinship carer enjoys an advantageous position.

Any suggestion by a local authority that a kinship carer is on a level playing field with a local authority foster carer should be speedily rebutted by reference to this decision and that in *Re W & X*. It is suggested that any assessment undertaken by a local authority that is predicated upon the notion that kinship carers must be as proficient as local authority foster carers is based on what the courts have stated to be a false premise. Whether the courts have gone so far as to establish a legal presumption in favour of family placement is a moot point. If that position has not yet been reached, we would suggest that it may well be close at hand.

Funding

Of course, legal proceedings can be expensive and lengthy. The parents, any other person with parental responsibility and the child are entitled to non-merits and non-means tested public funding. Prospective kinship carers are not. In the present climate the Legal Services Commission is normally willing to fund a family member's application for permission to join in care proceedings/seek a residence order. If the permission is granted the funding certificate is normally extended to cover the remainder of the proceeding. The problem lies more in the fact that the kinship carers are means tested. Although in many cases this does not present a problem there is a not inconsiderable number of cases where family members must either expend substantial amounts in legal costs or represent themselves.

The consequent reduction in the means of a family that elects to do the former can often have adverse implications, both in respect of the material provision for the child concerned and in terms of the additional stresses imposed upon the family. For the family that chooses to proceed without legal representation the reality is that the prospects of success are likely to be far lower by reason thereof.

This is clearly an unsatisfactory situation which will only be fully resolved by an amendment to the funding regulations. One possible mechanism, exists, however, to bring a kinship applicant within the class of those entitled to non-merits and non-means tested public funding. S 2 (9) Children Act 1989 states:

> *A person who has parental responsibility for a child may not surrender or transfer any part of that responsibility to another but may arrange for some or all of it to be met by one or more persons acting on his behalf.*

Whilst clearly, parental responsibility cannot be transferred to a member of the family, an arrangement can be made for some *or all* of it to be met. In those circumstances the Legal Services Commission might be open to the argument that the kinship applicant to whom the exercise of parental responsibility has been delegated pursuant to s 2 (9) is a person with parental responsibility for the purposes of the funding regulations and therefore entitled to funding without any means or merit assessment. It is unlikely that even if the child is subject to an interim care order, the local authority will be able to argue that the making of arrangements for someone else to exercise parental responsibility is in itself an exercise of parental responsibility. If it were the provisions of s 33 (3) Children Act 1989 which give the local authority the power to determine the extent to which a parent of the child may meet their parental responsibility for them, would enable the local authority to prevent the making of arrangements for another to meet the parental responsibility for a child in its care.

Such a situation would be analogous with the circumstances in *Re X (Parental Responsibility Agreement: Children in Care)* [2000] 1 FLR 517, where the court held that a local authority could not prevent a mother from entering into a parental responsibility agreement with the putative father of a child who was subject to a care order. What will be essential, however, will be a genuine delegation of parental responsibility. A parent may need to accept, unequivocally, that they have no future role in the child's care before the Legal Services Commission accepts that there has been a genuine delegation of parental responsibility (rather than simply a device through which to gain the benefit of public funding). A possible consequence of establishing that such a situation exists is that the funding of the parents is withdrawn on the basis that they have delegated their parental responsibility to someone else. In reality, each case would have to be dealt with on its own facts. Any application for public funding on this basis should always be accompanied by a copy of the arrangement for the kinship carer to exercise parental responsibility.

Despite this one possible means of securing legal representation for kinship carers whose means take them outside public funding, the absence of automatic, non-means tested public funding (and the consequent lack of effective legal representation) for some kinship applicants remains a cause of considerable concern amongst practitioners and the judiciary alike.

Conclusions

We conclude this discussion by making various suggestions as to how the position of kinship carers might be improved by the courts and the legislature. The following proposals all merit consideration:

(a) Recognition of the benefits to children of placement within their natural families by creating a legal 'presumption' in favour of kinship care where parental care has been excluded *and so long as the kinship placement*

proposed is consistent with the welfare of the child concerned. Accordingly, the presumption, as in the case of parental care, can be displaced if the child's welfare demands it.

(b) An amendment to the Fostering Services Regulations in order to create a distinction, so far as the type of assessment and the type of placement approval are concerned, between local authority foster carers and members of the child's wider family.

(c) One relatively simple means of achieving this would be to take kinship carers outside the scope of the Fostering Services Regulations and place them instead within the class of persons to whom the Placement of Children with Parents etc Regulations 1991 apply. If this were done, the kinship carer would not have to be approved as a local authority foster carer and approval of the placement, if the plan is for a care order, need only be given by a senior member of social services management.

(d) In the absence of such a removal of kinship carers from their scope, the restoration of a disapplication provision in the Fostering Services Regulations in order to permit the Court to make care orders in cases where kinship carers have been rejected as foster carers. As Hedley J stated in *Re W & X*, 'One might perhaps regret that the power of the court to disapply the regulations was not included in these regulations as it had been in their predecessor, after, of course, due diligent enquiry by the court.'

(e) The removal of the requirement that close family members, particularly grandparents, should seek prior permission before being permitted to participate in care proceedings/apply for a residence order.

(f) An amendment to the funding regulations to ensure that if a prospective kinship carer is involved in pubic law proceedings as a full party they are entitled to non-merits and non-means tested funding.

In order to be fully effective the measures that we have suggested will require the legal representatives of kinship applicants to ensure that applications are made early and that the full range of the court's powers are employed in their endeavour to keep children within their families. A combination of new measures and effective representation for kinship carers may well result in the 'very large number of potential kinship carers' identified by Hedley J as capable of providing an adequate standard of care successfully persuading the courts to place the child or children concerned with them and thereby retain the all important family connection referred to in other parts of this work.

The provisions of s 1 (f) Adoption and Children Act 2002, introduce a clearly defined statutory duty to give close consideration to the child's relationship with its wider family members whenever a court or an adoption agency is coming to a decision relating to the adoption of a child. It is to be hoped that underlining the need to do so, in the most extensive piece of child legislation since the Children Act 1989, might herald the adoption of a new professional mindset amongst those involved in this field, which is predicated upon the benefits (which the Courts have so clearly identified) of kinship care. The Courts, often accused of responding too slowly to society's changes, appear, in this particular context, to be leading the way.

Chapter Five

Kinship Placement and Parents With Intellectual Disabilities

Sadie Young

Introduction

Over the last three decades, there have been radical shifts in social policy concerning people with intellectual disabilities. The early 1970s saw the dawning of 'care in the community' and the gradual de-institutionalisation of large mental handicap hospitals (Wolfensberger, 1992). More recently, an integration policy for education in schools encourages mainstream education, where possible, for all children including those with special needs (DES, 2004). This progressive legislation has meant that people with low intellectual functioning are no longer to be contained and separated from society, but are included and supported in their local communities (DoH, 2001). People with intellectual disabilities are now born into a world where it is their right to make informed choices, including the right to marry and to have children, and many choose to exercise this right.

It is anticipated that the number of parents with intellectual disabilities is set to rise, as increasingly, members of this population seek to achieve the parental role. Consequently, there is a welcome diversity of research interest developing on the topic of parents with intellectual disabilities including: parental cognitive limitation, child outcome studies, parenting interventions, consumer perspectives, and social research (Murphy and Feldman, 2002). However, this sector of the population are amongst the most socially and economically disadvantaged groups and are more likely to make heavy demands on child welfare services and have their children looked after by the local authority (DoH, 2001). Furthermore, it is becoming clear from the number of families involved in child protection proceedings that the demands of parenthood challenge the coping abilities of many parents with intellectual disability, and that a lack of care often arises not out of an intention to harm but out of an omission of care and limited insight. It is accepted that the focus of professional input to a family is child centred and it is not unusual for

the special needs of the parents to go unnoticed. It is not until the child begins to show clear signs of need or distress that attention turns to the ability of the parents not only to provide but to maintain adequate care. Circumstances, such as when a child fails to thrive, or does not meet the expected developmental milestones in the period between birth and the second year of life, are common occurrences; however, by this stage of their development the child and family attachments are well established. The intellectual limitations experienced by the parents have reached their ceiling and for some the concept of support and intervention has unfortunately, arrived too late. The only option is a reactive response to a crisis and the child or children are frequently removed into an alternative placement. But, if we are to consider the support, attachment and emotional stability proposed by Broad (2001) and the notion of 'enabling' as opposed to 'approval' (Waterhouse, 2001) where we are assessing a triad of child, parent and family (Hegar and Scannapieco, 1999), should we not first explore the possibility of a kinship placement?

Parenting

Parenting in general, can be considered in terms of its function, relationship or nature. As a function, parenting can be viewed as an occupation that requires particular ways of adapting to and coping with children. This responsibility requires management strategies together with a satisfactory level of coping skill. Such a skills-based approach to parenthood has often been used for people with learning disabilities and examples are found in Craft (1993) who describes five programmes adopted in the USA, and McGaw and Sturmey's (1994) work, *The Parental Skills Model* is illustrative of similar developments in this country.

The role of parent implies by its very essence a relationship between an adult and a child. It is the role of caregiver and protector to a dependent person who is completely reliant on the adult for their physical, social and emotional needs. The relationship is enduring and when successful the child emerges as a socially integrated adult with the ability to form attachments and provide care for future generations. Conversely, where poor role models of parenting are evident, generations of unhappy childhoods can follow and impact not only on the immediate family system but on society at large. Despite the nature of this key concept, any attempt to define parenting in a neat and precise manner has proved to be too great a challenge, and general agreement on what constitutes the dimensions of parenting has failed to result in agreement on what comprises minimal acceptable standards of good-enough child care (Booth and Booth, 1994: 11).

The decision to become a parent need not involve the act of actually giving birth. It may be because a person spontaneously enjoys the behaviour associated with the parental role or, for various reasons to be found in that person's past experiences, they decide to take on the responsibilities of becoming a parent. The route to parenthood, of course, is not necessarily planned or socially recognised. It may be that one becomes a mother or father because that is what happens – because that is the natural course of affairs.

Kinship care has featured across cultures and classes for centuries and diversity in care arrangements should be recognised and understood. Just as there are no strict recommendations in the UK concerning the number of children any one parent should have, there are no strict guidelines concerning the number of parents any one child may experience, but it is generally agreed that a child's development is best met in an environment that provides nurture, stimulation, stability and security. It follows that in order to provide a child with these important developmental ingredients we need to provide an appropriate care environment. It is, therefore, sadly ironic that despite this knowledge being available to us, a child may today enter the UK care system and experience many parental changes that can result in a lifelong negative impact on their emotional and cognitive well-being. Instability for 'looked after' children is a major difficulty and can present with enduring consequences.

In the UK it is currently the case that children are removed from their parents when the level of care provided is deemed to be inadequate or inappropriate and a criteria of likely or actual significant harm to the child has been reached. This situation is not an infrequent scenario when the parent or parents have intellectual disabilities and lack the personal resources to parent successfully. As Ward (1993) observes, 'they are regularly confronted with the fear of losing their child to care'.

According to the government White Paper, *Valuing People: A New Strategy for the 21st Century* (DoH, 2001), the number of people with learning disabilities who are forming relationships and having children has steadily increased over the last 20 years. It is also acknowledged that this group is amongst the most socially and economically disadvantaged of the general population. Consequently, improved support and better developed services are advocated, but as numbers increase with limited specialist provision available, many of these families will have to face stressful and lengthy legislative procedures and alternative care will need to be secured for their children. It would seem that ever increasing pressure will be placed on an already beleaguered fostering and adoption service that operates primarily by providing non-kinship placements. So, should we begin to consider the advantages of children being placed within their natural families where ties, culture and relationships can be maintained?

Kinship Placement

'Kinship' is defined as a blood relationship or a sharing of characteristics or origins and is associated with such words as affinity, connection, understanding, empathy, similarity and tie. In the context of care placements for children a 'kinship placement' suggests that kin may be able to offer privileged or special care to a child by virtue of their family or friendship ties. Consequently, people who are connected, whether they are sisters, brothers, aunts, uncles, cousins, grandparents or friends of the child, are to be considered differently from those who are remote.

An examination of kinship placement literature shows that most research and publication has been conducted in the United States. Therefore, many of the early notions around kinship placement have a culturally specific resonance to the United States and a cautious approach is needed, although there is congruence with the emerging British research findings. It is important to make interpretations within the pertinent cultural and institutional framework in order to assess the transferability to the parameters of institutional practice of the UK.

In a thoughtful and discursive article, Brown et al. (2002) writing in a special issue devoted to the topic, argue that the foster care model does not do justice to the concept of kinship care (see Chapter 10). A close examination of the family histories of 30 young people in kinship care, as well as the household where they reside reveals a more complex picture. Brown's initial position is to critically examine the predominance of a nuclear family model consisting of a 'two-parent mother-and-father dyad caring for children' (op cit.: 54) which, in her opinion, fails to capture the adaptive and flexible nature of these families, which are particularly found in African American families 'and other American families who struggle against social and economic adversity' (op. cit.: 55). Indeed, one could argue that the nuclear family is itself a construct that emerged at a particular time in history and there is nothing natural about it; this concept is further questioned by Broad, 2001; Broad, 2004; Greeff, 2001.

Brown et al.'s qualitative study (op. cit.) has interesting and valuable conclusions. Kinship care families might look chaotic as they don't resemble the idealised nuclear family but the families studied by Brown et al. do provide an adaptive and accommodating framework with flexible roles. Practitioners need to work with their perceptions of chaos to recognise when children's needs are genuinely being met in kinship placements.

Where do we, in the UK, locate kinship placement in the framework of child care? This subject is discussed in detail elsewhere, but put simply when the need arises to remove a child from their birth parents consideration is usually given to two prime alternatives; fostering or adoption, although in some cases family placement may also be considered and indeed this was supported in legislation brought about by the Children Act 1989 (DoH, 1989). Much will depend on the circumstances of the child and their family but adoption is the more permanent option and more suited to infants requiring permanent care, whereas, fostering can provide either short-term or long-term care for older children. In the USA 'kinship care' involves the concept of family foster care where children are placed with foster parents who are biologically

related to them. 'Fostering' here refers to bringing up a child with parental care. Such an activity has been frequent enough, on an informal basis, throughout history[1] and across cultures, but the difference nowadays in this usage is that there is a legal and contractual obligation involved.

Who are kinship carers? Grogan-Kaylor (2000) cite Berrick et al. (1994) who found that, in the USA, kinship foster parents were more likely to be older, to be African American, and to have lower incomes than non-kin foster parents. Grogan-Kaylor (2000) was interested in which characteristics of children and their families would best predict whether the child was placed in kinship foster care or just foster care. He used administrative child welfare data from California and found that for example ethnicity did predict kinship care, confirming the results of Berrick et al. (1994). Latino and African American children are more likely to be placed in kin care. But children from families with one indicator of poverty (Aid to Families with Dependent Children eligibility of the family from which children were removed) were less likely to be placed with kin. Another concerning result was that infants were less likely to be placed with kin although there are good grounds for assuming that the more vulnerable need and deserve the quality of care that perhaps is better found in relatives than strangers.

The literature also suggests that kinship placements are gradually increasing in the USA and in the UK. There appears to be push as well as pull factors. The decline in licensed foster homes in the US is well documented (Grogan-Kaylor, 2000) and this resource is becoming less available. At the same time the attractiveness of kin placements in the eyes of the courts is recognised and guidelines in the USA (Pecora et al., 1992) suggest placement with relatives and in settings like families. Additionally, there are financial inducements so that in the US kinship foster parents are entitled to the same payment as non-relative foster parents. It is assumed that relatives come from a similar cultural background to that of the child and cultural similarity has become an important factor to consider in foster placement decisions.

As of 1998 kinship care in the US accounted for about one-third of all children in the formal foster

---

[1] According to the Oxford English Dictionary (OED electronic edition), the first occurrence of this term cited with a 'parenting' meaning was in a text from about AD 1205.

care system across the nation (Testa, 2002: 145). According to Testa (2002) there are certain advantages in assigning the role of carer to a private family and not the least of these is that the case can be closed and money saved. He quotes a figure of 50 per cent that can be saved per child in Illinois. The culture benefits of kinship placement are also stressed – not only are there likely to be shared cultural values thus making the transition into care less fraught with problems of learning new values and norms, but the roles are already established where the new guardians retain their identities as grandparents, aunts, and uncles.

Children of intellectually disabled parents

Children born to parents with learning disabilities span a wide range of intellectual potential. It is not a foregone conclusion that they too will experience similar intellectual problems to their parents. It is often the case that, although a diagnosis of learning or intellectual disability may be made for a parent, there may be no obvious or clear explanation as to the cause of the problem. In fact, it is useful at this point to consider just what is meant by the specific term of learning disability and the alternative term, intellectual disability. A comprehensive definition is that, 'Learning disability includes the presence of: a significantly reduced ability to understand new or complex information, to learn new skills (impaired intelligence), with; a reduced ability to cope independently (impaired social functioning); which started before adulthood, with lasting effect on development' (DoH, 2001). It follows that intellectual ability, social functioning and communication skills must all be considered when determining need. Standardised intelligence tests are the traditional means for identifying low intellectual functioning. However, the use of strict cut-off points can exclude some of the most vulnerable parents and lead to tensions amongst service providers (McGaw, 2000: 11). Although it is generally accepted that most adult learning disability services in the UK use a criterion of an IQ of 70 or below, some specialist services choose to have a broader range of IQ scores such as an IQ measure below 85 (Bradley et al., 2000: 9). It is felt by the writer that the label intellectual disabilities better suits the broader range option, and the advantage of including those parents whose

intellectual functioning is within the borderline range provides an improved response to need. However, the relationship between low intellectual functioning and low socio-economic factors becomes increasingly blurred. The difference between the congenital and environmental causes of poor parenting become less clear and can impede an early diagnosis of any developmental problems that may be present in the children involved. Where there is uncertainty for the professionals concerning the abilities of the parents there is also uncertainty concerning any delays shown by their children.

School performance of children in kinship placements

If children whose parents have intellectual disabilities are to achieve their full cognitive potential it is essential that they receive the necessary parental care. In the USA Sawyer and Dubowitz (1994) conducted the first comprehensive assessment of the school performance of children placed in kinship care. The vast majority of the group (91 per cent) were African-American and this fact limits the generalisability of the findings. Certainly, an analysis of children in kinship care suggests that they have serious school performance difficulties when compared with their peers, as shown by standardised achievement test scores. However, it is noted that Sawyer and Dubowitz (1994) did not compare children in kinship care with other groups such as children in foster care and argued that any comparison would be confounded because the severity of maltreatment and family dysfunction would probably differ substantially among these groups. In other words, there is no way of knowing whether any observed difference in school performance is a consequence of the difficulties and deficit the children bring to that group as part of the selection process or as a result of the treatment and service they receive when a member of that group.

In another paper based on the same data (Dubowitz and Sawyer, 1994) a further statistical analysis leads to the conclusion that '. . . children in kinship care manifest more school behaviour problems than their classroom peers' (p 905) with the caveat that there is considerable variability with children on the indices used. So although one can describe the groups in general terms, it would still be difficult to predict whether an individual child would benefit or not in terms of school performance from kinship placement.

A study by Leslie et al. (2002) reported on an analysis of data obtained with the Developmental Screening and Evaluation Project (DSEP) in California. Young children aged from 3 to 36 months who had been removed from their home after allegations of maltreatment and who were subsequently placed in various settings including kinship care, were examined using standard psychological tests. There was no difference in developmental delay between the groups of children in kinship care and in non-relative foster care. However, a closer examination of the data led Leslie to conclude that children raised in kinship care may have similar needs as children raised in non-relative care but may receive fewer services; a conclusion that is supported by other studies (Berrick and Barth, 1994; Broad et al., 2001; Broad, 2004; Dobowitz et al., 1994; Gleeson and Craig, 1994). Why? Leslie et al. argue that in the USA there are barriers to access such services and these barriers will include family functioning, insurance status, and decreased care supervision. Uncorroborated clinical experience in the UK would lead the writer to support the view that kinship carers are also likely to receive fewer services than other foster carers, and this is clearly endorsed by the British research of Bob Broad and his colleagues.

Support for kinship carers

Though it is generally acknowledged that parents with intellectual disabilities experience relationship difficulties and social isolation (Feldman et al., 2002; Llewellyn et al., 1995) it has been argued that they seldom parent in the absence of any support. Booth and Booth (1998) suggested that most families receive some paid or unpaid support through 'distributed competence' where back-up child care is provided by others. However, access to and provision of this support will depend to some degree on the competing market and available resources. There are few specific services for parents with intellectual disabilities despite an increasing literature that identifies support as a key to successful parenting for this population (Espe-Sherwindt and Kerlin, 1990; Seagull and Scheurer, 1986; Stenfert Kroese et al., 2002). Interestingly, the level of support necessary to maintain an adequate care situation has been described as 'that offered by a well-meaning extended family system' (Seagull and Scheurer, 1986). In spite of this, in instances known to the author, where family members have taken on the parental role for their relative with intellectual disabilities, they have struggled to secure services and have been denied access to financial support simply because they were kin carers. These issues are illustrated by the following vignette (case illustration 1) where confidentiality has been maintained and detail modified to protect identities.

Hawkins and Bland (2002) evaluated a programme in Texas called the Comprehensive Relative Enhancement Support and Training (CREST) project. The goal was to promote safety, permanency, and the well-being of children

---

Case illustration 1

Kate and David both had intellectual disabilities. They were married and had three children but were struggling to cope. Social services had become involved when their youngest child had failed to thrive as an infant but following a brief intervention the situation improved and the case was closed. The case was later re-opened when the family again began to struggle and multi-agency support was provided but the family failed to engage. The behaviour of the youngest child began to show clear signs of emotional disturbance. It was suggested that she be removed into voluntary foster care to allow further assessment. Consequently, the maternal aunt who was childless came forward to offer a kinship placement. She and her husband, who were themselves experiencing illness and financial hardship, underwent full assessment as foster carers. The child was placed with them and she quickly began to show significant improvement. A Residence Order was made in favour of the maternal aunt, and they were granted a Residence Order allowance. Other support, such as a link social worker, was not forthcoming and the case was closed by the child's social worker. Two voluntary agencies subsequently refused to offer financial support on the grounds that it was a kinship placement.

through care by relatives and support both in terms of (limited) financial assistance, management help, and some tuition. (Texas doesn't provide reimbursement or training to relatives who are caregivers.) This package was assessed for effectiveness using both qualitative and quantitative methods and results showed that there was a distinct enhancement effect with all major stakeholders in focus group investigations expressing appreciation and respect for the programme. The authors conclude that the additional benefits in terms of reduced costs as a result of such relatively cheap interventions compared with the expensive alternative of foster care presents a viable and acceptable option in a conservative political environment like the state of Texas.

The amount of support a family receives appears to be a crucial issue not only for carers but it also impacts on the children in those placements. Johnson-Garner and Meyers (2003) looked at issues in kinship care with African American children who represent a disproportionate number of children in kinship care (Berrick et al., 1994). They identified a subset of children who thrived in kinship care homes and attributed that to a quality they term 'resilience' which is a mixture of personal attributes and aspects of the broader social environment. All of these can interact so that good communication can be seen as a family characteristic that promotes its development in individual members. Johnson-Garner and Meyers (2003) identified this group of children as resilient. What makes a family and the child receiving kinship care 'resilient'? The availability of broad support is important and caregivers of resilient children often rely on extended family members for a variety of support functions including financial, emotional, and general advice and help. Close relations within the family, emphasising loyalty and interdependence are important; most importantly the ability to adjust to family roles in response to change. In summary, family strengths are key when kinship care is discussed.

Grandparent kinship placement

Lawrence-Webb et al. (2003) looked at a particular kind of kinship care – grandparent caregiving – using qualitative data with low-income African-American providers. Although

the data is limited to an analysis of the transcripts of two focus groups, an interesting theme that emerged was that grandparents need assistance in fully understanding the learning limitations and behavioural problems shown by the children. These older care providers own experience as parents are from a generation ago where some of the problems such as AIDS and crack cocaine were unknown.

Consequently, it is difficult to provide help or advice for these people.

Gibson (2002) addressed the issue of grandparenting and looked at the accounts 12 African American grandmothers gave of their experiences of looking after children where the parents were absent from the household. Five interrelated themes emerged and these were:

- *Traditions of kinkeeping*
  This refers to what one grandmother called 'a bonded family' which reflects a tradition of extended family caregiving.
- *Relationship with grandchildren*
  This theme reflects an involvement and investment in providing quality care for the grandchildren – succinctly put in the following quote:
  > I never wanted to see one of my loved ones in the care of someone they don't know because children don't ask to come into this world
  >   (op. cit.: 39)
- *Grandmother as the grandchild's only resource*
  This theme is characterised by a sense of inevitability where the grandmother takes over and has to – there is no choice – because the parents won't or can't and foster care just isn't an option.
- *Religious support*
  Faith has an important role to play in this community and 'the Lord' is called on as divine helper in intervention and decision-making.
- *The 'other' grandmother*
  And finally there is the other grandmother who may be unwilling or incapable of taking on the responsibility of looking after the child.

Although the information provided in this paper is specific to the small sample examined and cannot be generalised to other communities, such qualitative research does provide a rich source of feelings, justifications, and responses that can inform the experiences of grandparent carers. Interestingly, it is the experience of the writer, that where grandparents have offered kinship placements, there have been a wide variety of emotions evident. The added complexity of a parent with intellectual disabilities needs to be carefully considered. Feelings such as guilt, anger, love, obligation and the need to maintain family ties all appear to play a part. Case illustrations 2 and 3 (below) where again confidentiality has been maintained and detail modified to protect identities, describe clinical experience.

It is also worth considering the young people's views of kinship care summarised by Broad et al (2001) in particular, not wanting to be sent to a stranger, sustaining a sense of who they are and not being moved around and subject to disruption.

Although the above two examples appear tidy solutions to family problems, neither were straightforward decisions on the part of the respective grandparents. In the former case, the grandmother initially appeared torn between her own needs and those of her daughter and grandchild. In the latter case the grandparents had difficulty in communicating their wishes clearly, and only with the support of George's guardian were they able to do so. This suggests that child placements may well be located within the child's natural family but there is an obvious need to develop the appropriate facilitation, counselling and support to enable a positive and desired outcome.

In both of the instances described above, the level of stress encountered was considerable and this is further described in a study by Kelley et al. (2000) who examined the predictors of psychological distress in grandmother kinship care placements. Although there are fairly obvious ones that are well-documented, such as poor physical health, social isolation, and financial problems there are also less recognised factors

---

Case Illustration 2

Janet was a 19 year old single mother with intellectual disabilities. Following a residential assessment, it became apparent that even with significant support, she was unable to parent a child. A family conference was held and it was clear that the maternal grandmother wished for the baby to remain with its natural close-knit family. Although the grandmother did not feel able to offer a placement herself at this time, she was active in identifying a maternal cousin who agreed to offer a kinship placement. Contact between the child, the mother and grandmother was frequent and informal and included regular stays at the grandmother's home. When the child attained the age of three years circumstances within the family changed and the cousin remarried. At this point the grandmother felt able to come forward herself to offer a placement resulting in little disruption and emotional trauma to the child. The qualities within this family are representative of the strengths necessary to produce a 'resilient' child as identified by Johnson-Garner and Meyers (2003); close relations within the family and the ability to adjust to family roles in response to change.

Case Illustration 3

Maggie and Peter both had intellectual disabilities and were the parents of a four year old child, George. Maggie's elder child, Adam was in a kinship placement with the maternal grandparents, who were both in their seventies. Maggie had a large extended family that provided respite care to Adam as a means of supporting their parents. Over time Maggie and Peter's home gradually became an unsuitable environment for a child and they began to neglect George. He was removed from their care and placed with the maternal grandparents who offered a kinship placement. The grandfather was unwell and there was much debate about the appropriateness of the placement given the ages of the grandparents. However, other factors were considered such as longevity within the family, extended family support, and the fact that George's half-brother was with him. It was agreed that Maggie would have daily contact with George and play an active role in taking him to and from school. This arrangement allowed for a protective environment but maintained strong family ties.

which involve, for example, the circumstances surrounding the onset of care, change in role demands, conflict with the children's parents, behaviour problems with the grandchildren themselves, and issues relating to public policies and legal matters. So an older person, in perhaps already failing health, is suddenly called on in circumstances relating to the inadequate parenting of her son or daughter to assume a role she thought she had discharged some years ago and to redefine their relationship to their grandchild. This example may be considered extreme for most families but it serves to illustrate some of the problems that can arise particularly where the parent or parents have intellectual disabilities. Kelley et al. found, not surprisingly, that '. . . grandmothers who reported fewer resources, less social support, and poorer physical health tended to experience higher levels of psychological distress' (p319). Almost 30 per cent of this sample had psychological distress scores in the clinical range indicating need for clinical intervention.

Are parents with intellectual disability a special case for consideration?

Parents with intellectual disability are a wide and diverse population and their learning needs should not immediately indicate poor parenting. Many factors will contribute to an assessment of need, not least the level of support that might be available to them. It is unclear how intellectual disability in itself impacts on the ability to parent and different strategies may be needed to cope with the environmental conditions in which they frequently live (Stenfert Kroese, 2002). However, it is the case that in the UK parents with intellectual disabilities are frequently represented in the legislative child care system; a system that struggles to adapt to the needs of these parents and one where the parents themselves are challenged to comprehend the process. We should not make generalisations and assumptions based on their membership to a particular group. But, their vulnerability is recognised and this often means a need to assess their parenting skills in a safe and supportive environment. These assessments tend to focus on the mother and are frequently conducted in generic mother and baby units or special mother and child foster placements which involve unfamiliar surroundings and social networks. Whatever the prognosis in these situations is

there will be an unavoidable need for further planning and disruption to the parent and child or children. Would it not be more appropriate, at least in some cases, to first consider a natural home-based assessment with support from both professional and family sources? It is of course acknowledged that, for some parents with intellectual disabilities, extended family support will be inappropriate and traditional care placements may be inevitable, but where possible we should be taking a more pro-active and innovative approach to this difficult challenge.

Scannapieco and Hegar (2002) describe how kinship care is a way of meeting children's needs in the USA and is becoming a more established way of meeting the needs of children in care in other western countries (Greeff, 2001). They argue that kinship care providers should be empowered to identify their support and intervention needs and that they should do this in partnership with their social worker. A family decision-making model is viewed as the best vehicle for promoting the triadic relationship of child, parent and family and undoubtedly this model provides a useful assessment tool for families where one or both parents have intellectual disabilities.

It can be argued that the child protection issues that arise for parents with intellectual disabilities are precisely the same issues that arise for all families that are struggling to cope with the parental role and that they do not warrant special status. They are simply exacerbated by the fact that the parents are of low intellectual functioning. To some extent this is of course true, however, as noted earlier parents with intellectual disability seldom show any intention of harm to their child or children. They frequently have a strong desire to parent but it is through an omission of care brought about by their intellectual limitations that they may ultimately lose their parental rights.

If the option of kinship placement were to be considered for parents with intellectual disabilities at the outset of their parental careers, as a matter of course, and prior to serious concern, then in appropriate cases an extended family system could emerge that would serve to cushion and protect its members in times of crisis. This, in turn, would lead to a smoother transition of roles if subsequently the birth parents were ultimately unable to cope. The child or children would be the responsibility of a wide kinship network rather than cared for by isolated individuals within that family system.

References

Berrick, J. and Barth, R.P. (1994) Research on Kinship Foster Care: What do we Know? Where do we go From Here? *Children and Youth Services Review.* 16: 1, 1–5.

Berrick, J.D., Barth, R.P. and Needell, B. (1994) A Comparison of Kinship Foster Homes and Foster Family Home: Implications for Kinship Foster Care as Family Preservation. *Children and Youth Services Review.* 16, 33–63.

Booth, T. and Booth, W. (1994) *Parenting Under Pressure: Mothers and Fathers With Learning Difficulties.* Milton Keynes: Open University Press.

Booth, T. and Booth, W. (1998) *Growing-Up with Parents Who Have Learning Difficulties.* London: Routledge.

Bradley, R., Toft, S. and Collins, G. (2000) Parenting Assessments. *Learning Disability Practice.* 2: 5, 9–11.

Broad, B. (Ed.) (2001) *Kinship Care: The Placement Choice for Children and Young People.* Lyme Regis: Russell House Publishing.

Broad, B., Hayes, R. and Rushforth, C. (2001) *Kith and Kin: Kinship Care for Vulnerable Young People.* London: NCB and Joseph Rowntree Foundation.

Broad, B. (2004) Kinship Care for Children in the U.K: Messages from Research, Lessons for Policy and Practice. *European Journal of Social Work.* 7: 2, 211–27.

Brown, S., Cohon, D. and Wheeler, R. (2002) African American Extended Families and Kinship Care: How Relevant is the Foster Care Model for Kinship Care? *Children and Youth Services Review.* 24: 1, 53–77.

Craft, A. (1993) Parents With Learning Disabilities: An Overview. In Craft, A. (Ed.) *Parents with Learning Disabilities.* Kidderminster: BILD.

Department of Education and Skills (2004) *Removing Barriers to Achievement: The Government's Strategy for SEN.* London: HMSO.

Department of Health (1989) *The Children Act 1989.* London: HMSO.

Department of Health (2001) *Valuing People: A New Strategy for Learning Disability for the 21st Century.* London: HMSO.

Dubowitz, H. et al. (1994) Children in Kinship Care: How do They Fare? *Children and Youth Services Review.* 16, 85–106.

Dubowitz, H. and Sawyer, R.J. (1994) School Behaviour of Children in Kinship Care. *Child Abuse and Neglect.* 18: 11, 899–911.

Espe-Sherwinde, M. and Kerlin, S. (1990) Early Intervention With Parents With Mental Retardation: Do We Empower or Impair? *Infants and Young Children.* 2, 21–8.

Feldman, M.A. et al. (2002) Relationship Between Social Support, Stress and Mother-Child Interactions in Mothers with Intellectual Disabilities. *Journal of Applied Research in Intellectual Disabilities.* 15, 314–24.

Gibson, P.A. (2002) African American Grandmothers as Caregivers: Answering the Call to Help Their Grandchildren. *Families in Society: The Journal of Contemporary Human Services.* 83: 1, 35–43.

Gleeson, J.P. and Craig, L.C. (1994) Kinship Care in Child Welfare: An Analysis of States' Policies. *Children and Youth Services Review.* 16, 7–31.

Greeff, R. (2001) Family Dynamics in Kinship Foster Care. In Broad, B. (Ed.) Kinship Care: The Placement Choice for Children and Young People. Lyme Regis: Russell House Publishing.

Grogan-Kaylor, A. (2000) Who Goes Into Kinship Care? The Relationship of Child and Family Characteristics to Placement Into Kinship Foster Care. *Social Work Research.* 24: 3, 132–41.

Hawkins, C.A. and Bland, T. (2002) Program Evaluation of the CREST Project: Empirical Support for Kinship Care as an Effective Approach to Permanency Planning. *Child Welfare.* LXXXI: 2, 271–92.

Hegar, R.L. and Scannapieco, M. (1999) *Kinship Foster Care: Policy, Practice and Research.* New York: OUP.

Johnson-Garner, M.Y. and Meyers, S.A. (2003) What Factors Contribute to the Resilience of African-American Children Within Kinship Care? *Child and Youth Care Forum.* 32: 5, 255–69.

Kelley, S.J. et al. (2000) Psychological Distress in Grandmother Kinship Care Providers: The Role of Resources, Social Support, and Physical Health. *Child Abuse & Neglect.* 24: 3, 311–21.

Lawrence-Webb, C., Okundaye, J.N. and Hafner, G. (2003) Education and Kinship Caregivers: Creating a New Vision. *Families in Society.* 84: 1, 135–42.

Leslie, L.K. et al. (2002) Developmental Delay in Young Children in Child Welfare by Initial Placement Type. *Infant Mental Health Journal.* 23: 5, 496–516.

Llewellyn, G., McConnell, D. and Bye, R. (1995) *Parents with Intellectual Disability.* Sydney: University of Sydney.

McGaw, S. and Sturmey, P. (1994) Assessing Parents With Learning Disabilities: The Parental Skills Model. *Child Abuse Review*. 3, 36–51.

McGaw, S. (2000) *What Works for Parents With Learning Disabilities?* Basingstoke: Barnardo's.

Murphy, G. and Feldman, M.A. (2002) Parents with Intellectual Disabilities. *Journal of Applied Research in Intellectual Disabilities*. 15, 281–4.

Pecora, P.J. et al. (1992) *The Child Welfare Challenge*. New York: Aldine de Gruyter.

Sawyer, R.J. and Dubowitz, H. (1994) School Performance of Children in Kinship Care. *Child Abuse and Neglect*. 18: 7, 597.

Scannapieco, M. and Hegar, R.L. (2002) Kinship Care Providers: Designing an Array of Supportive Services. *Child and Adolescent Social Work Journal*. 1: 4, 315–27.

Seagull, E.A. and Scheurer, S.L. (1986) Neglected and Abused Children of Mentally Retarded Children. *Child Abuse & Neglect*. 10, 493–500.

Stenfert Kroese, B. et al. (2002) Social Support Networks and Psychological Well-being of Mothers with Intellectual Disabilities. *Journal of Applied Research in Intellectual Disabilities*. 15, 324–40.

Testa, M.F. (2002) Subsidized Guardianship: Testing an Idea Whose Time Has Finally Come. *Social Work Research*. 26: 3, 145–58.

Ward, L. (1993) Partnership with Parents. In Craft, A. (Ed.) *Parents with Learning Disabilities*. Kidderminster: British Institute of Learning Disabilities.

Waterhouse, S. (2001) Keeping Children in Kinship Placements Within Court Proceedings. In Broad, B. (Ed.) *Kinship Care: The Placement Choice for Children and Young People*. Lyme Regis: Russell House Publishing.

Wolfensberger, W. (1992) Deinstitutionalisation Policy: How is it Made, by Whom and Why? *Clinical Psychology Forum*. January, 7–11.

Chapter Six

Towards an Empirical Basis for Domestic Violence Risk Assessment

Calvin Bell

Introduction

Much of the population of 'looked after' children have lived in families where domestic violence has been present. Research has consistently found a relationship between child abuse and domestic violence. There is evidence that 90 per cent of violent instances occur when children are present or near to the attack and that one in three children attempt to intervene to protect their mothers, (Rowsell, 2003). The assessment of potential kinship placements needs to consider whether violence has been present, the impact on the child and the capacity of carers to protect from physical or emotional harm. The focus of this chapter is assessment. For a discussion on definition and prevalence see Rowsell (2003) and Calder (2004).

The increasing appearance of the issue on political and social agendas has led to a growth in demand for domestic violence risk assessments. However, as Calder and Hackett (2003) point out, the *Assessment Framework* (DoH, 2000) provides no guidance on assessing for domestic violence and the framework triangle itself is flawed in that it collapses mothers' and fathers' roles into one when considering parenting capacity. This chapter draws on the growing body of literature to consider the limitations of current risk assessment technology. It identifies the key demographic and psycho-social variables which place an individual at an elevated risk of domestic violence perpetration, as well as those factors associated with elevated vulnerability to domestic violence. It is hoped that assessors of kinship placements will have essential empirical information available to equip them to ask the relevant questions in the assessment process.

Assessor performance

Professional evaluators have been criticised for impressionistic assessments based on clinical interview rather than on an examination of an individual's established record of behaviour that offers by far the most reliable indicator of risk (Moore, 1996).[1] Probabilistic error in risk assessments thus commonly involves the inflated salience of clinical or impressionistic assertions at the expense of under-rating base-rate significance (Campbell, 1995). Researchers therefore recommend that clinical evaluation be regarded as a mechanism for revision (usually modest except in very exceptional circumstance) of the basal empirically-based risk estimate upward or downward (Beaumont, 1999) and warn against opinion which markedly departs from the empirically-based assessment unless such variations are capable of thorough justification (Hall, 2001).

Reliability

The more infrequent an individual's past violence, the less chance of predictive accuracy (MacDonald and MacDonald, 1999; Webster et al., 1994). The more serious forms of violence are generally the least frequent. The usefulness of risk assessments is therefore more likely to be at its greatest in relation to common events rather than to low-probability but potentially high-cost events which may cause public protection agencies far more concern (Beaumont, 1999). Infanticide and spousal homicide, for example, are both difficult to predict because of their relative rarity compared with other forms of domestic violence. Conversely, all other factors considered, the more often behaviour occurs, the more likely it is to be repeated (Moore, 1996).

The likely *severity* of an individual's violent behaviour is important in informing judgements about acceptable levels of risk: *seriousness* should be inversely related to the level of risk which may be deemed acceptable. Intervention measures to protect a child may well be warranted, for example, where the risk of harm occurring is identified as being low or moderate but where the injuries resulting from any violence are likely to be severe or life-threatening. The probability that an individual will act in a way that is likely to cause harm in the future is therefore not necessarily the same as the probability that they will cause *serious* harm (Wald and Woolverton, 1990).

Despite a plethora of predictive instruments and screening tools, risk assessment remains an *estimation of probabilities* (Webster et al., 1994) and at best a 'good guess' (Kemshall, 1996): it is an interpretive task, *an informed judgement under uncertainty*. Commentators therefore seem to concur that standardised instruments, attitudinal scales or questionnaires offer no substitute for the painstaking task of examining an individual's background, past behaviour, mental and social functioning and personal circumstances (especially since there is no profile of a typical domestic violence perpetrator). Risk assessment is therefore a more complex task than the dominant models in the literature assume (MacDonald and MacDonald, 1999) there is, as yet, no 'gold standard' for domestic violence risk assessment (Beaumont, 1999).

Risk factors for men's perpetration of domestic violence

Though the dominant feminist discourse in the field continues to assert that domestic violence is a cross-cultural phenomenon which occurs (more or less equally) across all social groups, the growing body of literature exploring the relationship between domestic violence and social exclusion makes it increasingly clear that it is not equally widespread. In addition to an individual being male,[2] factors that put a man at an increased risk of domestic violence perpetration when compared with the population at large include:

- **Being under 30 years of age.** Contemporary research identifies men aged between 18 and 30 years as being at greatest risk of committing domestic violence (Bowker, 1983; Brisson, 1981; Gelles et al., 1994; Roberts, 1987).
- **Military personnel or veterans.** Some research points to the considerably higher level of domestic violence perpetrated by military men than by their civilian counterparts (Prigerson et al., 2002; Shupe et al., 1987).
- **Poorly educated men.** Again, no doubt linked to other social exclusion indicators, men's low

educational attainment and occupational status has been identified as increasing the risk of their behaving violently to their partner (Bowker, 1993; Gelles et al., 1994; Hotaling and Sugarman, 1990, 1986) especially when inferior to that of their partners' (Steinmetz, 1979).

- **Being currently unemployed or on low income.** It is not known[3] why being without a paid job in itself increases risk (Heise, 1998) but the fact remains that men who are unemployed, unable to sustain permanent employment or on low income are identified in numerous studies (Campbell, 1995, 1986; DeKeseredy et al., 2004; Gelles, 1997; Gelles et al., 1994; Stuart and Campbell, 1989) as posing an increased risk of domestic violence perpetration, including murder (Dobash et al., 2002).
- **Being in a casual or co-habiting relationship (as opposed to being married).** Men in casual ('dating') or cohabiting relationships have been found to be at greater risk of committing both lethal and non-lethal domestic violence than their married counterparts (Brownridge and Hallis, 2001; DeMaris and Jackson, 1987; O'Leary et al., 1994).
- **Experience of abuse in family of origin.** There is some truth to the commonly held belief in the intergenerational cycle of violence. Whilst not all boys who are abused grow up to be violent, experience of violence as a child is positively correlated with partner abuse by men (Browne et al., 1999; Fagan et al., 1983; Hamberger and Hastings, 1991; Hotaling and Sugarman, 1986; Yexley et al., 2002).
- **Exposure to an abusive parental role model.** Exposure to domestic violence in one's childhood is not a *prerequisite* for future abuse.[4] However, comprehensive reviews of studies reveal that by far the most robust risk marker for the subsequent perpetration of violence toward an intimate partner is witnessing or otherwise being exposed to family violence and abusive role models as a child or adolescent. This is particularly pertinent to boys who witness their father abusing their mother (Bell, 1995; Campbell, 1995; Dobash et al., 2002; Gelles et al., 1994; Silverman and Williamson, 1997).
- **Childhood conduct problems.** A consistent research finding is that boys with a history of family disruption or those who exhibit early antisocial behaviour are at elevated risk of

perpetrating violence in adulthood (Dutton, 1988; Quinsey et al., 1998; Skilling et al., 2001; Widom, 1989). Other researchers also found that in longitudinal studies, early antisocial behaviour was a strong predictor of violence within intimate relationships (Capaldi and Crosby 1997; Magdol et al. 1998).

- **Substance misuse.** Among the most prominent risk factors for violence toward a partner cited in the literature is a man's history of (especially chronic) misuse of drugs or alcohol (Dobash and Dobash, 1998; McCloskey, 2001; O'Keefe, 1997; Sharps et al., 2001; Symons et al., 1998; Thompson et al., 2003).

- **Mental health.** Though individuals who suffer from minor mental health difficulties are no more likely to commit violent acts than the population at large (Swanson et al., 1990), there are established links between severe mental health problems, personality disorders[5] and para-suicide and an increased risk of violence within intimacy (Saunders, 1995, 1993; Straus, 1993; Goldsmith, 1990; Stuart and Campbell, 1989).

- **Criminal activity.** Various studies indicate that a prior criminal record for offences *unrelated* to partner abuse or involvement in a 'criminal life-style' (Saunders, 1995) puts a man at increased risk of violence in general and partner violence (including murder) in particular (Dobash et al., 2002; Gondolf, 1988; Klein, 1993; Kropp et al., 1995; Sonkin et al., 1985; Straus, 1991).

- **Breach of bail or court order conditions.** Criminologists have established that violent offenders who have breached their bail, probation or parole orders (regardless of the nature of the original offence) are more likely than their compliant counterparts to continue to behave violently (Andrews et al., 1990; Hart, Kroppe and Hare, 1988).

- **Generalised aggression.** Although the majority of domestically abusive men restrict their violence to intimate relationships, there is widespread agreement among researchers that men with a history of physical violence outside the context of the home and intimacy are at increased risk of assaulting a partner and that those who are 'pan-violent' or 'generally violent' are among the most dangerous of domestically violent men (Campbell et al., 1998; Hanson et al., 1997; Hilton et al., 2001; Quinsey et al., 1998; Saunders, 1995, 1992; Tweed and Dutton, 1998).

- **Cruelty towards animals.** Experts in the field increasingly recognise a correlation between cruelty to animals and domestic violence (Arkow, 1996; Ascione et al., 1997; Lerner, 1999; Metropolitan Police, 2003; Straus, 1993).

- **Aggression towards another family member.** Violence toward a sibling or other member of one's family emerges as a risk factor for perpetration against a partner. Many researchers have found that men who have previously assaulted a family member (other than their children or partners) are at increased risk of repeating violence within the home (Dutton, 1998; Dutton and Hart, 1992; Hotaling and Sugarman, 1986; Peacock and Rothman, 2001; Saunders, 1992).

- **Aggression towards a previous intimate.** Actual or attempted assault against an intimate puts an individual at increased risk of violence perpetration within another relationship. It seems clear that the majority of domestically assaultive men are violent in more than one relationship (e.g. Dutton, 1995; Saunders, 1995; Woffordt et al., 1994). In their study, Woffordt et al. (1994) found that over half of men who were violent to a partner went on to abuse a second woman.

- **Aggression towards a child.** Though mistreating a child's primary carer invariably causes harm to both, the *direct* abuse of a child is a risk factor for the perpetration of domestic violence toward a partner (and *vice versa*). Mullender and Morley (1994) and other researchers (e.g. Appel and Holden, 1998; Kelly, 1996; Gelles et al., 1994; Straus, 1993, 1991, 1983; Saunders, 1995, 1994) have identified that where a man has abused a child, especially violently (generally defined as more severe than a 'spanking'), there is the strong likelihood that he will also have abused the mother (and vice versa).

- **Violence within a current relationship.** Universal among violence researchers is the view that those individuals who have acted violently in the past are much more likely to do so again when compared with those who have not. A previous (even minor) assault against a partner therefore constitutes one of the most robust risk markers for future violence perpetration within that (and other) relationships. It is also commonly accepted in the field that once physical violence is introduced into a relationship it is likely to escalate over time both in frequency and severity (Campbell, 1995; Dobash and Dobash, 1979; Dutton, 1995; Fagan et al., 1983; Saunders, 1995; Sonkin, 1987; Straus et al., 1980).

The cessation of aggression is also seen as least likely in those men who have perpetrated *severe* violence against a victim: the use and threat of weapons, serious injury inflicted, sadism, credible death threats, attempts to strangle and violence during pregnancy are among those regarded by researchers and practitioners alike as powerful indicators of high risk (Campbell, 1995; Edwards, 1997; Goodman et al., 2000; Weisz et al., 2000).

- **Domination**. Male dominance may be the most widely mentioned risk factor for the use of physical violence against an intimate partner (Browne, 1987; Campbell, 1995; Garrity and Baris, 1995; Hamby, 2001; Straus, 1993).
- **Sexual assault.** Generally associated with the most dangerous of domestically violent men is their sexual assault of or forced sex against a partner, acquaintance or stranger (Bergen, 1999; Campbell, 1995; Garrity and Baris, 1995; Saunders, 1992; Straus, 1993).
- **Mental abuse.** Emotional and psychological abuse is highly correlated with physical violence and is a strong longitudinal predictor of physical aggression (O'Leary and Maiuro, 2001; Murphy and Hoover, 2001).
- **Proprietariness.** Those men who have exhibited obsessional behaviour, delusional or extreme sexual jealousy or high possessiveness towards a partner or who attempt to isolate a partner or otherwise restrict her freedom are seen as posing a high risk to their victims (Browne, 1987; Campbell, 1995; Garrity and Baris, 1995; Hart, 2001; Straus, 1993; Wilson and Daly, 1999, 1995, 1993).
- **Post-separation harassment.** Of particular concern are those men who have continued their attempts to control (or punish) their partner through harassment, violence, hostage-taking and/or stalking[6] *after* separation or divorce. With this type of offender, it is the very period during and following a couple's separation that poses the greatest threat to their victims (including friends, family members and those who help them leave), especially when it is the woman who has initiated the end of the relationship (Bancroft and Silverman, 2002; Hardesty, 2002; Sever, 1997; McMahon and Pence, 1993; Dobash and Dobash, 2001; Gelles, 1997; Browne, 1987).

Weighting of factors

Whilst the existence of any factor is seen as an indicator of risk, the co-existence of several indicators holds far greater predictive power than any single one. Particular 'volatile combinations' (Holder and Corey, 1993) also denote especially high risk of domestic violence: for example, the combination of witnessing paternal violence to one's mother and of directly suffering parental abuse is especially highly correlated with the perpetration of domestic violence against a partner in adulthood (Campbell, 1995; Chapters 4 and 5, Saunders, 1993).

Vulnerability factors for women[7]

A perpetrator's personal and offence profile provides a much more robust risk indicator than the characteristics of the victim, and there is little evidence to suggest that the personalities of women contribute to their own victimisation.[8] Nevertheless, there are various demographic, developmental and environmental factors that increase the risk of a woman becoming or remaining a victim of domestic violence. These are important considerations during the process of the assessment of kinship placements. The level of a mother's vulnerability is an important factor when considering risks to her and therefore to her children.[9] The presence of the following vulnerability factors increases the likelihood that a woman will be subjected to domestic violence when compared with the population at large:

- **Being under 25 years.** Smaller scale studies and national surveys invariably find that youth appears as a constant risk factor for victimisation by domestic violence (Alpert et al., 1997; Anderson, 1997; Klein et al., 1997; Mirrlees-Black, 1999; O'Donnell et al., 2002; Rodgers, 1994; Walby and Allen, 2004).[10]
- **Low educational attainment.** According to researchers such as O'Donnell et al. (2002), women who are educationally disadvantaged are at higher risk of exposure to domestic violence.
- **Subjection abuse or harsh parenting as a child.** Harsh corporal punishment and/or sexual abuse during childhood has been shown to substantially elevate the probability of a woman being subjected to domestic violence by a boyfriend or spouse as an adult (Black et al.,

2001; Coid, 2000; Downs et al., 1992; Ehrensaft et al., 2003; Marshall and Rose, 1990; Riggs et al., 2000; Schumacher et al., 2001; Simons et al., 1993; Weaver and Clum, 1996).

- **Exposure to violence between one's parents.** Research shows that witnessing domestic violence as a child puts a woman at substantially elevated risk of victimisation as an adult (Ehrensafet et al., 2003; Gillioz, 1997; Rodgers, 1994; Jackson, 1996).
- **Previous sexual or physical assault.** Previous sexual or physical assault as an adolescent or adult is associated with a high risk of repeat assault (Bosch, 2002; Rodgers, 1994; Roscoe and Benaske, 1985; Weaver and Clum, 1996).
- **The woman's own use of violence within the relationship.** Riggs et al. (2000) point to research which highlights aggression on the part of a woman as being positively associated with subsequent violence perpetration on the part of her male partner. It remains unclear whether this link reflects women's use of violence in self-defence or some form of 'mutual combat' but regardless of the dynamics involved, a woman's own use of aggression places her at risk of future victimisation with the relationship.
- **Disability.** Although in its infancy, research into the prevalence of domestic violence against women with disabilities suggests that physical, sensory or mental impairment puts women at increased risk of domestic violence victimisation (Chenoweth, 1997; Rodgers, 1994).
- **Poor health.** In the British Crime Survey (2004) women who self-reported being in poor health suffered domestic violence at more than twice the rate of their healthy counterparts.
- **Mental health difficulties.** Women with mental health difficulties are at increased risk of sexual and physical assault according to Acierno et al., 1997; Brown, 1997; Goodman et al., 1995; Jacobson and Richardson, 1987; Kelley and Moore, 2000; and Rodgers, 1994.
- **Pregnancy.** According to Jasinki (2004) whether the risk of domestic violence increases during pregnancy remains unclear. However, other research reveals that domestic violence often starts (typically 30 per cent of cases) or intensifies during pregnancy (Bowker and Maurer, 1987; Curry and Harvey, 1998; McFarlane et al., 1995; Mezey, 1997).
- **Substance abuse**. Women's alcohol and drug use is strongly associated with exposure to domestic violence (Mears et al., 2001; Melchior et al., 1999; Mirrlees-Black, 1999).
- **Prostitution.** A study of prostitutes in Bradford found that 42 per cent had been victims of violence from their boyfriend (Streets and Lanes Project). Farley and Barkan (1998) found a strong link between prostitution and sexual abuse. These women may also be less able to seek help and less willing to do so because of the fear of prejudice.
- **Women on benefit or low income**. Whilst there is evidence that abused women living in more affluent households are less likely to inform the police and to seek medical help (e.g. Walby and Allen, 2004), numerous studies reveal that women living in poverty experience domestic violence at disproportionately high rates. Mirrlees-Black (1999) reported that families in financial difficulties were two to three times more at risk of domestic violence than those who were financially secure.[11]
- **Not working outside the home**. Women who are unemployed or 'housewives' are more than twice as likely to face domestic violence than their employed counterparts (Mirrlees-Black, 1999; Walby and Myhill, 2001). The risk of exposure is also regarded as being a function of the *amount* of time spent in the home.
- **Absence of an active social network, or living in a rural or isolated community**. The absence of an active social network or isolation from one's community, extended family and other support can be seen as an aggravating factor in inter-spousal violence as it restricts access to potential resources such as emotional support, information, transport and legal and professional assistance (Stuart and Holtzworth-Munroe, 1995).
- **Being in rented accommodation**. No doubt linked to a household's income and stability, housing tenure also appears as a risk factor for women's exposure to domestic violence. British Crime Surveys (Mirrlees-Black, 1999; Walby and Allen, 2004) have revealed that, for women, the highest risk of domestic violence is found among those living in the social rented sector, followed by the private rented sector and least among owners or co-owners of their own homes.
- **Overcrowding.** The cumulative effect of other factors and overcrowding (often interpreted as more people in a dwelling than the number of habitable rooms) can lead to substantially

increased stress levels and therefore increased risk of domestic violence occurring.

- **An ethnic minority background.** Where minority women do face increased risk, it often appears to be associated with poverty and isolation (Browne, 1997; Jewkes, 2002). Nevertheless, many women from ethnic minorities are likely to face increased vulnerability to abuse because of their greater difficulty in accessing services because of discrimination among service providers and the barriers provided by language and other cultural differences (Morley and Mullender, 1994; Pilspa, 2002; Richards, 2004).
- **Immigrant women, especially those with an insecure immigration status.** American studies suggest that 'foreign-born' women are at greater risk of homicide; risk factors for immigrant women include the stress that immigration places on relationships, a greater fear of seeking help outside the family (especially if in the country illegally), difficulty in finding services, ignorance of rights and language barriers (Mama, 1989).
- **Dating, co-habiting and separated (as opposed to married) women.** The British Crime Survey, Gelles et al. (1994) and O'Donnell et al. (2002) and Walby and Allen (2004) found that women who were separated, divorced or co-habiting were at greater risk of domestic violence than those who were married: those who are separated being at greatest risk.
- **Financial dependence on a partner.** Kalmus and Straus (1982) argued that the rate of severe violence was nearly three times higher among maritally dependent women (e.g. the women's lack of independent income or where the husband earned more than 75 per cent of the couple's income).
- **Age disparities.** An age gap of at least ten years – especially young women married to older men – appears as a risk factor for lethal domestic violence (Aldridge and Browne, 2003; Wilson et al., 1998, 1993). The risk appears to increase with the extent of the age disparity.
- **Power imbalances (such as physical strength, class, status, education).** Domestic violence is also at its highest in inegalitarian households. Relative power imbalances (e.g. the couple's class, status or physical strength) and women's dependence have been found to augment considerably the incidence and

severity of domestic violence (Walby and Myhill, 2001).

- **Having (particularly pre-school) children, especially if from a prior union.** According to Walby and Allen's (2004) analysis of the British Crime Survey, the presence of children in the household nearly doubles the risk of domestic violence for women. This reinforces the need to consider the vulnerabilities of women and children together. Stanko et al. (1998) found an even higher association with rates over twice as high for women with children.
- **Repeated separations and reconciliations or ongoing conflict.** Couples who have a history of separation and reconciliation, ongoing or unresolved marital conflict and verbal aggression have been cited as among the strongest correlates of physical abuse (Aldorado and Sugarman, 1996; McKenry et al., 1995; O'Leary et al., 1994; Wilson and Daly, 1993). High risks of violence have also been identified by some researchers in cases where the woman wants the relationship to end but the man is unwilling to separate or the man is living apart from his partner but wants to resume co-habitation despite the woman's resistance (McNeil, 1987; Sonkin et al., 1985; Wilson et al., 1993).

The impact of domestic violence on children

It is important that those conducting the assessment have some insight into the range of effects children exposed to domestic violence experience. The links between marital conflict (as opposed to violence) and children's poor development have been the subject of widespread clinical interest and research for many years (Holden et al., 1998). However, though social scientists are fully cognisant of the emotional harm experienced by children who have suffered direct physical abuse, the effects on children of exposure to *marital violence* have been surprisingly far less widely reported. Nevertheless the psychological and behavioural sequelae are now beginning to be well documented (see Bancroft and Silverman, 2002; Gleason, 1995; Hester et al., 2000; Jaffe et al., 1990; Kolbo et al., 1996; Mullender and Morley, 1994), as are the effects on children's social worlds, such as their interpersonal relationships with teachers and friends (see Holden et al., 1998).

Post-traumatic stress

Research at the Royal Free Hospital in London has confirmed the traumatic impact on most children of witnessing extreme and sudden violence. Pynoos and Nader (1987) illustrated the extent of the emotional and behavioural disturbance of these children concluding that their behaviour was similar to children suffering post-traumatic shock. Mertin and Mohr (2002) suggest that a proportion of children who regularly witness domestic violence do meet the criteria for Post Traumatic Stress Disorder as did Brandon and Lewis (1996) who also maintained that witnessing domestic violence during childhood is a risk factor for greater psychological distress in adulthood. Silvern and Kaersvang (1989) propose that children who are repeatedly exposed to violence in the family indeed perceive each incident as a traumatic episode needing resolution before the child can resume normal functioning. Since in some families these incidents occur many times a week, the children may still be reeling from the effects of observing one traumatic episode and unable to recover before they witness another.

In fact, a review of the available research shows that children who witness violence between their parents have emotional and behavioural difficulties that mirror those of children currently identified as being abused (Carroll, 1994). Also of interest are the research findings by Sternberg and colleagues (1993) who found that children who were exposed to the abuse of their mothers exhibited the same level of symptomatology as those who had themselves been abused by a parent *and* been exposed to abuse of their mothers. Jaffe et al. (1990) also maintain that children from domestically violent homes share much in common with children from families with an alcoholic mother or father or who witness homicide or other extremely disturbing events.

Exposure to aggression and abuse also harmful

Ballard and Cummings (1990) found that children responded as negatively to a parent's aggression towards objects (e.g. kicking something, smashing possessions) as they did to inter-parent abuse and research by Jouriles et al. (1996) and

Laumakis (1998) suggests that such behaviour and other forms of marital abuse such as threats, insults and swearing are each correlated with children's adjustment problems. For their part, Cummings and Zahn-Waxler (1992) evidenced that even expressions of anger between parents negatively affects children's emotional and behavioural development.

Emotional and behavioural difficulties

In their assessment of 1,069 cases of children from violent homes, Fantuzzo and Lindquist (1989) indicated that children who witnessed parental violence were generally more likely to exhibit *external* behavioural problems at home, school and in the community where they tended to be more aggressive (e.g. fights with siblings or other children) than children from non-violent homes, as well as *internalised* symptoms such as depression, suicidal ideation, specific fears and phobias, tics, enuresis and insomnia and low self-esteem (for pre-school age children), as well as low levels of social competencies, impaired concentration spans, difficulties with school work and significantly lower than average scores of verbal, motor and cognitive abilities.

Hurley and Jaffe (1990) Jaffe et al. (1990) and Robertson and Bush (1994) also describe how children who witness marital violence tend to show lower self-esteem and poorer social competence; to feel confusion, shame, guilt, fear, sadness, helplessness and isolation and to exhibit a range of 'maladaptive' behaviours (including sleep disturbance, aggression, disobedience, lying, bullying and an inability to concentrate). Cummings (1987) explored the effects on children varying in age from one to adolescence and found that even very young infants exhibited signs of distress, dispelling the myth that babies are too young to notice and be effected by such events taking place around them. Hughes (1992) also found that many school-age children for the sake of social desirability belied their inner experience by putting on a 'brave face'. However, when interviewed, they quickly revealed their profound emotional distress. For many children, too fearful or embarrassed for their friends to witness the violence or abuse at home, social relationships are impaired since they prefer to keep their home life separate from their outside life.

Difficult children

Research by Brandon and Lewis (1996) revealed that the impact for some children leads to poor conflict resolution skills or to the avoidance of conflict itself and, moreover, that even when the violence had ended it still seemed to pre-occupy many of the children. The subsequent behaviour of the children in their study earned them labels of disapproval since many were regarded by their parents as 'disobedient', 'difficult', 'complaining', 'playing up', 'aggressive', etc. and the backdrop of violence was ignored by most of the adults concerned when attempting to explain the children's actions. Their findings also concluded that the children's need for respite from the violence and for some acknowledgement of the confusion and harm it caused rarely featured in the detail of child protection plans.

Some children fluctuate between extreme passivity and sudden outbursts of aggression. Others express feelings of severe anxiety, powerlessness and guilt at not contacting police or neighbours or at their inability to prevent assaults. Research by McGee (1997) also suggests that arguments about child-rearing are a major precipitating factor in parental conflict and violence. Assaults which appear to be triggered by the behaviour or mere presence of the child can serve as a powerful reinforcer of self-blame for a child who believes that they are somehow responsible for the family's predicament or at fault for not protecting their mother. Some children exhibit the hypervigilance (Mertin and Mohr, 2002) and watchful behaviour typical of an abused child; others are always tired, simply from being awake at night (Carroll, 1994). All children are individuals and will react differently to distressing experiences. However, Hague et al. (1996) list the most common difficulties experienced by children in Women's Refuges as follows:

- aggression/tantrums 40 per cent,
- introversion and withdrawal 37 per cent,
- disruption of routines 29 per cent,
- fear/insecurity 21 per cent,
- acceptance of violence 10 per cent,
- missing father 9 per cent, copying/mimicking father 7 per cent.

They also reported particular health problems such as bed-wetting, nightmares, headaches, stomach upsets, delayed development, lack of concentration, poor performance at school, truanting, self-harm and eating disorders.

Children's social development

Graham-Bermann (1998) also demonstrates how children exposed to domestic abuse are at risk of early problems in social development, in their interpersonal relationships with people in the home, with parents and siblings and outside the home (such as friends and peers). Findings by Dube et al. (2002) revealed that, compared with those who grew up with no domestic violence, adults who were exposed as children were at substantially increased risk of exhibiting health deficits from other adverse childhood experiences such as neglect or household dysfunction. There was also a positive graded risk for self-reported alcoholism, illicit drug use, intravenous drug use and depressed affect as the frequency of witnessing domestic violence increased. Hughes' study (1992) revealed that the children who were both abused and had witnessed violence displayed the most distress, especially for pre-school age children.

The intergenerational cycle

Among others, Bell (1995) has highlighted the risk of an intergenerational cycle of violence for children exposed to marital abuse. Sugarman and Hotaling (1989, 1986) also found these children are at risk of acting violently both within and outside the home in adulthood. In particular, research has consistently demonstrated that boys exposed to domestic violence in childhood are at substantially increased risk of abusing their own partners as adults (e.g. Silverman and Williamson, 1997; earlier review in Hotaling and Sugarman, 1986). Osofky (1998) also cites various studies which hold that such children learn that:

- Violence is an appropriate way to resolve conflicts.
- Violence is part of family relationships.
- The perpetrator of violence in intimate relationships usually goes unpunished.
- Violence is a way to control people.

Others still (e.g. Carlson, 1990; Koss et al., 1994; Wolfe, 1994) found a link between exposure to domestic violence and delinquency in adolescence.

Delayed symptoms

It must also be emphasised that some children initially exhibit no overt signs of psychological distress, in fact taking some time before showing any reaction (often only after they have been removed from the violence), their observable responses thus belying their emotional distress and inner experience. The absence of symptoms, especially in the short term, should not therefore be taken to mean that children are unaffected. Moreover, the degree of emotional distress and behavioural disturbance, for example, is not entirely dependant upon the extent and severity of any violence or abuse observed. It is therefore important to recognise that each child's experiences are unique, as are their perceptions and responses.

Protective and mediating factors

The growing body of research findings thus confirm that living with marital violence has far-reaching effects for children's emotional, cognitive and behavioural functioning and educational and social development in many different ways. However, not all children seem adversely affected (see Hughes et al., 2002). Professionals are therefore advised not to pathologise all children living in these circumstances (Brandon and Lewis, 1996). Cleaver and colleagues (1999) Jaffe et al. (1990) and Moore et al. (1990) for example, found children's responses do vary and are mediated by child-based factors such as their age, sex, developmental stage and role within the family as well as by their self-esteem levels, general temperament and by their ability to adjust to new situations; by family factors such as the mother's mental health (see also Hughes and Luke 1998), the warmth and support the child may receive from the non-abusive parent and overall parental competence (see also Graham-Bermann and Levendosky, 1997) and by community factors, especially for adolescents, such as the degree of support from peers or relatives outside the family.

Hughes et al. (2002) also report that children's resilience is at its greatest in families where the levels of verbal and psychological abuse between the parents and towards the children themselves have been low. Children's perception of the violence they witness also seems to play a large part in their reactions to it. Hester et al. (2000) maintain that there is growing consensus in the literature that providing support and protection for mothers is an effective way to improve the welfare of their children. Kelly (1994) also stresses that, though there are still gaps in our knowledge, 'one simple and key principle from which we can begin is that woman protection is frequently the most effective form of child protection' (p53).

Aggravating factors

Stressors which tend to increase the psychological impact and impair children's long and short-term functioning include the nature and frequency of the violence and abuse, the frequency of separations and moves, parental psychopathology and substance abuse, general level of marital discord, the extent of economic and social disadvantage the family faces and any special needs a child may have. Individual variations in how children respond are also therefore partly a function of the nature and social context of their parent's associated problems. Although there is considerable evidence to suggest that children can be protected from the adverse effects of parent's mental health problems and drug and alcohol misuse, there is little or no evidence for this in the case of domestic violence. In fact, it is the association with domestic violence that is most frequently cited as presenting the greatest risk of causing significant harm to children when parents suffer from mental health difficulties or substance misuse (Cleaver et al., 1999). Apart from witnessing or being exposed to the physical and sexual abuse of the mother, factors which are identified (see Cleaver et al., 1999; Grych and Fincham, 1999; Hamner, 1989; Jaffe et al., 1990) as aggravating the impact of domestic violence on children are:

- The combination with parental alcohol or drug misuse.
- Feeling 'caught up' in the conflict.
- Being drawn into participating in the abuse of a parent.
- Colluding in the secrecy and concealment of the violence.

• Abuse which is frequent, intense and physical.

The Social Research Unit at Dartington also confirm the common-sense view that poor outcomes for children increase where families are low on warmth and high on criticism (DoH, 1995). Finally, children exposed to domestic violence often have to contend with the additional psychological impact associated with the separation of their parents (see Buchanan et al., 2001 for review of effects). Their comprehensive review of over 200 current research reports, (Rodgers and Prior, 1998) for example, found the children of separated parents to be twice as likely to display behavioural or emotional problems, than children from families whose parents remained together.

Conclusion

This chapter has considered a substantial body of literature of pertinence to assessment work and has offered findings in respect of heightened risk of perpetration and of elevated vulnerability. Following decades of campaigning and consistent research evidence, domestic violence is becoming increasingly recognised on social agendas. Many children at the core of kinship assessments will have experienced domestic violence, and this may well have been a long-term exposure, making a significant impact on the child's attachments and on their emotional, physical and sexual welfare. Kinship placements must be safe for children and viable for their carers. The matter of domestic violence, therefore, must be properly explored.

Notes

1. In his oft-quoted seminal work, Monahan (1981) warns that inappropriate evaluation methods can impair the assessment task and cites four key areas of clinical error:
   • The lack of specificity in defining the target behaviour.
   • The overwhelming tendency for practitioners to ignore statistical base-rates despite their centrality in arriving at reliable assessments.
   • The reliance upon illusory correlations.
   • The failure to consider situational variables and applied risk.

Those who pose a risk to their partners and children are often very difficult to distinguish from those who do not: abusive men come from all socio-economic backgrounds and from all personality groups, from loud and aggressive to mild and passive. There are risks that mental health practitioners may be seduced into under-rating the degree of risk posed by those who have previously offended because of their capacity to:
   • Present themselves as mild-mannered, reasonable people.
   • Appear as though they share the interviewer's humane perspectives and values.
   • Construe past incidents of domestic violence as being isolated and uncharacteristic, or resulting from 'mutual combat' or from uniquely occurring situational stressors.
   • Convince others that they have 'learned their lesson' or 'put their past behind them'.
   • Overstate the deterrence value of future punishment or other consequences.

2. Despite the current controversy about whether domestic violence is a gendered phenomenon, there are powerful arguments that it is heterosexual men who are the predominant perpetrators of severe domestic violence (Dobash et al., 1998, 1992; Davidson et al., 2000; Hamberger et al., 1997; Hester et al., 2000; Gleaver et al., 1999; Malloy et al., 2003; Mullender, 1996).

3. DeKeseredy et al. (2004) suggest that unemployed men may seek to rebuff aversive feelings associated with being economically disenfranchised through substance use or other risk-augmenting activities such as increased contact with peers, which research suggests often promote attitudes supportive of woman abuse (DeKeseredy et al., 2003; Raphael 2001). Men's inability to achieve their traditional superiority in earning-capacity within relationships may also lead to their employing compensatory ways of retaining the balance of power. Conflict (and therefore an increased risk of violence) may also exist within relationships because of women's continued emphasis on a man's bread-winning capacity as an important quality in a prospective husband.

4. In her sample of domestically violent men, Caesar (1988), found that 38% had neither

witnessed nor experienced violence as a child.

5. Men with 'personality disorders' (typically characterised by high impulsivity and anger, inability to sustain intimate relationships, dramatic mood swings etc.) for example, are over-represented among domestically violent offenders (Dutton, 1995; Dutton and Kerry, 1999; Dutton et al., 1997; Gondolf, 1997; Hamberger and Hastings, 1993, 1988; Hart et al., 1993; Oldham et al., 1985) and are associated with an increased risk of violent recidivism (Hilton et al., 2001). Swanson et al. (1990) found that the risk of violent behaviour increased with the number of psychiatric diagnoses which met Diagnostic and Statistical Manual (DSM IV) criteria and that the interaction between substance misuse and major psychopathology is a statistically significant predictor of violence. Lidz et al. (1993) found a substantially elevated prevalence rate for intimate violence among recently released psychiatric patients.

6. Stalking (following or spying, sitting in car outside victim's home or place of work etc) is strongly associated with both lethal and sub-lethal violence to women by an ex-partner (Campbell, 2003; Coleman, 1997; Meloy, 1998; Metropolitan Police, 2003). McFarlane et al. found that over 90% of the women who faced attempted murder by an ex-partner had reported being stalked. In their study of offenders charged with stalking and related offences, Reid et al. (2001) found that prior sexual intimacy with the victim was the primary predictor of violence.

7. The concept of 'vulnerability' is used here in a particular sense. It is not intended to implicate the individual concerned by implying that she exhibits pathological or dysfunctional traits nor to extract her from her social context but rather to identify factors which increase the likelihood that she will experience violence and abuse as a consequence of interconnected personal and social factors which are mediated by powerful socio-political and economic inequities (see Perry and Whiteside, 2002).

8. Pilspa 2002 (cited in Barnish 2004). According to Hotaling and Sugarman (1986), dysfunctional behaviour in victimised women appears to be the product of abuse rather than the cause.

9. This may be because:
   - A woman with limited personal, financial or community resources is less likely to have been able to take precautions for the safety of her children, to defend herself, to recover from maltreatment and to marshal protective legal remedies.
   - Vulnerable women are more likely to be targeted by abusive men, many of whom seek relationships with such women in order to feel important and to satisfy a desire for control.
   - The 'life-generated' vulnerabilities of many women are exploited by abusive men to increase their control.
   - The childhood difficulties of many vulnerable women leave them with significant attachment deficits and a tendency to harbour fantasies of idealised romance and family life which they are desperate to live out (for themselves and for their children). Many find life alone unbearable. This can cloud a women's judgement about partner choice and make ending a relationship with a violent spouse especially difficult.
   - Women who grew up in an environment of family violence are more likely to associate with men with similar backgrounds. In turn, these men are more likely to behave violently to their spouses than men from non-abusive homes.

10. The 2001 British Crime Survey also found that the younger the person is the more likely they are to be subject to domestic violence. The study by (Walby and Myhill (2000), revealed that the percentage of women assaulted by a partner in the previous year was over twice as high as the average (4.2%) for women aged between 16 and 19 (10.1%) and between 20 to 24 (9.2%).

11. The British Crime Surveys have found that people living in poor and financially insecure households were more likely to suffer from domestic violence (Walby and Allen, 2004; Walby and Myhill, 2001, 2000) the latest of which found that women in households with an income of less than £10,000 were three and a half times more likely to suffer domestic violence than those in households with an income of over £20,000.

References and bibliography

Aldorado, E. and Sugarman, D.B. (1996) Risk Markers of the Cessation and Persistence of Wife Assault. *Journal of Consulting and Clinical Psychology.* 64: 5, 1010–9.

Alpert, E., Cohen, S. and Sege, R. (1997) Family Violence: An Overview. *Academic Medicine Supplement.* S72(1), S3–S6.

Anderson, K. (1997) Gender, Status and Domestic Violence: An Integration of Feminist and Family Violence Approaches. *Journal of Marriage and the Family.* 59: 3, 655–69.

Andrews, D.A. et al. (1990) Correctional Treatment Work? A Clinically Relevant and Psychologically Informed Meta-analysis. *Criminology.* 28: 369–404.

Appel, A.E. and Holden, G.W. (1998) The Co-Occurence of Spouse and Physical Child Abuse: A Review and Appraisal. *Journal of Family Psychology,* 12, 578–99.

Archer, J. (1999) Assessment of the Reliability of the Conflict Tactics Scales: A Meta-Analytic Review. *Journal of Interpersonal Violence,* 14, 1263–89.

Arkow, P. (1996) The Relationship between Animal Abuse and other Forms of Family Violence. *Family Violence and Sexual Abuse Bulletin,* 12: 1, 29–34.

Ascione, F.R., Weber, C.V. and Wood, D.S. (1997) The Abuse of Animals and Domestic Violence: A National Survey of Shelters for Women who are Battered. *Society and Animals: Journal of Human-Animal Studies* (internet: www.psyeta.org) 5: 3.

Ballard, M.E. and Cummings, E.M. (1990) Response to Adults' Angry Behaviour in Children of Alcoholic and Non-Alcoholic Parents. *Journal of Genetic Psychology.* 151: 195–210.

Bancroft, L. and Silverman, J. (2002) *The Batterer as Incest Perpetrator.* In Bancroft, L. and Silverman, J. CA: Sage.

Barnish, M. (2004) *Domestic Violence: A Literature Review.* HM Inspectorate of Probation.

Beaumont, B. (1999) Assessing Risk in Work with Offenders. In Parsloe, *Risk Assessment in Social Care and Social Work,* op. cit.

Bell, C. (1995) Exposure to Violence Distresses Children and may Lead to Their Becoming Violent. *Psychiatry News.*

Bergen, R.K. (1999) *Marital Rape.* Vawnet: www.vaw.umn.edu/Vawnet/mrape.htm

Black, D.A., Heyman, R.E. and Smith Step, A.M. (2001) Risk Factors for Male-to-female Partner Sexual Abuse. *Aggression and Violent Behaviour.* 6: 2–3, 269.

Bowker, L. (1993) *Beating Wife Beating.* Lexington, MA. Lexington Books.

Bowker, L. and Maurer, L. (1987) The Medical Treatment of Battered Wives. *Women and Health.* 112: 1, 25–45.

Brandon, M. and Lewis, A. (1996) Significant Harm and Children's Experiences of Domestic Violence. *Child and Family Social Work.* 1: 33–42.

Brisson, N. (1982) Helping Men who Batter Women. *Public Welfare,* 40, 28–34.

Brown, V. (1997) *Breaking the Silence: Violence/Abuse Issues for Women Diagnosed With Serious Mental Illness.* LA: Prototypes Systems Change Center.

Browne, A. (1987) *When Battered Women Kill.* London: Collier Macmillan.

Browne, A. (1997) Violence in Marriage: Until Death Do Us Part? In Cardarelli, A.P. (Ed.) *Violence Between Intimate Partners.* London: Allyn and Bacon.

Brownridge, D.A. and Hallis, S.S. (2002) Double Jeopardy? Violence Against Immigrant Women in Canada. *Violence and Victims.* 17: 455–71.

Buchanan, A. et al. (2001) *Families in Conflict: Perspectives of Children and Parents on the Family Court Welfare Service.* The Policy Press, University of Bristol.

Caesar, L.P. (1988) Exposure to Violence in the Families of Origin Among Wife Abusers and Maritally Non-Violent Men. *Violence and Victims.* 3: 1, 49–63.

Calder, M.C. (2004) *Children Living with Domestic Violence.* Lyme Regis: Russell House Publishing.

Calder, M.C. and Hackett, S. (2003) Assessment in Childcare: Using and Developing Frameworks for Practice. Lyme Regis: Russell House Publishing.

Campbell, J. et al. (1998a) Empowering Survivors of Abuse: Health Care for Battered Women and their Children. In Campbell, J. (Ed.) London: Sage.

Campbell, J.C. (Ed) (1995) *Assessing Dangerousness: Violence by Sexual Offenders, Batterers, and Child Abusers.* London: Sage.

Campbell, J.C. et al. (2003) Risk Factors for Femicide in Abusive Relationships: Results From a Multisite Case Control Study. *American Journal of Public Health.* 93: 7, 1089–97.

Capaldi, D.M. and Crosby, L. (1997) Observed and Reported Psychological and Physical Aggression in Young, At-Risk Couples. *Social Development,* 6, 184–206.

Carlson, B. (1990) Adolescent Observers of Marital Violence. *Journal of Family Violence.* 5: 285–99.

Carroll, J. (1994) The Protection of Children Exposed to Marital Violence. *Child Abuse Review.* 3: 1, 6–14.

Chenoweth, L. (1997) Violence and Women With Disabilities: Silence and Paradox. In Coo and Bessant (Eds.) *Women's Encounters With Violence. Australian Experiences.*

Cleaver, H., Unell, I. and Aldgate, J. (1999) *Children's Needs-Parenting Capacity: The Impact of Parental Mental Illness, Problem Alcohol and Drug Use, and Domestic Violence on Children's Development.* London: Stationery Office.

Coid, J. (2000) *A Survey of Women's Experience of Domestic Violence Attending Primary Care in East London.* Conference Report: Domestic Violence a Health Response: Working in a Wider Partnership. London: Department of Health.

Coleman, F.L. (1997) Stalking Behaviour and the Cycle of Domestic Violence. *Journal of Interpersonal Violence.* 12: 3, 420–32.

Cummings, E.M. (1987) Coping with Background Anger in Early Childhood. *Child Development.* 58: 976–84.

Cummings, E.M. and Zahn-Waxler (1992) Emotions and the Socialisation of Aggression: Adults' Angry Behaviour and Children's Arousal and Aggression. In Fraczek, A. and Zumley, H. (Eds.) *Socialisation and Aggression.* NY: Springer-Verlag.

Curry, M.A. and Harvey, S.M. (1998) Stress Related to Domestic Violence During Pregnancy and Infant Birth Weight. In Campbell, J.C. et al. (Eds.) *Empowering Survivors of Abuse.*

Davidson, L. et al. (2000) What Role Can the Health Service Play? In Taylor-Browne, J. (Ed.) *Reducing Domestic Violence: What Works?* Home Office.

DeKeseredy, W., Alvi, S. and Schwartz, M.D. (2003) Curbing Woman Abuse and Poverty: is 'Welfare' the Cure? Paper Presented at the Trapped by Poverty/Trapped by Abuse Conference, Austin Texas.

DeKeseredy, W. et al. (2004) Separation/Divorce and Sexual Assault in Rural Ohio: The Contribution of Patriarchal Male Peer Support. Paper presented at the Annual Meeting of the American Society of Criminology.

DeMaris, A. and Jackson, J.K. (1987) Batterer Report of Recidivism After Counselling. *Social Casework,* 68, 458–65.

Department of Health (1995) *Child Protection: Messages from Research.* London: HMSO.

Department of Health (2000) *Domestic Violence. A Health Response: Working in a Wider Partnership.* Conference Report. London: HMSO.

Department of Health (2000) *Domestic Violence: A Resource Manual for Health Care Professionals.* London: HMSO.

Department of Health (2000) *Framework for the Assessment of Children in Need and Their Families.* London: HMSO.

Dobash, R.E. et al. (1992) The Myth of Sexual Symmetry in Marital Violence. *Social Problems.* 39: 1, 71–91.

Dobash, R.E. et al. (2002) *Homicide in Britain.* University of Manchester: Department of Applied Social Science.

Dobash, R.P. and Dobash, R.E. (1979) *Violence Against Wives: A Case Against the Patriarchy.* New York: Free Press.

Dobash, R.E. and Dobash, R.P. (1998) *Rethinking Violence Against Women.* Sage.

Dobash, R.E. and Dobash, R.P. (2001) Risk, Danger and Safety. *SAFE: The Domestic Abuse Quarterly,* Winter, 7.

Dobash, R.P. et al. (1998) Separate and Intersecting Realities. A Comparison of Men's and Women's Accounts of Violence Again. *Violence against Women; An International and Interdisciplinary Journal.* 1–3.

Downs, W.R. et al. (1992) Long Term Effects of Parent-to-Child Violence for Women. *Journal of Aggression, Maltreatment and Trauma.* 5: 2, 73–104.

Dube, S.R. et al. (2002) Exposure to Abuse, Neglect and Household Dysfunction Among Adults Who Witnessed Intimate Partner Violence. Violence and Victims. 17: 1, 3–17.

Dutton, D. (1995) *The Domestic Assault of Women: Psychological and Criminal Justice Perspectives.* Vancouver: UBC Press.

Dutton, D.G. (1988) Profiling of Wife Assaulters: Preliminary Evidence for a Trimodel Analysis. *Violence and Victims,* 3: 1, 5–29.

Dutton, D.G. and Hart, S.G. (1992a) Risk Markers for Family Violence in a Federally Incarcerated Population. *International Journal of Law and Psychiatry,* 15, 101–12.

Dutton, D.G. et al. (1997) Wife Assault Treatment and Criminal Recidivism: An 11-year Follow-up. *International Journal of Offender Therapy and Comparative Criminology,* 41, 9–23.

Dutton, D.G. (1998) *The Abusive Personality: Violence and Control in Intimate Relationships.* New York: Guilford.

Dutton, D.G. and Kerry, G. (1999) Personality Profiles and Modi Operandi of Spousal Homicide Perpetrators. *International Journal of Law and Psychiatry*, 22: 3, 287–300.

Edwards, S.S. (1997) *The Law and Domestic Violence*. In Bewley, S., Friend, J. and Mezey, G. (Eds.) *Violence Against Women*.

Ehrensaft, M.K. et al. (2003) Intergenerational Transmission of Partner Violence: a 20 year Prospective Study. *Journal of Consulting and Clinical Psychology*. 71: 4, 741–53.

Fagan, J.A., Stewart, D.K. and Hansen, K.V. (1983) Violent Men or Violent Husbands? Background Factors and Situational Correlates. In Finkelhor, D. et al. (Eds.) *The Dark Side of Families: Current Family Violence Research*. Newbury Park. CA: Sage.

Fantuzzo, J., and Lindquist, C. (1989) The Effect of Observing Conjugal Violence on Children: A Review and Analysis of Research Methodology. *Journal of Family Violence*. 4: 1, 77–94.

Farley, M. and Barkan, H. (1998) Prostitution, Violence and Post-Traumatic Stress Disorder. *Women and Health*. 27: 37–49.

Garrity, C. and Baris, M. (1995) Custody and Visitation: Is it Safe? *Family Advocate*, 17: 3, 40–5.

Gelles, R.J. (1997) *Intimate Violence*. Sage.

Gelles, R.J., Wolfner, G.D. and Lackner, R. (1994) Men who Batter: the Risk Markers. *Violence Update*, 4, 1.

Gillioz, L. (1997) Domination and Violence Against Women within the Couple. European Strategies to Combat Violence Against Women.

Gleason, W.J. (1995) Children of Battered Women: Developmental Delays and Behavioural Dysfunction. *Violence and Victims*. 10: 2, 153–60.

Goldsmith, H.R. (1990) Men who Abuse their Spouses: An Approach to Assessing Future Risk. *Journal of Offender Counseling Services and Rehabilitation*, 15, 45–56.

Gondolf, E.W. (1997) Batterer Programs: What we Know and Need to Know. *Journal of Interpersonal Violence*, February 12. 1, 83–98.

Gondolf, E.W. (1988) The State of the Debate: A Review Essay on Woman Battering. *Reponse to the Victimization of Women and Children*, 11: 3, 3–8.

Gondolf, E.W. (1998) A Comparison of Four Batterer Intervention Systems: Do Court-referral, Program Length, and Services Matter? *Journal of Interpersonal Violence* (In press).

Goodman, L.A., Bennett, L.E. and Dutton, M.A. (1999) Obstacles Battered Women Face in the Prosecution of their Batterers: The Role of Social Support. *Violence and Victims*, 14, 427–44.

Graham-Bermann, S. and Levendosky, A.A. (1997) The Social Functioning of Pre-School Aged Children Whose Mothers are Emotionally and Physically Abused. *Journal of Emotional Abuse*. 1: 1, 57–82.

Grych, J.J. and Fincham, F.D. (1999) The Adjustment of Children from Divorced Families: Implications of Empirical Intervention. In Galatzer-Levy, R.M. and Kraus, L. (Eds.) *The Scientific Basis of Child Custody*.

Hague, G. et al. (1996) *Children, Domestic Violence and Refuges: A Study of Needs and Responses*. Bristol: Women's Aid Federation.

Hall, H.V. (2001) Violence Prediction and Risk Analysis: Empirical Advances and Guidelines. *Journal of Threat Assessment*, 1: 3, 1–39.

Hamberger, L.K. and Hastings, J.E. (1988a) Exposure to the Families of Origin Among Wife Abusers Maritally Nonviolent Men. *Violence and Victims*, 3, 49–63.

Hamberger, L.K. et al. (1997) An Empirical Classification of Motivations for Domestic Violence. *Violence Against Women*, 3: 4, 401–23.

Hamby, S.L. (2001) The Dominance Scale: Preliminary Psychometric Properties. In O'Leary and Maiuro, *Psychological Abuse in Violent Domestic Relations*. Springer, NY: 61–76.

Hamner, J. (1989) Women and Policing in Britain. In Hamner, J., Radford, J. and Stanko, E.A. (Eds.) *Women, Policing and Male Violence: International Perspectives*. London: Routledge.

Hanson, R. Karl et al. (1997) Correlates of Battering Among 997 Men: Family History, Adjustment, and Attitudinal Differences. *Violence and Victims*. 12: 3, 191–208.

Hardesty, J.L. (2002) Separation Assault in the Context of Post-divorce Parenting: An Integrative View of the Literature. *Violence Against Women*. 8: 5, 597–625.

Hart, B. (2001) *Assessing Whether Batterers Will Kill*. PCADV. www.mincava.umn.edu/hart/parenta.

Hart, S., Dutton, D. and Newlove, T. (1993) *The Prevalence of Personality Disorders Among Wife Assaulters. Journal of Personality Disorders*. 7, 329–41.

Hart, S.D., Kropp, P.R. and Hare, R.D. (1988) Performance of Male Psychopaths Following Conditional Release From Prison. *Journal of Consulting and Clinical Psychology*. 56: 227–32.

Heise, L. (1998) Violence Against Women: An Integrated, Ecological Framework. *Violence Against Women.* 4: 3, 262–90.

Hester, M., Pearson, C. and Harwin, N. (2000) *Making an Impact: Children and Domestic Violence, a Reader.* London: Jessica Kingsley.

Hilton, N.Z. et al. (2001) Predicting Violence by Serious Wife-assaulters. *Journal of Interpersonal Violence.* 16: 5, 408–23.

Holden, G.W. et al. (1998) Parenting Behaviours and Beliefs of Battered Women. In Holden, G.W. Geffner, R. and Jouriles, E.N. (Eds.) *Children Exposed to Marital Violence.*

Holden, G.W., Geffner, R and Jouriles, E.M. (Eds.) (1998) *Children Exposed to Marital Violence.* Washinton DC: American Psychological Association.

Holder, W. and Corey, M. (1993) *Child Protection Services Risk Management: A Decision-Making Handbook.*: Charlotte, NC: Action for Child Protection.

Home Office (2004) *British Crime Survey.* London: Home Office.

Hotaling, G.T. and Sugarman, D.B. (1986) An Analysis of Risk Markers in Husband to Wife Violence: The Current State of Knowledge. *Violence and Victims.* 1: 101–24.

Hotaling, G.T. and Sugarman, D.B. (1990) A Risk Marker Analysis of Assaulted Wives. *Journal of Family Violence.* 5: 1–13.

Hotaling, G.T., Strause, M. and Lincoln, A.J. (1990) Intrafamily Violence and Crime and Violence Outside the Family. In Strause, M and Gelles, (Eds.) *Phisical Violence in American Families.*

Hughes, H. (1992) Impact of Spouse Abuse on Children of Battered Women. *Violence Update.* 1: 9–11.

Hughes, H.M. and Luke, D.A. (1998) Heterogeneity in Adjustment Among Children of Battered Women. In Holden, G.W. et al. (Eds.) *Children Exposed to Family Violence.* Washinton DC:

Hughes, H.M., Graham-Bermann, S. and Gruber, G. (2002) Resilience in Children Exposed to Domestic Violence. In Graham-Bermann, S. and Edleson (Eds.) *Domestic Violence in the Lives of Children.*

Hurley, D.J. and Jaffe, P. (1990) Children's Observations of Violence 11: Clinical Implications For Children's Mental Health Professionals. *Canadian Journal of Psychiatry.* 35: 471–6.

Jackson, J.A. (1996) Observational Experiences of Intrapersonal Conflict and Teenage Victimization: A Comparative Study. *Journal of Family Violence.* 11: 191–203.

Jacobson, A. and Richardson, R. (1987) Assault Experiences of 100 Psychiatric Impatients: Evidence for the Need for Routine Inquiry. *American Journal of Psychiatry.* 144: 908–13.

Jaffe, P. G., Hurley, D. J., and Wolfe, D. (1990) Children's Observations of Violence: 1. Critical Issues in Child Development and Intervention Planning. *Canadian Journal of Psychiatry.* 35: 6, 466–70.

Jaffe, P.G., and Wilson, S.K. (1990) Children of Battered Women. *Developmental Clinical Psychology and Psychiatry.* 21: 8039.

Jasinki, J.L. (2004) Pregnancy and Domestic Violence: A Review of the Literature. *Trauma, Violence and Abuse.* 5: 1, 47–64.

Jewkes, R. (2002) Abstract: Preventing Domestic Violence . . . *BMJ.* 324: 7332, 253–4.

Jewkes, R. (2002) Intimate Partner Violence: Causes and Prevention. The Lancet, April 20, 359: 1423–9.

Jouriles, E.N. et al. (1996) Physical Violence and Other Forms of Marital Aggression: Links with Children's Behaviour Problems. *Journal of Family Violence.* 11: 223–34.

Kalmus, D.S. and Straus, M.A. (1982) Wife's Marital Dependency and Wife Abuse. *Journal of Marriage and the Family.* 44: 2, 277–86.

Kelly, L. (1996) When Woman Protection is the Best Kind of Child Protection. *Administration,* 44: 2, 118–35.

Kemshall, H. (1996) Offender Risk and Probation Practice. In Kemshall and Pritchard, *Good Practice in Risk Assessment and Risk Management.* op. cit.

Klein, A.R. (1993) *Spousal/Partner Assault: A Protocol for the Sentencing and Supervision of Offenders.* Swampscott, MA: Production Specialities.

Kolbo, J.R. et al. (1996) Children Who Witness Domestic Violence: A Review of Empirical Literature. *Journal of Interpersonal Violence.* 11: 2, 281–93.

Koss, M.P. et al. (1994) *No Safe Haven: Male Violence Against Women at Home, at Work and in the Community.* Washington, DC: American Psychological Association.

Kropp, P.R. et al. (1995) *Development of the Spousal Assault Risk Assessment Guide.* Paper presented at Mental Disorder and Criminal Justice Conference.

Laumakis, M.A., Margolin, G. and John, R.S. (1998) The Emotional, Cognitive and Coping

Responses of Pre-adolescent Children to Different Dimensions of Marital Conflict. In Holden, G.W. et al. (Eds.) *Children Exposed to Marital Violence: Theory, Research.*

Lerner, M. (1999) From Safety to Healing: Representing Battered Women with Companion Animals. *Domestic Violence Report.* 4: 2, 28.

MacDonald, K.I. and MacDonald, G.M. (1999) Perceptions of Risk. In Parsloe: *Risk Assessment in Social Care and Social Work.* op. cit.

Magdol, L. et al. (1998) Developmental Antecedents in Partner Abuse: A Prospective Longitudinal Study. *Journal of Abnormal Psychology.* 107, 375–89.

Malloy, K.A. et al. (2003) Women's Use of Violence within Intimate Relationships. *Journal of Aggression, Maltreatment and Trauma.* 6: 2, 37–59.

Mama, A. (1989) *The Hidden Struggle: Statutory and Voluntary Sector Responses to Violence Against Black Women in the Home.* London: London Race and Housing Research Unit.

Marshall, L.L. and Rose, P. (1990) Premarital Violence: The Impact of Family of Origin Violence, Stress, and Reciprocity. *Journal of Family Violence.* 5: 51–64.

McCloskey, L.A. (2001) The 'Medea Complex' Among Men: The Instrumental Abuse of Children to Injure Wives. *Violence and Victims,* 16: 1, Feb, 19–37.

McFarlane, J., Parker, B. and Soeken, K. (1995) Abuse During Pregnancy: Frequency, Severity, Perpetrator and Risk Factors of Homicide. *Public Health Nursing.* 12: 284–9.

McGee, C. (1997) Children's Experience of Domestic Violence. *Child and Family Social Work.* 2: 13–23.

McKenry, P.C., Julian, T.W. and Gavazzi, S.M. (1995) Toward a Biopsychosocial Model of Domestic Violence. *Journal of Marriage and the Family.* 57: 2, 301–20.

McMahon, M. and Pence, E. (1993) Doing More Harm than Good? Some Cautions About Visitation Centres. In Peled, E. et al. (Eds.) op. cit.

McNeil, M. (1987) Domestic Violence: The Skeleton in Tarrasoff's Closet. In Sonkin, D.J. (Ed.) *Domestic Violence on Trial: Psychological and Legal Dimensions of Family Violence.*

Mears, D. et al. (2001) Reducing Domestic Violence Recidivism: The Effects of Individual and Contextual Factors and Type of Legal Intervention. *Journal of Interpersonal Violence.* 16: 12, 1260–83.

Melchior, L.A. et al. (1999) Evaluation of the Effects of Outreach to Women with Multiple Vulnerabilities on Entry into Substance Abuse Treatment. *Evaluation and Program Planning.* 22: 269–77.

Meloy, J.R. (1998) *The Psychology of Stalking: Clinical and Forensic Perspectives.* San Diego, CA: Acad.

Mertin, P. and Mohr, P.B. (2002) Incidence and Correlates of Post-traumatic Symptoms in Children from Backgrounds of Domestic Violence. *Violence and Victims.* 17: 5, 555–67.

Metropolitan Police Service (2003) *Findings from the Multi-agency Domestic Violence Murder Reviews in London.* Prepared for the ACPO Homicide Working Group. Racial and Violent Crime Task Force, New Scotland Yard.

Mezey. G.C. (1997) Domestic Violence in Pregnancy. In Bewley, S., Friend, J. and Mezey, G. *Violence Against Women.* RCOG Press.

Mirrlees-Black, C. (1999) *Domestic Violence: Findings from a New British Crime Survey Self-Completion Questionnaire.* Home Office Research Studies 191.

Monahan, J. (1981) *Predicting Violent Behaviour. An Assessment of Clinical Techniques.* Beverly Hills CA: Sage.

Moore, J. (1990) Confronting the Perpetrator. *Community Care.* 12.

Moore, B. (1996) *Risk Assessment: A Practitioner's Guide to Predicting Harmful Behaviour.* Whiting and Birch.

Morley, R. and Mullender, A. (1994) Domestic Violence and Children: What do we Know From Research. In Mullender, A. and Morley, R. (Eds.) *Children Living With Domestic Violence: Putting Men's Abuse of Women on the Child Care Agenda.* London: Whiting and Birch.

Morley, R., and Mullender, A. (1994) *Preventing Domestic Violence to Women.* Police Research Group: Crime Prevention Unit Series.

Mullender, A. and Morley (Eds.) (1994) *Children Living with Domestic Violence: Putting Men's Abuse of Women on the Child Abuse Agenda.* Whiting and Birch.

Mullender, A. (1996) *Rethinking Domestic Violence.* London: Routledge.

Murphy, C.M. and Hoover, S. (2001) Measuring Emotional Abuse in Dating Relationships as a Multifactorial Construct. In O'Leary, K.D. and Maiuro, R.D. *Psychological Abuse in Violent Domestic Relations.* NY: Springer.

O'Donnell, C., Smith, A. and Madison, J.R. (2002) Using Demographic Risk Factors to Explain

Variations in the Incidence of Violence Against Women. *Journal of Interpersonal Violence*. 17: 12, 1239–62.

O'Keefe, M. (1997) Predictors of Dating Violence Among High School Students. *Journal of Interpersonal Violence*. 12: 4, 546–68.

O'Leary, K.D., Malone, J. and Tyree, A. (1994) Physical Aggression in Early Marriage: Prerelationship and Relationship Effects. *Journal of Consulting and Clinical Psychology*. 62: 3, 594–602.

O'Leary, K.D. and Maiuro, R.D. (Eds.) (2001) *Psychological Abuse in Violent Domestic Relations*. NY: Springer.

Oldham, J. et al. (1985) A Self Report Instrument for Borderline Personality Organization. In McGlasham, T.H. (Ed.) *The BorderLine: Current Empirical Research*. Washington, DC: American Psychiatric Press.

Osofsky, J.D. (1999) The Impact of Violence on Children. *Domestic Violence and Children*. 9: 3, 33–49.

Peacock, D. and Rothman, E. (2001) *Working with Young Men who Batter: Current Strategies and New Directions*. Internet: Vawnet.org/VNL/library/general/AR_juvperp.html, Nov.

Perry, D. and Keszia-Whiteside, R. (2002) *Recontextualising Violence: Children, 'Disability' and Gender*. People 1st Programme (PIP).

Piispa, M. (2002) Complexity of Patterns of Violence Against Women in Hetrosexual Relationships. *Violence Against Women*. 8: 7, 973.

Prigerson, H.G. et al. (2002) Population Attributable Fractions of Psychiatric Disorders and Behavioural Outcomes Associated with Combat Exposure among US men. *American Journal of Public Health*. 92, 59–63.

Pynoos, R.S. and Nadar, K. (1987) Children Who Witness the Sexual Assaults of Their Mothers. *Journal of the American Academy of Child and Adolescent Psychiatry*. 27: 5, 567–72.

Quinsey, V.L. et al. (1998) *Violent Offenders: Appraising and Managing Risk*. Washington, DC: American Psychological Association.

Raphael, J. (2002) Public Housing and Domestic Violence. *Violence against Women*. 7: 6, 689–706.

Resnick, H. and Kilpatrick, D (1997) Health Impact of Interpersonal Violence: Prevalence Rates, Case Identification and Risk Factors. *Behavioural Medicine*. 23: 53–64.

Richards, L. (2004) *Getting Away With it: A Strategic Overview of Domestic Violence Sexual Assault and 'Serious' Incident Analysis*. London: Metropolitan Police.

Riggs, D.S., Caulfield, M.B. and Street, A.E. (2000) Risk for Domestic Violence: Factors Associated with Perpetration and Victimization. *Journal of Clinical Psychology*. 56: 10, 1289–316.

Roberts, A.R. (1987) Psychosocial Characteristics of Batterers: A Study of 234 Men Charged with Domestic Violence Offences. *Journal of Family Violence*. 2: 1, 81–93.

Robertson, D. and Busch, R. (1994) Not in Front of the Children: The Literature on Spousal Violence and its Effects on Children. *Butterworths Family Law Journal*. 107.

Rockvills, M.D. (1981) *The Clinical Prediction of Violent Behavior*. The National Institute of Mental Health.

Rodgers, B. and Prior, J. (1998) *Divorce and Separation: the Outcome for Children*. Joseph Rowntree Foundation.

Rodgers, K. (1994) Wife Assault: the Findings of a National Survey. *Juristat Service Bulletin of the Canadian Center for Justice Statistics*. 14: 9, 1–22.

Roscoe, B. and Benaske, N. (1985) Courtship Violence Experienced by Abused Wives: Similarities in Patterns of Abuse. *Family Relations*. 34: 419–24.

Rowsell, C. (2003) Domestic Violence and Children: Making a Difference in a Meaningful Way for Women and Children. In Calder, M. and Hackett, S. *Assessment in Child Care: Using and Developing Frameworks for Practice*. Lyme Regis: Russell House Publishing.

Saunders, D.G. (1992) A Typology of Men who Batter: Three Types Derived from Cluster Analysis. *American Journal of Orthopsychiatry*. 62: 2, 264–75.

Saunders, D.G. (1993) *Husbands who Assault: Multiple Profiles Requiring Multiple Responses. Legal Responses to Wife Assault*. Newbury Park, CA: Sage.

Saunders, D.G. (1994) Helping Battered Women in Child Custody Disputes. *Violence Update*. 5, 1–24.

Saunders, D.G. (1995) Prediction of Wife Assault. In Cambell, J.C. (Ed) *Assessing Dangerousness: Violence by Sexual Offenders, Batterers and Child Abusers*. Newbury Park: Sage.

Saunders, D.G. (1992) Woman Battering. In Ammerman, R.T. and Hersen, M. (Eds.) *Assessment of Family Violence: A Clinical and Legal Sourcebook*. New York. Wiley.

Schumacher, J.A. et al. (2001) Risk Factors for Male-to-Female Partner Physical Abuse. *Aggression and Violent Behavior*. 6: 281–352.

Sever, A. (1997) Recent or Imminent Separation and Intimate Violence Against Women. *Violence against Women*. 3: 6, 566–89.

Sharps, P.W. et al. (2001) The Role of Alcohol Use in Intimate Partner Femicide. *American Journal on Additions.* 10: 2, 1–14.

Shupe, A. et al. (1987) *Violent Men, Violent Couples.* Lexington MA: Lexington Books.

Silverman, J. and Williamson, G. (1997) Social Ecology and Entitlement Involved in Heterosexual Battering by College Males: Contributions of Family and Peers. *Victims and Violence.* 12: 2, 147–64.

Silvern, L., and Kaersvang, L. (1989) The Traumatised Children of Violent Marriages. *Child Welfare League of America.* 84: 4, 421–36.

Simons, R.L. et al. (1993) Explaining Women's Double Jeopardy: Factors that Meditate the Association Between Harsh Treatment. *Journal of Marriage and the Family.* 55: 713–23.

Skilling, T. et al. (2001) *The Assessment of Persistently Antisocial Offenders.* Quoted in Hylton et al.

Sonkin, D.J. (1987) The Assessment of Court-mandated Male Batterers. In Sonkin, D.J. (Ed.) *Domestic Violence on Trial: Psychological and Legal Dimensions of Family Violence.* New York: Springer.

Stanko, E.A. et al. (1998) *Counting the Costs: Estimating the Impact of Domestic Violence in the London Borough of Hackney.* Swindon: Crime Concern.

Steinmetz, S.K. (1979) Violence Between Family Members. *Marriage and Family Review.* 1: 1–16.

Sternberg, K.J. et al. (1993) Effects of Domestic Violence on Children's Behaviour Problems and Depression. *Developmental Psychology.* 29: 44–52.

Straus, M.A. (1991) Discipline and Deviance: Physical Punishment of Children and Violence and other Crime in Adulthood. *Social Problems.* 38, 133–54.

Straus, M.A. (1993) Identifying Offenders in Criminal Research on Domestic Assaults. *American Behavioral Scientist.* 36: 5, 587–600.

Straus, M.B. (1991) Physical Punishment of Children and Violence and other Crime in Adulthood. *Social Work.* 133–55.

Straus, M.A. (1993) Husband Abuse and the Woman Offender are Important Problems. In Gelles and Loseke (Eds.) *Current Controversies in Family Violence.* Newbury Park: Sage.

Straus, M.A. et al. (1980) *Behind Closed Doors: Violence in the American Family.* New York: Garden Press, Anchor Press/Doubleday.

Stuart, E.P. and Campbell, J.C. (1989) Assessments of Dangerousness with Battered Women: The Danger Assessment. *Issues in Mental Health Nursing.* 10: 3, 245–60.

Stuart, G.L. and Holtzworth-Munroe, A. (1995) Identifying Subtypes of Maritally Violent Men: Descriptive Dimensions, Correlates and Causes of Violence and Treatment Implications. In Smith, S. and Straus, M. (Eds.) *Understanding Partner Violence: Prevalence, Causes, Consequences and Solutions.* Minneapolis. National Council on Family Relations.

Sugarman, D.B. and Hotaling, G.T. (1986) An Analysis of Risk Markers. *Violence and Victims.* 1: 101–24.

Sugarman, D.B. and Hotaling, G.T. (1989) Violent Men in Intimate Relationships: An Analysis of Risk Markers. *Journal of Applied Social Psychology.* 19: 1034–48.

Swanson, J., Holzer, C., Ganju, V. and Jono, R. (1990) Violence and Psychiatric Disorder in the Community: Evidence from the Epidemiological Catchment Area Surveys. *Hospital and Community Psychiatry,* 41, 761–70.

Symons, R., Lin, K-H. and Gordon, L. (1998) Socialisation in the Family of Origin and Male Dating Violence: A Prospective Study. *Journal of Marriage and the Family,* 60: 2, 467–78.

Thompson, M., Saltzman, L. and Johnson, H. (2003) A Comparison of Risk Factors for Intimate Partner Violence-Related Injury Across Two National Surveys on Violence Against Women. *Violence Against Women,* 9: 4, 438–57.

Tweed, R.G. and Dutton, D. (1998) A Comparison of Impulsive and Instrumental Subgroups of Batterers. *Violence and Victims,* 13: 3, 217–29.

Walby, S. and Allen, J. (2004) *Domestic Violence, Sexual Assault and Stalking: Findings from the British Crime Survey.* Home Office Research 276.

Walby, S. and Myhill, A. (2001) Assessing and Managing Risk. In Taylor-Browne, J. (Ed) *What Works in Reducing Domestic Violence?* Whiting and Birch, 307–34.

Walby, S. and Myhill, A. (2000) *Reducing Domestic Violence . . . What Works? Assessing and Managing the Risk of Domestic Violence.* Crime Reduction Research Series. Policing and Reducing Crime Unit, Home Office Research, Development and Statistics Directorate, London.

Wald, M. and Woolverton, M. (1990) Risk Assessment: The Emperor's New Clothes? *Child Welfare,* 69: 6, 483–512.

Weaver, T. and Clum, G. (1996) Interpersonal Violence: Expanding the Search for Long-term

Sequelae within a Sample of Battered Women. *Journal of Traumatic Stress*. 9: 783–803.

Webster, C.D. et al. (1994) *The Violence Prediction Scheme*. Centre of Criminology, University of Toronto: Canada.

Weisz, A.N., Tolman, R.M. and Saunders, D.G. (2000) Assessing the Risk of Severe Domestic Violence: The Importance of Survivors' Predictions. *Journal of Interpersonal Violence*. 15: 75–90.

Widom, C.S. (1989) Does Violence Beget Violence? A Critical Examination of the Literature. *Psychological Bulletin*, 106, 3–28.

Wilson, M. and Daly, M. (1999) Lethal and Non-lethal Violency Against Wives and the Evolutionary Psychology of Male Sexual Proprietariness. In Dobash, R.E. and Dobash, R. (Eds) *Rethinking Violence Against Women*. Sage. London.

Wilson, M., Daly, M. and Wright, C. (1993) Uxoricide in Canada: Demographic Risk Patterns. *Canadian Journal of Criminology*, July, 35: 3, 263–91.

Wilson, M., Johnson, H. and Daly, M. (1995) Lethal and Non-lethal Violence Against Wives. *Canadian Journal of Criminology*, 37, 331–61.

Woffordt, S. et al. (1994) Continuities in Marital Violence. *Journal of Family Violence*, 9: 3, 195–204.

Yexley, M., Borowsky, I. and Ireland, M. (2002) Correlation between Different Experiences of Intrafamilial Physical Violence and Violent Adolescent Behaviour. *Journal of Interpersonal Violence*, 17: 7, 707–20.

Chapter Seven

Multiple Child Abuse that Involves Wider Kin and Family Friends Within Intergenerational Networks: A Theoretical Model

Pam Freeman and John Ingham

Introduction

The presumption of the Children Act 1989 is to maintain children at home with their parents wherever possible and failing this, to explore placements within the extended family. There are, however, a number of circumstances when this is neither possible nor desirable. Child sexual abuse is one such context where detailed assessment coupled with caution is required. To date, little attention has been given to the specific contra-indication of intergenerational sexual abuse. This chapter seeks to address this gap in knowledge and practice, moving towards a theoretical model for the understanding of intergenerational abusive networks and associated implications for practice.

Despite the many advantages of kinship care, it does not come with a risk-free guarantee. As such, kinship care must sometimes be viewed with caution and cognisance, and detailed examination undertaken in relation to the inherent risks posed by close family members and friends. Such placements are most likely to be made by practitioners unwittingly, where substantial and specific risk assessment have not been undertaken thoroughly but executed in a hasty, routine manner, based on the assumption that children will *inevitably* benefit from the proximity of family links.

A number of salient child deaths in the UK, resulting in child abuse inquiries, should alert us to the fact that outcomes in kinship care placements have not always been deemed successful. Examples of high profile cases where kinship placements have resulted in tragedy, exacerbated by failures in agency practice, are that of Maria Colwell, Tyra Henry and more recently, through the erroneous perception of kinship links of an 'Auntie' figure, in the case of Victoria Climbié. Families are not always safe. There is considerable research literature warning of the perpetuation of the 'cycle of family

violence', describing the family unit as a potential source of multiple forms of child maltreatment. Broad conclusions from this mainly clinical literature, would lead to the belief that, without successful therapeutic interventions, a sub-group of such child victims may go on to become sexual or violent offenders. This stated, it must be indicated that there remains a paucity of research studies that address the normative, non-clinical populations within the topic of intergenerational abuse. There are research gaps for example, surrounding an ecological context and the mechanisms that influence normative patterns of abuse within family life in communities where child sexual abuse is perceived as an integral part of ordinary adult behaviour.

This chapter addresses some of these knowledge gaps, by alerting the reader to the dangers posed to children who are placed with, or returned to family systems of this pattern, namely, where a normative culture of endemic and multiple child abuse and neglect exists. Some families and communities perpetuate a context where connected core families may operate, often with impunity, to abuse multiple numbers of children over the long term. Although these families are often recognised by child protection agencies as chaotic or dysfunctional, and where long-term niggling child protection concerns may have surfaced in 'a career of suspicion', the true extent of their inability to protect children and actively abuse, can be overlooked (Cleaver and Freeman, 1995). The 'career of suspicion' related to family patterns may consist of largely unsubstantiated allegations or concerns about existing children, accrued often over family generations. Differing statutory agencies may have overlooked or failed to identify the significance of shared information about family linkage as a consequence of poor interagency co-ordination (see *The Laming Report*, 2003). Thus, abusive child rearing practices coupled with a lack of thorough practitioner assessment can place children in an environment that may expose them to further risk. Poor practitioner decisions may also be a consequence of avoiding delay, of scarce resources or the toleration of unacceptable parenting. The evidence also suggests that mistakes have occurred in practitioner cultures where even supervision or monitoring of such families has not acknowledged the wider social context or links between families. Effectively, practitioners can fall into the trap of collusion via desensitisation/acculturation with families who have become over familiar to their caseloads. Thus, there has sometimes been a failure to explore and identify the nature of a normative family culture that exposes children to extreme risks of long-term and chronic child abuse and neglect, within core family alliances where family members and friends are drawn in, with the intent of entrapping and abusing children.

Towards a theoretical model

Cleaver and Freeman (1996) and Freeman (2003) have attempted to develop a cautionary, descriptive, theoretical model from research evidence that has examined the nature, the characteristics and modus operandi of intergenerational abuse family networks. This model inevitably challenges the notion of kinship care as the most positive remedy. The evidence has been collated from a variety of sources: namely, statutory agency investigations, anecdotal sources, case file research detailing histories, mapping linkage, cross referencing chronologies, interviews with participants of networks including criminal operations, research interviews with disclosing child or adult victims and the analysis of an adult sexual abuse helpline.

This model describes the nature of reinforcement of an informal normative family culture through practices of secrecy and intimidation of children, with the extensive geographic spread of abusive family networks based on consanguinity and kinship ties. Such a family culture appears to emanate from a normative, endemic social context of multiple forms of child abuse and neglect. It is transmitted through social learning processes across generations, based initially on incestuous core family memberships. These link together, with a common interest of enmeshing children across communities in a network formation (or discreet

cell like structures) with the purpose of abusing children, physically and specifically sexually (Cleaver and Freeman, 1995; 1996). True to a network formation model, the numerical and geographic extent of the scale of the network will be hidden from each participant, thus secrecy is ensured. There appears to be no formal leadership, nor a sophisticated paedophiliac organiser. Emphasis is thus on links being made *informally* on the basis of a common interest in children. To this extent, the pattern differs in nature from more systemic, organised abuse or sex rings. This child abuse pattern is based firmly on informal linkages between core family alliances within different communities.

There has been some disbelief or some resistance to the acceptance that this form of child abuse exists in community life, despite the harrowing evidence of disclosures by child or adult (usually female) victims. Practitioners, with memories of the over-zealous pursuit of 'ritual abuse' in the early 1990s have sometimes failed to accept this could be happening within their family case loads. The implications for time and resources are enormous. General disbelief, even initially from statutory persons engaged in investigations, has been focused on the numbers of targeted children, their gender, ethnicity, or age of victims (babies onwards) and the determination of adult family members to abuse any children coming within their sphere. The first breakthrough of a more public 'suspension of disbelief' was as a result of the West family publicity, still passed off by some, as a pathological aberration rather than a social phenomenon that society must confront. If analysed in more depth, the West family's, links across locations and the intergenerational chronological history could be tracked back to reveal the nature of a deviant normative culture of child abuse. Recently the Pitcairn Island trial (2004) and the Angers French sex ring trials of 62 adults (July, 2005) has further publicly vindicated the descriptive model put forward in respect of the normative culture of interconnecting familial abuse (*The Independent*, 2004).

Although the characteristics of family abusing networks may be interpreted as likely to be associated most with the social isolation often found within rural communities, subsequent research in the mid 1990s, has also demonstrated that inner cities were not immune to a culture of family based abusing networks. These are clearly linked together, and cross social class boundaries (Cleaver and Freeman, 1996). Moreover, it is increasingly recognised to be a cross-cultural phenomenon, with evidence emerging from child abuse studies globally. By nature, however, it is a hidden concern and thus difficult to estimate in terms of prevalence rates, although the endemic nature of such a culture is recognised and how it spreads. Comparable sociological theories of networking operations such as the functioning of organised crime, drug sub-cultures, and more recently, global terrorism often suggest similar characteristics, such as cellular formation and family based origins.

The abusing family networks demonstrate similar characteristics of secret complicity, selective targeted marriages or serial partnerships with blurred sexual boundaries based on blood ties or core family alliances. The predilection for multiple child sexual abuse in this ingrained culture is so great that this activity overrides all other. Family and friendship alliances are formed on the basis of targeting vulnerable fertile women and children who in turn are caught up in the network. The networks appear resilient and tenacious. The adults within the circles seem to have omnivorous sexual appetites with neither age nor gender protecting children from being targeted. Adults will infiltrate any child focused organisations or use opportunities by any means possible, in order to make contact with children, from ice cream van driver, fairground attendant, lorry driver, teacher, baby sitter or foster carer. The networking model ensures no *one* individual abuser knows the extent of the geographic spread. However, there is disconcerting evidence to suggest that many core alliances and friendship formations were established historically, in residential care settings or prisons, where adults formed early alliances.

Within the linked social networks, power relationships are turbulent and dynamic with control often exerted by older males supported by strong matriarchal figures that maintain closed family systems. Crossing sexual generational boundaries, the abusers (perpetrators) become indistinguishable from the abused (victims). The transmission of this type of normative culture thus perpetuates in both a vertical and horizontal manner to include siblings who abuse each other, thus becoming socialised as both victims and perpetrators simultaneously, and repeating the ingrained patterns into the next generation of children. More alarming are the numbers of adult perpetrators who remain non-convicted of any sexual offences against children. Attempts at

criminal prosecutions have notoriously failed or collapsed through an insufficiency of evidence from children or vulnerable witnesses who cannot withstand the scrutiny of the adversarial court system (Ceci and Bruck, 1995).

Crucial and unique to this model, are the activities of female sexual abusers who are as proactive and complicit in many ways with the predatory males and involved in the grooming, recruitment and prostitution of children. We argue that the females, active matriarchal figures such as grandmothers or mothers, act as 'recruiters' in the network. They groom or pimp children for sexual abuse to relatives, family friends or lone 'satellite men' (some convicted Schedule 1, paedophiles). These men circle and cluster around the family based network. They are known to ply children with alcohol, drugs or relaxants in order to facilitate child rape. Children in this environment fear disclosure to the authorities as a consequence of threats and intimidation. For example, a child may suddenly 'lose' a favourite pet, be beaten or imprisoned in the home if they appear to be 'wobbling'. Chronic parental neglect of these children must also be emphasised as a concomitant feature. Originally targeted themselves, and victims of incest and intergenerational abuse, the mothers are frequently vulnerable. They are subject to learning disability, chronic health problems, severe domestic violence, serial pregnancies, unsuitable partnership, and premature child deaths, some of which remain unexplained. However, they are frequently active in the abuse episodes and cannot protect their children.

There is unequivocal evidence that few of this population of children will escape this form of abuse and neglect. They are born and brought up in a normative multiple sexual exploitative culture that sexualises them from babyhood onwards. In this respect, they may not show the overt signs of sexualised behaviour that is generally associated with the professional identification of child sexual abuse. Full and coherent disclosures from these children are rare, vague or chronologically confused: a consequence of long-term trauma. Thus, attempts at disclosure to teachers or social workers may frequently be ignored or misunderstood and corroboration of evidence of abuse by other child victims is hard to achieve. It would seem that children in these circumstances might remain intimidated and unprotected throughout childhood unless there is an effective timely intervention.

Although these families operate in extremis, the actual prevalence and spread of the family based networks remains unknown even when core families within a community are identified. It is, therefore, highly challenging for child protection agencies to manage and maintain vigilance. The evidence suggests much geographical movement, specifically of the adult males with considerable lateral spread in many known communities where family groups may reform when there has been exposure. Thus, the statutory agencies may attempt identification and prosecution through joint police and social services operations, to address known core families, but this will usually be just the beginning of identifying a more widespread geographic linkage to another normative culture where multiple child abuse has equally been well established. The social and geographic linkage between abusing family networks therefore presents major challenges for the statutory agencies in terms of supervision and monitoring as does the constant movement and use of aliases in tracking offenders.

The above descriptive model has major implications for children being removed or returned from care to such family networks because research evidence suggests that few children will escape being victims in this family culture of multiple child abuse or neglect. This can be despite a rigorous surveillance by the statutory agencies. It also has implications for disclosing child victims removed to care or within the court forum who need to be well protected from any contact with family members who will intimidate the children. This may risk the retraction of disclosures. The abusing adult may apply for contact or resident orders, increasingly used in kinship arrangements. There are also inherent dangers of practitioners becoming complacent, where cases have reached the court forum. Successful convictions of male perpetrators and registration on the sex offenders register should not lull professionals into a false sense of security as there is ample evidence that sexual activities will continue, accompanied by aliases or changes in location. They will cluster upon yet another vulnerable linked family, once again regenerating the potential of the network formation.

Children living within kinship placements, or being assessed for potential placements, may face a range of individual or multiple risks from their family and community. These are identified below:

The grandparents

Many grandparents may, by virtue of age, appear to be benign, posing little threat to grandchildren, even though in the past, they may have been perceived as dysfunctional in parenting their own children. However, our research evidence indicates that often these are the active 'Old Guard' of powerful abuse networks that recruit and prostitute grandchildren to the younger males and friends. 'Old habits seem to die-hard'. They are no respecters of sexual boundaries, resulting in confused biological boundaries that add to the complexity of abuse patterns. For example, it is not uncommon to find that a female 'grandchild' is actually a daughter of a 'grandfather' and thus considered 'fair game'. These matriarchal sets of women, in particular, have admitted to intense cruelty and highly active intent in assisting the grooming and multiple sexual abuse incidents. In one case history, known to the writers, the disclosing female adolescent victim was more frightened of such a matriarchal person than any of the males in the network in which she had been repeatedly raped.

The mothers

Mothers are non-protecting in the respect that they have also been victims, drawn into, and socialised within abuse circles. The myth should be dispelled, however, that they are passive recipients of the abuse that is conducted in these environments. There is evidence to suggest the active involvement in the abuse of their own children. It is difficult to ascertain whether there is any unease about the abuse. There is limited evidence emerging from historical disclosures within adult therapy which indicates damage and trauma but also a reported sense that this abuse was their 'lot' in life. However, it is apparent that mothers are prepared to sacrifice their children in favour of their adult male partners.

The siblings

Sibling perpetration is also a further risk to be taken into account, once again, crossing gender boundaries. There is considerable debate from research on this issue, sometimes described as 'Contagion Theory', in which young abused children have also been victims of abuse

(Freeman-Longo,1986; Hackett, Print and Dey, 1998). Whilst caution is urged in reaching conclusions about direct causal relationships, the research undertaken by the writers over a number of years, using evidence from case material research has indicated that there are few, if any, exceptions, to moving along the continuum of abuse (victim) to abusing (perpetrator). The normative intergenerational impact of victimisation, its intensity and long-lasting nature seems to perpetuate into the next generation of abusers (Hummel et al., 2000; Rutter, 1995). In addition, children are frequently likely to be victims of uncles, aunts, cousins, step-parents and other permutations of kinship relationships.

Infiltrating adult male friends

The final group of perpetrators that targets vulnerable children in these settings are the infiltrating male family friends, who circle and link the family clusters together in a culture that is extensive and active. Undoubtedly the children are prostituted to them for favours or money and potentially also the making of pornography (videos etc.). There are some grotesque examples from the case stories collated even in the writers' geographic location, of the numbers of men that participate in multiple rape, using empty houses, or remote farms, or, city estates. Children have been taken by car to a distant locality, much of which involves considerable numbers of children of varying gender and disability. It can only be conjectured that as access to these numbers of children depletes (as a result, for example, through removal into care, or there is a seeping of information through disclosure) the males move off to target another cluster of fertile females and offspring. Thus, once again, the network is extended to incorporate the 'new guard'.

Implications for practice

There are many legal, ethical and practical dilemmas posed by this social phenomenon, to which agency practitioners and society in general, have been slow to confront or respond. Many ramifications of confronting and managing this problem are too numerous to mention at this juncture. Neither is it the purpose of this chapter to exaggerate or implicitly suggest that most

kinship care placements will generally be of this nature and description. Our plea is for thorough assessment which is responsive to risk. Nevertheless it is the responsibility of those professionals involved in permanency planning to consider the possibility that kinship care placements may pose risks to children. There are ways forward and practical methods that can assist the identification of abusing family networks and risk analysis across service areas and these can be used to safeguard children more effectively.

Case studies

This section will provide some case studies written to identify risk factors. These consist of ecological assessments through the use of genograms, the careful recording of case material, and protocols on the sharing of information. These can be used to help to identify and track family and extended kinship networking.

Most of the tools to establish if an abusive family network exist, are not new, nor complex to implement. It is, however, time consuming, with many local authority social workers struggling to find the space to use them effectively. They need to be accessed in an organised, structured way with one technique following on from another. It is very useful to obtain a full genogram, covering at least, three generations. Most families are prepared to co-operate with this, and engage easily in discussing memories of kinship relationships. The more information that can be collected in this process, the more effective it can be: for example, names, or name changes or (aliases) dates of birth, current addresses, and anecdotes about individual roles and expectations within the family are helpful. The family member being assessed, can be encouraged to draw the family tree as they go along or the assessor can do this with or for them. The resulting mapping can be reproduced using a computer disc, (readily and cheaply available in the shops, in the expanding home genogram industry). The extended family tree is an essential source material in identifying risks and family patterns of parenting across generations. It can also provide suggestions about family support for foster placements, or even reveal further placement options.

Case example A demonstrates what a substantial pool of information can be gleaned through the use of this process, citing the

---

Example A. The use of extensive genograms

Rupert aged five years, had been in the care system for 18 months on an interim care order, whilst various assessments of his mother and maternal grandmother were undertaken. His mother had significant mental health difficulties, and had experienced a turbulent adolescence, finishing up in a secure unit. Whilst there, she had made allegations of sexual abuse against her paternal grandfather and an uncle, later retracting them. None of the court material that had been presented had contained a family tree. However on the completion of this procedure with an aunt, the results revealed a large extended family system. The grandmother, who had been previously hostile to the process, partly because her own legal application to care for Rupert had been rejected, became more amicable. She was encouraged to add considerable detail about family links that provided new sources and options around the potential support for a kinship care placement. It also allowed the local authority to check their records to see if there were patterns of abuse in the wider family that were similar to the ones they had faced with Rupert and his immediate carers. This included investigating another significant feature of the case, namely whether other family members from the wider family, had made sexual abuse allegations against the same or other persons within the linked family network.

---

extended family system, initially thought to be very sparse of significant family relationships.

Allied with the simple use of genograms, is the Eco-map, an important and accessible tool long established as a technique in fostering and adoption assessments. The use of this tool should reveal the participant's view of the positives and negatives of their current family relationships and friendship circles, including those that are significant to them and others where relationships are characterised by tensions or conflict. This technique can identify frequent visitors to the household. Friends who the family have most contact with outside the home can be established. The participant family member can be asked to include anyone with whom they were friendly and explain why the contact dwindled or ceased. This gives an in depth assessment of movements in or around the family household and may help to locate weak links in an abusive system, namely members who are more willing to disclose abuse through reasons of revenge, protection, or vulnerability.

Once this basic material is available, the next stage in the information collation is accessing local authority records. This process is highly recommended as a means of double checking information to verify whether others identified as significant from the family tree, especially those being proposed as potential carers or their close associates, have been previously known to the statutory agencies. In one sense the original direct approach to families to collate information is done 'blindly' without this back up information.

Naturally there must have been a serious child protection concern or strong suspicions in order to trigger the investigation at this depth, and it is not suggested that this process is used on all and sundry service users, unless there are such grounds for concern.

The secondary search of past historic case files may wield alternative results: they may confirm known information, reveal wider unease of allegations and repeated suspicion or other new significant material. This could be a family member having a sex offending conviction that may have got 'lost' to the system. It must be stated however that finding or accessing previous case files is not always an easy process and may involve a considerable amount of time, patience and detailed research. Some may be found in archives in town or county halls, some have been stored by independent companies, and many have been microfilmed. Others remain in district offices linked to relevant current files, misfiled, on their own, in boxes of old material in basements or under stairwells or at the worst, missing or destroyed.

Local authority protocol is to retain case files on children who have been in the care system for many years (up to 75 years) but in reality retention periods vary enormously. Similarly, management can make different interpretations of the rules about how long child protection files should be kept. Some local authorities follow the maxim of keeping the file until the youngest child in the family on the child protection register is 18 years old. Files recording social services input outside these 'heavy end' criteria are often retained for much shorter periods, with a two or five year cut off point before final destruction not being uncommon. This does not enhance the possibility of making useful links between core family alliances.

Traditionally local authorities have not been effective in establishing or recording linkage or alliances between varying core families that are well known to them (see example B below). Anecdotally, social work team members covering specific geographic locations are often aware of these links between families in their 'patch', with information being retained mentally by members of staff. However, some may have drawn up elaborate diagrams of relationships between family systems. It is notoriously difficult to keep these updated in the light of constant movements of suspected offenders, changing relationships, serial marriages and so on. Equally from a professional perspective, it is hard to obtain sufficient time from management who may not perceive this form of 'research' as a major priority vital to the course of a case. In addition, the early local authority computerised systems tended to focus mainly on financial information. Whilst maintenance of case information is now more usual, it still tends to be unsophisticated in demonstrating potential links between extended family core alliances or friendship circles

Having located relevant case files, reading them is very time-consuming. Examining records of key meetings, such as various case conferences, core group meetings or LAC reviews, is a useful starting point before delving into the case running sheets. These are often hand written, and can be barely legible. It is, however, important to do this work rigorously as substantive themes or major incidents can often emerge from the typed records of child protection conferences, and can be elaborated on from the detail of the case recording. It is important therefore at this stage that the 'researcher' records key incidents on rough notes that may form a historical chronology, equally utilising photocopies of particular material or using a dictaphone for written recording later.

The chronology can be done in different forms. They are increasingly routine in child care social work and are now presumed by the courts citing in public law proceedings. Simple chronologies show the date, the source of the material, and brief details of the incident. More elaborate ones, for example, those first used by the Bridge Project in special case reviews, also have a column about injuries or developmental concerns surrounding the index children involved. This format is especially helpful as there is a further column describing what a child actually stated about a particular incident. A poignant concern is that this is usually the column with the least in it, as historically children were not always asked directly for their explanations of abuse experiences. Unfortunately, despite the rhetoric given to the importance of eliciting the children's voice within the Children Act 1989 this may still

---

Example B. The linking of cases by local authorities

Angela (aged 11) had not lived with her father for some years, but he was now being assessed as a possible kinship carer. The father lived with Angela's paternal grandmother and step-grandfather in a different part of the country. On visiting Angela's mother to discuss her views of the possible placement, the assessor was gradually told of a number of serious child sexual abuse allegations from the maternal side of the family. The male partner of mother's best friend had recently been convicted of sexually interfering with his own children. This man had previously babysat Angela and her half-sister. The mother's brother had been in court for sexual abuse of a stepchild, but had been found not guilty. The children of the mother's sister were currently on the child protection register for neglect and also at risk of sexual abuse (from their mother's boyfriend). When the social worker made enquiries of the local authority concerned, they had no idea that these three cases were linked within the same family system. The cases were currently being worked in three different local district social services offices. However, when the social services department's computerised records were accessed, no connections between differing family members had been recorded. This is a classic example of the social workers presumably focusing discreetly on their own core family case without discussing the extent of the other family relationships. In the event, neither would the computerised records have made any necessary connection for them.

Example C. Intergenerational parenting: patterns of neglect

Elaine had her two young boys taken into care due to their chronic neglect, poor school attendance, and strong suspicions of child sexual abuse by visitors to the household. She had difficulties in creating consistent boundaries for both boys and they could be found wandering down the street at 5-6 am before the neighbourhood was up. The elder boy was profoundly deaf and had great difficulty communicating or understanding instructions. Elaine had health problems as a result of obesity and was further restricted in the little effort she made to manage the boys, through her own lack of mobility. In an effort to control them, she had persuaded the local authority's occupational therapy department to build a high fence around the garden to keep them in. She had also managed to convince the housing department to put locks on their bedroom windows to stop them climbing out. Consequently, when a fire started in one of the boy's bedrooms early in the morning, it was very fortuitous that a passer-by raised the alarm and then lead the family to safety. This specific incident had triggered their entry into the care system.

Subsequently the maternal grandmother, Betty, had requested the care of both boys. The discovery of some very old files of Elaine and her siblings during their childhood, revealed some intriguing similarities. Betty, along with a punitive but mainly absent husband had been unable to cope with their children. She had resorted to restricting the movement of most of her five children by locking them in rooms, or cupboards. This was an entrenched parenting pattern. As babies and toddlers they had also been tied into prams, pushchairs or beds, so that she could maintain control of their movements. Predictably, all had suffered differing degrees of developmental delay. Elaine had responded to similar parenting difficulties using different controlling methods and manipulating service providers to support her response to the behaviour of her children. It was a matter of conjecture how much her obesity and lack of mobility was also associated with her early childhood. Needless to say, Betty was firmly rejected as a kinship carer, indeed becoming a central figure later in a major police enquiry and criminal prosecution surrounding extensive and multiple abusive networks.

---

not be the case, as manifested on some occasions by virtue of age or poor practice.

With chronologies or information on as many members of the extended family as may appear relevant, the analysis of this becomes a crucial stage. Patterns of parenting behaviour and traits of multiple forms of inter-generational abuse can be identified. Patterns of neglect, lack of emotional warmth, or domestic violence appear to be often transmitted from one generation to the next without effective intervention, although there will be family members who prove more resilient. Case example C suggests an intergenerational pattern of behaviour transmitted from mother to daughter but manifesting itself in a different manner. Example D is an analysis of a more complex set of events within an extended family structure.

Discussion

These examples demonstrate how a collation of initial information obtained from case files is an essential ingredient in identifying links between cases. The next part of the process, the engagement and discussion of these observations with the family members may prove even more challenging; for example, the family may not accept the professional assessment surrounding parenting patterns. Alternatively, within their family, they may be able to provide new information or perceptions that differ from the profile that has emerged from former case records. If the evidence of serious deficiencies or significant risk of harm is overwhelmingly strong however, a fundamental issue in the assessment becomes the family's willingness and ability to recognise and acknowledge this. They must be able to demonstrate they are able to operate differently in the future.

The theoretical model outlined earlier in this chapter as well as empirical and practical experience based on many risk assessment and child protection enquiries, would suggest that the more a potential kinship carer remains involved with abusive family members, then the less chance there is for a safe, successful placement. If the kinship carer's main support network

---

Example D. Establishing patterns of child or adult sexual abuse across the wider extended family system

Carol was a 32 year old woman who has had four children removed on care orders as a consequence of her chronic inability to parent effectively. Other concerns related to the children's exposure to domestic violence, and the risk posed of child sexual abuse from an ever increasing number of different male partners. The fifth child was removed at birth and a permanent alternative placement sought. Whilst she rarely talked of the events and had never disclosed her own childhood sexual abuse, previous assessments by practitoners perceived Carol's own dysfunctional childhood as the root cause of her difficulties. One of Carol's sisters, Janet, and her husband, offered to bring up the new baby and initially this looked potentially an attractive proposition to maintain links within the family of origin. The couple were successfully parenting two children of their own, and the health visitor and school talked favourably of them. However, an extensive research of old court papers retained by the local authority legal department and historic case files describing a particular incident, changed this initial perception. The case notes revealed that Carol's mother, Sheila, had frequently taken Carol and her sisters out of school to visit an 'uncle'. This man was not related to the family and was a Schedule 1 offender. The old notes implied that Sheila was aware of this and knew exactly what she was doing in having contact with this man. A child protection enquiry had been started at the time but proved inconclusive.

Coincidentally, around the same time as this case was being explored by the assessor, Carol's 16 year old half-brother, Luke, was convicted of sexually interfering with a three year old niece whilst he was babysitting. Luke was sentenced to a supervision order, and continued to live at home with his mother Sheila. Interestingly, the youth offending team, oblivious of this previous history, had drawn up a 'Family Safety' contract using Sheila as the principal day to day supervisor to ensure Luke was barred from family babysitting, and did not have unsupervised contact with younger children.

The notion of a 'career of suspicion' acts as a trigger to identify other concerns, and further research was done. This research was undertaken on Carol's five adult siblings and their children. Whilst they had not all been known to social services, some concerns were identified about inappropriate sexual behaviour amongst the current generation. There were also recorded concerns about some previous partners with abuse allegations made against them from their former partners. It also became apparent that all the adult siblings were in frequent contact with each other, regularly visiting each other's houses. For example they all saw Sheila, the grandmother, on a weekly basis and she appeared to be at the hub of the family wheel. It became apparent that Luke had babysat for most of their children in the past. It transpired that Janet and her husband had previously applied through private law proceedings to care for the baby of another sister when her relationship had run into difficulties. This application had been rejected. Within the family system, it would appear that she was perceived by the family to have been the most successful sibling and was viewed as the 'family rescuer'.

It is interesting in the light of theories of normalisation, to comment on the reactions of this family to the allegations. When the implications of this investigation were discussed with Janet and her husband, they denied Sheila's role in any past abuse. Whilst they did not wish to retain Luke as a baby sitter at the time they would not concede that he could be a long term risk to their children in general. The assessor concluded that relationships in the extended family were so enmeshed, and the couple's attitude to the sexual boundaries of the family so uncertain, that this was not a safe, long term placement for Carol's baby. Despite opposition from other parties in the court case this view was also accepted by the court.

---

remains within the abusive network and if they were also past child victims, the harder it will be to negate the family network's normative influence and patterns of behaviour.

With historical allegations of child abuse, it is important that focus is not only on the outcome of an enquiry. Some allegations may have been made when the victim became an adult, and there may not be any earlier childhood investigations into the family. There is also a likelihood that original allegations were not properly investigated at the time by practitioners. This could be as a consequence of the hindrance and obstruction of the families themselves or through pressure of work of the investigating statutory agencies. It is a well known fact that only a tiny number of child sexual abuse allegations ever reach the court, let alone produce a conviction. In trying to map connections, it is essential to identify the alleged perpetrator and their relationship to other alleged perpetrators. For instance, if an uncle is alleged to have been an abuser during adolescence, an assessment would involve assessing whom the likely abuser may have been to his generation of the family. This may also involve establishing a specific *modus operandi* common to family members such as hanging around school playgrounds, working as carers and so on. It is important to identify the core family members who are non-protecting parents, often in less powerful positions in the family network and frequently (although not exclusively) female. Another question is about whether there are family members who appear to always be at the hub of the family wheel, to which everyone in the family relates back to in some way. Are they the individuals that always seem to know what is going on alternatively condoning, facilitating or actively participating in abuse? Sheila, in Example D, is almost certainly such a person.

Many of the above techniques used to investigate such families rely on there being local authority records available to peruse, but this is not always the case. There can alternatively be other sources of information. Even in an age of staff mobility, within individual offices, there are often staff members with memories of previous events or of informal knowledge of complex family relationships. These are not always social workers, and could be managers who have long since left the front line, family support workers or clerical staff who may have typed minutes of meetings or case notes. Whilst memories and anecdotal evidence should not inevitably be used as a reliable source in its own right, they can be useful in providing major leads about links, and directions where further formal evidence might be sought.

The staff of other agencies can also be a source of much historical material. It is not uncommon for health visitors to remain in the same geographical area in some capacity. One example was a child protection nursing manager, currently offering consultation to local health visitors, who had previously practised in the same area. She had been the health visitor for many of the mothers now caring for their own children when they had been babies themselves. She had extensive knowledge of the local community, little of it documented, but had rarely been asked to contribute to any assessments.

It is also possible for assessors to access the records of other agencies where there are identified child protection concerns without falling foul of the Data Protection Act. Health visiting, school nursing and education department records are regularly contained in child protection minutes. Relevant medical notes are also present whether from GPs or hospital consultants. All of these can be sought if necessary as part of an assessment. If informal approaches or letters of consent from applicants are met with refusal, then ultimately a court order may be necessary if the matter seems significant enough.

Potentially the police with their criminal investigation role often hold the most resources to pursue an enquiry along these lines, as compared to other agencies outside social services. Most local authorities and CAFCASS now have protocols of how this information can be accessed including data protection protocols. As is known from the events in Soham and the subsequent report this can be a 'hit and miss' affair. A check on the criminal records of any potential carer should always be asked for. However in our experience, in providing this information, the police child protection teams sometimes reduce this to their own definitions of what constitutes a child protection matter. The assessor should seek the full criminal record and make their own judgements. For example past offences of violence against adults, or misuse of alcohol or drugs, even cruelty to pets should not be excluded and can be very relevant. Again the court would be the final arbitrator of any disputes in this area.

Although only recently introduced with more detail, the heightened emphasis on the recording of police call outs to incidents of domestic disturbances, can be crucial information. For this tracking to be effective an accurate record is needed from carers of all their previous addresses. Domestic violence that has taken place with one or more partners is usually a contra-indicator to the suitability of a kinship placement (see Chapter 6). Recent work has suggested that repeat victimisation or perpetration can also become an established pattern in relationships with different permutations of partners (Freeman, 2005). Similarly, what the police describe as 'intelligence' can be very revealing, although harder to obtain, and not always accurate. For example, in one case, intelligence revealed that a stepfather, who had two children temporarily placed with him by the local authority, had been stopped by patrol cars on three occasions in the early hours of the morning, cruising around an industrial estate. On two occasions, both children had been asleep in the back of the car. The police suspected that, given his past history of offending, he was looking for premises to burgle. With no one else to care for them, he claimed, he had been forced to take the children with him on two occasions. (This begged the question as to where they were on the third occasion and what he was up to). Unfortunately, the father's belligerent and defensive response to the police investigation led to the early removal of the children from his care, whatever the truth of the matter was.

The purpose of all these techniques of mapping and checks are not to restrict the potential use of kinship care placements across the board. It behoves practitioners, however, to subject family members to the same degree of scrutiny as stranger foster placements, without making the assumption that all family members will care non-abusively for 'their own'. It is necessary to establish whether there are issues within a family member applicant's past that will significantly compromise their ability to safely meet the needs of a child in the future. Just as the financial, practical and emotional support available to kinship placements should be on the same level playing field as long term fostering or adoption placements so does the quality and depth of the assessment undertaken by professionals with carers. It is not in any children's best interests to move them from one part of an abusive family network, only to set them up in another part of the same extended family system.

References

BBC News *France Sentences Sex Ring Members.* news.bbc.co.uk/2/Li/europe/4719751.stm.

Ceci, S.J. and Bruck, M. (1995) *Jeopardy in the Courtroom: A Scientific Analysis of Children's Testimony.* Washington: American Psychological Association.

Cleaver, H. and Freeman, P. (1995) *Parental Perspectives in Cases of Suspected Child Abuse.* London: HMSO.

Cleaver, H. and Freeman, P. (1996) Child Abuse Which Involves Wider Kin and Family Friends. In Bibby. P. (Ed.) *Organised Abuse: The Current Debate.* Aldershot: Ashgate/Arena.

Freeman, P. (2005) *Attrition Rates in Domestic Violence.* Unpublished. ADVA Partnership.

Hummel, P., Thomke, V. et al. (2000) Male Sex Offenders Against Children: Similarities and Differences of Those With and Those Without a History of Sexual Abuse. *Journal of Adolescence.* 23: 305–17.

Rutter, M. (1995) Causal Concepts and Their Testing. In Rutter, M. and Smith, D. (Eds.) *Psychosocial Disorders in Young People: Time, Trends and Their Causes.* Chichester: Wiley.

Chapter Eight

The Impact of Parental Substance Misuse on Kinship Care and the Implications for Assessment

Brynna Kroll and Julie Cornwell

Introduction

... my mam's always there ... I know I can always fall back on my mam.

(Parent in Barnard, 2003: 297)

Parental substance misuse is now a significant feature in relation to children in need, presenting a range of challenges for professionals in child and family health and social care (Bates et al., 1999; Forrester, 2000; Harwin and Forrester, 2002; Kroll and Taylor, 2000, 2003) as well as adult services (Weir and Douglas, 1999). When parents misuse drugs or alcohol, there can be manifold consequences for child development, from pre-birth onwards, as well as implications for sound psychological and social development. In this chapter, we explore some of the key practice issues encountered in situations where children of substance misusing parents are cared for by grandparents or other extended family members. In particular we analyse some of the complex dynamics that can arise and their implications for assessment, specifically in relation to risk. Even in the best regulated homes, the 'sharing' of a child between carers can be complex; in these types of extended family arrangements, we encounter a situation where this sharing might be enforced rather than voluntary, where contact may be difficult due to substance misuse, and where loyalties may be tested to the limit. We must also consider the impact of the 'elephant in the living room' – a huge and significant family member whose presence is often denied by adults but who is very visible to the children and who can cast a long shadow (Kroll and Taylor, 2003; Kroll, 2004).

For the purposes of this debate, our use of the term 'substance misuse' is based on the definition provided by the Standing Conference on Drug Abuse (SCODA, 1997) which highlights a number of important points:

The terms drug use and misuse mean different things to different people. Drug use may be described as drug taking. In general misuse can be taken to mean the use of drugs which leads to harm (social, physical and psychological).

(SCODA, 1997: 36)

Here a useful distinction is made between 'use' and 'misuse'. What is also important is that the emphasis is not simply on definitions based solely on quantity, but on patterns, motivations and consequences, including the role played by the substance in managing a range of personal and inter-personal issues and the links between this and wider family dynamics. By 'substance' we mean both the licit (alcohol, prescribed drugs, including methadone and solvents) and illicit (heroin, amphetamines, cocaine, crack, cannabis, ecstasy etc.). At times drugs and alcohol will be discussed together. However, there are some significant differences between them in terms of impact and consequences and these will be highlighted, as and when they arise.

We will begin by examining what little we know about kinship care issues where there are drug and alcohol problems. A number of contextual issues will then be considered including some useful theoretical frameworks and what research can tell us about the impact of substance misuse on both child welfare and parenting capacity, within an environmental context. Against this backdrop, the implications for assessment will be examined, illustrated by case material.

Inevitably, this area of welfare practice poses almost unlimited questions, many of which may be impossible to answer, as we are effectively confronted with a set of Russian dolls, each concealing another doll within. How far is it useful to trace the aetiology of the substance problem to assess the extent to which it may be problem-solving behaviour, learnt at the parents' knee? If substance use or misuse is a characteristic of the family system, how helpful is it to place the children in this environment? Would it be better to remove them completely, depending on age and the extent of their exposure to the family drink or drug culture? Here of course we enter the realms of social engineering in which that long forgotten difference – class – rears its head. This is a contentious issue within the general kinship care literature in which the pros and cons of remaining within the same neighbourhood, community and school are often hotly debated particularly if there are negative peer group pressures (see for example Barth, 1999). Where there is substance misuse, and children have been subjected to bullying and vilification due to the unfortunate behaviour or appearance of parents with drug and alcohol problems, remaining in the same environment or, indeed, the same family may do more harm than good, depending on the attachment to and strength of the substance using subculture. These factors, combined with generational transmission of poor parenting – a regular assumption in assessment (Flynn, 1999) – need to be carefully balanced with the child's needs, in terms of identity, connectedness and safety. However the part played by class and its connection to substance of choice cannot be sidestepped, in our view. Would we cheerfully leave a child with a dedicated G and T swilling, educated, middle class family but robustly protest if the placement system was working class and characterised by unemployment and cocaine and heroin use, however well managed and controlled?

Irrespective of the class dimension, why is it that we view alcohol misuse less seriously than drug misuse, despite the wealth of evidence attesting to the damage it can cause and, as a consequence, leave children in the care of heavy drinkers for much longer than we should (Forrester and Harwin, 2004; Hayden et al., 2002)? How can we effectively assess the role played by the substance in managing attachment, loss, fear, feelings, difficult and painful history, and work with these issues throughout the family system so that children can find security within an extended family network, with all its implications for identity and cultural and genealogical connectedness (Owusu-Bempah and Howitt, 1997)?

Parental substance misuse: how many children are affected?

It is estimated that about a million children in the UK may be living with parents with problematic drinking patterns (see for example Brisby et al., 1997; Orford, 2001) and that between 250–350,000 are in the care of problem drug users (Advisory Council on the Misuse of Drugs, 2003). Not all

end up coming to the notice of the social welfare system, as many parents manage their drug and alcohol use in a way that minimises the impact on their children. However a substantial proportion can be found in the 'looked after' population with many requiring substitute care (Mather, 2004).

Although child protection registers and social services records have been used to gain a sense of the extent of parental substance misuse (see for example Forrester, 2000; Hayden et al., 2002; Kearney et al., 2000) this obviously only identifies people who have come to the notice of statutory services. Studies do not always distinguish between drug use, alcohol use or both and there are further complications where there is poly-substance use and a mental health problem (Kearney et al., 2000). In other words, there is often a constellation of problems that may skew the way in which data are categorised. In addition, many families present for services for problems other than substance misuse which may remain undetected or denied (Tunnard, 2000a; 2002b) and problems with alcohol, in particular, are often underestimated or under recognised by social workers (Hayden et al., 2002; Forrester, 2000; 2004). Figures emanating from studies based on social services' data vary considerably in relation to the proportion of families where substance misuse is an issue. Cleaver et al. (1999), for example, suggest that 20 per cent of child and family referrals feature substance misuse in some form, rising to 25 per cent at the case conference stage. Forrester (2000) however, in his study based in Southwark Social Services, found that substance misuse was an issue in 52 per cent of cases, and in their analysis of the care plans of 100 children Harwin et al. (2003) found it a major factor in care proceedings for 40 per cent of their sample of children subject to care orders. In a separate study of children on the child protection register, parental substance misuse was a factor for 62 per cent of children subject to care proceedings (Forrester and Harwin, 2002). A study based in Bolton found that over 30 per cent of children on the child protection register and 75 per cent subject to care proceedings had parents misusing substances (Murphy and Oulds, 2000), while a study based on four children and family-focused teams in Portsmouth found there was concern in almost 33 per cent of cases (Hayden et al., 2002).

Substance misuse: family support and kinship care – messages from research

The role of family support has received considerable attention in studies of the impact of both drug and alcohol misuse on children (Barnard, 2003; Hogan and Higgins, 2001; Laybourn et al., 1996; Velleman and Orford, 1999) as well as within a range of cultural contexts (Patel, 2000; Mayer, 2004). It has also been a major theme in the development of family focused intervention where there is substance misuse (Kroll and Taylor, 2003) consistent with the ecological context in which assessments must now be undertaken (DoH, 2000). What is in little doubt, from the available literature on the impact of parental substance misuse, is the important role that grandparents and other relatives can play in providing support and emotional sustenance to children as well as protecting them from the often dangerous consequences of chaotic lifestyles and other substance-related behaviours (Barnard, 2003; Hogan and Higgins, 2001; Laybourn et al., 1996). Ironically however, supportive kin can also undermine parents' motivation to tackle their substance problems, free them from responsibilities and thus appear to collude with a chaotic lifestyle and provide a significant barrier to both change and a continuing attachment to their children (Barnard, 2003).

Because of the links between substance misuse and 'significant harm' a considerable number of children who come to the notice of social services departments are unable to remain with their parents and kinship placements become an option in order to avoid entry into the 'looked after' system (Broad, 2001), and to enable children to remain within a familial network which will foster identity and genealogical connectedness. Kinship placements may have been initiated by carers themselves due to concerns, planned in advance with professionals or may have been in response to a crisis. In relation to grandparent intervention where there is drug misuse, figures are now considered to be 'substantial' (Barnard, 2003: 291), with many children in need of emotional permanence (Hunt, 2003). In relation to alcohol misuse, this is an under researched area although the situation is likely to be similar (Kroll and Taylor, 2003). This is consistent with the US literature which also reflects a high rate of

kinship placements where there is substance misuse. Indeed the US 'explosion' in kinship care was in response to maternal drug use (Hunt, 2003) – a problematic state of affairs in light of research that now suggests that kinship placements are less suitable for drug exposed infants pre-birth (Brooks and Barth, 1998). Gleeson and Hairston (1999) suggest that 80 per cent of kinship placements in their North American study were precipitated by drug and alcohol problems, a finding reflected by Beeman and Boisen (2000) where kinship care was found to be more likely in this context. Neglect was often a significant variable in relation to kinship placements (Hunt, 2003) and this is important in view of the firm links between neglect and substance misuse, as already indicated above. Barrio and Hughes (2000) emphasise the extent to which kinship placements are used as a cultural resource by African-American and Latino families managing substance misuse, as well to preserve ethnic identity (Flynn, 2002). The role played by grandparents in particular is highlighted (Kolar et al., 1994) although the complications caused by uncertain legal status, prior dysfunctional and conflictual relationships, the health, wealth and age of the carers, as well as the problems presented by children who may have suffered neglect, abuse and lack of control are also underlined (Jaudes et al., 1995; Kelley and Damato, 1995; Marcenko et al., 2000; Minkler at al., 1992).

In the UK context, there is very little research about kinship care placements and outcomes where there is substance misuse. Although Flynn (2002) provides an invaluable overview of research on kinship care over the last 20 years, the reasons for the placement are not examined in depth apart from an emphasis on the crucial area of kinship care and black families. It is fruitful, however, to examine the literature on parental substance misuse for references to the role played by family in general and grandparents in particular. Although kinship care is not explicitly addressed, it is apparent that grandparents provide a source of invaluable support. For parents, this often means practical and financial support and child care – the emotional support and oversight lacking at home (Elliott and Watson, 1998; Hogan 1997; Laybourn et al., 1996). In addition to providing continuity for children, it was also recognised in the study by Hogan and Higgins in Dublin (2001) that grandparents would be quick to notice non-school attendance and that, without their support, many parents would be unable to enter treatment for drug problems. However, there was an equal amount of evidence to suggest that grandparent involvement was not without its problems in terms of confusion for children about who was 'in charge' of them and conflict over parents' behaviour.

The most detailed available study is by Barnard (2003). Although focused on parents' perceptions of *their* parents' role in caring for and indeed protecting their children from harm, it undoubtedly has resonance for situations where it is alcohol misuse that is the problem. Part of a larger study that focused on children's experiences of drug misusing parents, which included interviews with parents too, an unexpected emerging theme was the role and level of family involvement in the care and protection of children and that, '. . . where they did not step into the breach, the most likely outcome was that the children would be looked after and accommodated' (Barnard, 2003: 298). The tensions, dilemmas and conflicts highlighted in the US literature were also reflected in this study.

What we do not have access to are accounts from kinship carers or children who have been in such placements and this is clearly an important area for future research. Meanwhile, general child care research certainly endorses the view that, in extremis, a significant emotional attachment to a reliable family member fosters resilience (Fonagy et al., 1994; Howe et al., 1999), as does a secure, permanent substitute placement (Mather, 2004). However, as the above findings show, in families where there is substance misuse, this level of attachment and security cannot always be assumed and kinship care is not without its problems.

The impact of parental substance misuse on child welfare: some theoretical frameworks

Not all parents who use alcohol or drugs mistreat their children (Barnard, 1999; Harbin and Murphy, 2000). However, research suggests that parental substance misuse can adversely affect attachment (Brooks and Rice, 1997; Flores, 2001; Howe et al., 1999; Klee et al., 1998), family dynamics, relationships and functioning (Cleaver et al., 1999; Harbin and Murphy, 2000; Velleman and Orford, 1999), and significantly increases the

risk of violence (Brookoff et al., 1997) (see Bell in Chapter 6). This can be exacerbated where there are also mental health problems (Mulvey, 1994) and the combination of maternal depression and alcohol misuse has been found to be a particularly high risk mix (Woodcock and Sheppard, 2002). Neglect and emotional, sexual and physical abuse have also been linked to substance misuse (Alison, 2000; Ammerman et al., 1999; Chaffin et al., 1996; Famularo et al., 1992; Jaudes et al., 1995), as has child homicide (Besharov, 1994; Reder et al., 1993; Reder and Duncan, 1999). The chaotic lifestyle often associated with drug misuse, the unpredictability of parents and the fact that parents may engage in criminal behaviour of different kinds in order to fund a drink or drug problem also have obvious consequences for the child's well-being. A range of financial, psychological, physical and environmental consequences inevitably flow from this, to a greater or lesser extent (Cleaver et al., 1999; Harbin and Murphy, 2000; Kroll and Taylor, 2003).

As a consequence, growing up with parental substance misuse can expose children to a range of problematic and frightening behaviours and experiences and this can cast a long shadow, as accounts from children suggest (Kroll, 2004). This experience can have significant implications for substitute care, particularly if care is provided within the extended family where substance use may effectively be a family member, whether actual or ghostly.

Central to this brief overview will be a number of key theories. The first is that substance problems do not develop in isolation but in response to circumstances, relationships, contexts; one of the most significant arenas in which it evolves is often the family (Velleman, 1993; Velleman and Orford, 1999). The literature on alcohol certainly emphasises this dynamic and there is no reason to assume that drug related problems evolve any differently. In this regard, the family could be seen as both the cause of the problems and the solution to them – a potentially powerful force for change and a source of support, but also a protective mantle, a smokescreen, an obfuscator, a repository of secrets. These contradictions have obvious significance for kinship care.

The second is attachment theory and its relevance not only for the child/parent/grandparent dynamic but also as a means of understanding the relationship between substance and user. Research suggests that parental substance misuse can significantly undermine the attachment between parents and children, since it can render parents psychologically unavailable, inconsistent (depending on levels of use, impact of withdrawal and so on), less sensitive to children's signals, needs and overall welfare, and often actually physically absent due to the demands that obtaining substances may make (Cleaver et al., 1999). This parenting experience, unless bolstered by support from other adult figures/attachment objects, can lead to insecure attachment patterns with implications for a child's internal working model and overall sense of self worth and identity (Kroll, 2004). Closely linked to this is the idea that substance misuse is based on an attachment relationship and if one's primary attachment is to drugs, alcohol or both, this has significant implications for the ability to attach to others (Kroll and Taylor, 2003). If we apply this in a generational context, hypothetically it could be possible that grandparents' use of drugs or alcohol could have impacted on their attachment to their child, who could in turn have developed a substance problem with implications for their own parenting capacity. Although it is possible that grandparents could have resolved their substance use and their attachment issues by the time they become substitute carers, these may be re-activated in the face of their child's inability to parent effectively. Even if substance misuse had never been a feature in the family of origin but had developed subsequently for reasons not obviously connected or indeed very separate, becoming carers for grandchildren could confront grandparents with their own complex attachment issues as well as allowing the substance to enter the family via the children's experience.

The final idea underpinning this analysis is based on systems theory. The substance either is or becomes a family member with the potential to impact on attachment styles and behaviours in relation to all concerned. It is here that we encounter the elephant in the living room.

Elephant: what elephant? Denial, distortion and secrecy

Secrecy and denial, with the resultant confusion, tensions and anxieties that arise, emerge clearly as issues for the children of substance misusing

parents (Kroll, 2004). The dynamic of denial, distortion, confusion and secrecy often results in the substance use becoming the 'central organising principle' of the family, with all the family members operating around it, and in relation to it (Brown, 1988) and 'whose rhythm is drawn from meeting the needs of a drug habit' (Barnard and Barlow, 2003). From the child's point of view, a 'don't talk' rule is imposed and children are encouraged, from an early age, not to 'tell'. If challenged, the child's perceptions of the realities of the family are called into question (Brooks and Rice, 1997).

> ... children know that the household revolves round something other than themselves but they are not allowed to know what it is and they are not allowed to ask what it is ... this persists even once children have worked out that drug dependency is at the heart of their family dynamic.
> (Barnard and Barlow, 2003: 52)

What seems to evolve for many of the children is 'a conspiracy of silence' where shame and fear of consequences effectively cut families off from both wider family and community (Laybourn et al., 1996: 71). This has obvious implications, in that children are effectively muzzled and isolated from potential sources of support which might foster resilience. Drug misuse, in particular, connects children and parents to a sub-culture in which secrecy is essential, due to anxieties about police raids, imprisonment and the consequences of criminal activity (Brisby et al., 1997; Hogan, 1997; Hogan and Higgins, 2001).

The longer this culture of denial and secrecy persists, the harder it is to penetrate, with children admitting to becoming mistrustful of outsiders, reluctant to confide and fearful of attempts to help, support or simply ask questions (Brisby et al., 1997; Brooks and Rice, 1997; ChildLine, 1996: Laybourn et al., 1996). Knowing but being forced into denying that you know, as Barnard and Barlow (2003) have argued, makes it difficult for the 'knowing' self to discuss that which is being denied. Hogan's (1997) study also suggests that parental secrecy breeds secrecy in children about more than just the drug use because of the atmosphere of furtiveness created in the home, due to locked doors and other types of suspicious behaviour. The experience of constantly feeling shut out and excluded, literally and metaphorically, contributes to children's sense of being unwanted, rejected and unimportant (Barnard and Barlow, 2003; Hogan and Higgins, 2001). Ironically, although they work hard to keep 'the secret', children also feel aggrieved because people do not try to discover the 'secret' or make attempts to find out what is wrong, although they acknowledged how difficult this would be (Robinson and Rhoden, 1998).

Here the elephant is encountered – a huge, significant, but secret presence which takes up a lot of space, uses considerable resources, and requires both a great deal of attention and the adjustment of all those in its vicinity. The image of the 'elephant in the living room', first used by Hastings and Typpo (1984) in relation to the impact of alcohol misuse, vividly evokes the sense of a huge and dominating presence impossible for children to ignore. The process of denial, where the adult has an emotional attachment to either drugs or alcohol (Flores, 2001; Kroll and Taylor, 2003), makes acknowledging the presence of the elephant very difficult. The elephant can also obscure the child, rendering them 'invisible' to those whose job it is to care for them (Kroll and Taylor, 2000):

A child would never overlook an elephant in the living room ('Hey there is an elephant in the living room. Doesn't anyone else see it?'). When adults behave as if there is no elephant, the child experiences a distorted reality.

(Brooks and Rice, 1997: 93)

The consequences of experiencing this 'distorted reality' can be manifold. Confusion about the elephant increases as does the child's capacity to trust their own perceptions – 'it must be me; there must be something wrong with the way I see things – I can no longer trust my own judgment'. The world, therefore, becomes an uncertain place, as the child ceases to know whether what they are seeing or experiencing is real or not – 'a world of mirrors where nothing is as it seems' (Barnard and Barlow, 2003: 54).

Alongside this is the issue of the child's management of the anxiety that is provoked by the 'elephant' which might be paraphrased like this – 'I don't like this elephant, but no one else ever admits it's there, so what do I do with my fear?' This in turn can lead to what Brooks and Rice (1997) refer to as the 'don't feel' rule which often means that children are not just discouraged from feeling but from talking about feelings as well. As one parent observed 'That was a big thing that I done . . . I never taught her

to be able to share honestly about her feelings or anything . . . I just taught her to hide things' (Barnard and Barlow, 2003: 51).

The issue of secrecy is likely to loom particularly large for ethnic minority groups when it comes to accessing services. Seeking help outside the community can be problematic for a range of cultural reasons, since admitting to substance problems may lead to exposure and censure. A range of assumptions are often made based on cultural stereotyping – certain groups are not 'supposed' to have such problems and so it is hard for them to be heard by others, including those providing services (Awiah et al., 1992; Brisby et al., 1997; Patel, 2000). These beliefs can lead either to the realities of children's lives being ignored or to assumptions being made about the way in which the extended family will swoop in and save them if need be.

The elephant, then, may be a secret shared by the extended family or kept within one small unit. Either way, children will probably have experienced persistent denial ('what elephant?') and may bring elephant-adaptive behaviours into the carer network. These will have to be managed and understood.

The impact of substance misuse on parenting

More an art than a science, parenting is a complex activity requiring patience, selflessness, tenacity, consistency, knowledge, understanding, physical and emotional availability and the capacity to place a child's needs before one's own. The 'good enough parent' (Bettelheim, 1987; Winnicott, 1964) should also provide a holding, containing environment based on a secure attachment in which the child can develop a secure internal working model (Howe et al., 1999) and separate appropriately, in response to developmental change. Parenting is not a free standing 'skill' which exists independently of context and environment; it has a dynamic quality in which state of mind, personality, character, history, structural and practical circumstances, and a host of unconscious processes all play their part. What follows should be considered in relation to both the child/parent dynamic and the relationship between the adult 'children' and their parents, particularly in view of some of the generational patterns of substance misuse that will be discussed later.

We all come to parenting with histories, anxieties, fantasies and stereotypes of what good fathers and mothers are supposed to do and be; the reality can be all we dreamed of, everything we feared or something in between. We also have complex motivations for having children and 'the meaning of the child' has been seen to have significance particularly when things go wrong (Reder et al., 1993; Reder and Duncan, 1999). A crucial determinant of parenting style is the parents' own internal working model – an inner sense of their own value derived from previous experiences of parents, carers and others, particularly the extent to which their needs were met and the trustworthiness and availability of others (Howe et al., 1999). This in turn affects attachment behaviour and the capacity to tolerate need and dependence in others. It may be here that the substance of choice begins to play a part. This brings us to what might be called collision of circumstances. In other words, parental substance misuse occurs for many reasons, and in many contexts. Poverty, social and structural disadvantage or exclusion, oppression, environment, mental health problems, domestic violence, emotional pain, anxiety, hopelessness, loss, identity dilemmas, problem childhoods, rejection and culture (familial, ethnic, racial or all three) can all contribute both to its onset and maintenance. There is also a strong correlation between problem drug use and social and individual deprivation (Barnard, 1999; Hepburn, 2000). These levels of complexity cannot be emphasised too much.

Whatever the reasons for the substance misuse, there is little doubt that it has the potential to affect all six dimensions of the parenting capacity domain of the Framework for the Assessment of Children in Need and their Families (DoH, 2000a) – basic care, ensuring safety, emotional warmth, stimulation, guidance and boundaries and stability. By the same token, it can impact upon the environmental domain in relation to family functioning, relationships with the wider family, housing, employment, income, social integration and community resources (Cleaver et al., 1999). Class, culture and gender also act as significant variables in relation to the degree of exposure, impact and intervention in families where there is substance misuse (Harbin and Murphy, 2000; Hepburn, 2000; Kearney, 1994; Kroll and Taylor, 2003; Klee et al., 1998) – all significant factors in assessment.

What has to be considered in this context is the role that the substance plays in the parenting task – what Elliott and Watson (2000) refer to as 'the deep association between drugs and coping'. This may include managing the pressures and tensions of bringing up children, providing a 'reward' to compensate for the demands of child care or helping to manage unresolved issues resurrected by being a parent. In addition, the substance may also have a role in managing relationship tensions with the other parent, partners or family, or in keeping difficult feelings, depression or other types of mental health problem at bay as well as helping to alleviate pressures and stress caused by day to day living (Elliott and Watson, 2000). What is significant to consider, then, is the *importance* attached to the substance misuse, its *role* in behaviour and the overall *effects* that it has on all those in its orbit.

Equally significant for the child is the atmosphere in which parenting takes place. A number of themes have emerged from the literature that seem useful to consider here – decreased involvement with children, increased irritability, more partner-related friction and the atmosphere of secrecy and denial that seems to pervade families as a consequence of substance misuse. Here we can see the impact of the substance as a family member as well as the central organising principle around which the family revolves. The focus of attention, rather than being the children and the overall well-being of the family unit, however construed and constructed, becomes the substance – obtaining it, using/drinking it, experiencing it and managing the effects of withdrawal, hangovers or sobering up. As one women observed 'I was a junkie first and a mother second' (Hogan, 1997: 28).

Parental substance misuse also has implications for what might be called the normal rhythms of family life and is often associated with a chaotic lifestyle which can have more of an impact than the substance use itself (Cleaver et al., 1999; Velleman and Orford, 1999). Rituals and daily functioning can be adversely affected, special occasions are often a source of concern due to uncertainty about parental behaviour, routines are upset or abandoned. Even being picked up from school or coming home for tea become fraught with anxiety (Brisby et al., 1997) – will they remember to collect me? Will they be home? If so, will they be OK? Public displays of problematic substance related behaviour at school or at other gatherings expose children to teasing, labelling, bullying and general all pervasive shame and misery. As a consequence, children are often isolated, cut off from other sources of support and consequently very vulnerable (Kroll, 2004). Neglect, strongly associated with substance misuse, has a range of consequences and risks ranging from poor hygiene, health risks, inadequate clothes and other basics to lack of educational resources, inadequate supervision, exposure to hazards in the home and access to substances (methadone, for example, has been accidentally ingested by a number of small children – see Bates et al., 1999). Children may be exposed to risky adult behaviour or be the subject of substance induced hallucinations or paranoid delusions (Coleman and Cassell, 1995; Klee et al., 1998). Indeed parents are often all too aware of their failure to protect their children from harm (Klee et al., 1998; McKeganey et al., 2001).

The impact of parental substance misuse: what children bring with them

What, then, is it like for children living in this environment? Children inevitably bring themselves with them to any new situation; this includes not only their gifts, talents, strengths and capacity for survival and resilience but also their coping strategies and learnt behaviours. However familiar and close kinship carers and children may appear to be to one another, curious and unexpected dynamics can develop as the legacy of previous experiences emerges. What challenges do children present to those who are trying to care for them, particularly when such carers are intimately and biologically connected to the parents themselves? Once again, only a brief overview can be provided with a particular focus on a small number of themes – attachment, loss, role reversal, role confusion and a model for problem solving.

To begin at the beginning . . . attachment

We have already looked at the role played by attachment in the adult/substance relationship and its centrality for sound emotional and psychological development in children. Here we move on to examine the relationship between parental substance misuse, attachment and the development of a secure internal working model

or inner template for the way that relationships should work and what one should expect from the world and the people in it (Howe et al., 1999). In other words, early experiences and the way in which our first primitive needs are met influence our capacity for emotional connectedness, our trust in those around us and our confidence in getting our needs met. Finding its earliest expressions in the work of Bowlby (1969, 1979, 1980) attachment was seen as an instinctive force essential for survival. More recently it has been argued that the attachment relationship also has an impact on the child's neurological system which contributes to the capacity for management of self and emotions (Archer, 2004; Schore, 1994, 2001).

In a sense, the process that culminates in attachment starts in the womb and so it is essential to consider in utero experience particularly in this context due to the impact that substance misuse can have pre birth. There is considerable research to suggest that alcohol and drug use, depending on its frequency and severity, can have an adverse impact on the health and development of the growing baby (Dore et al., 1995; Juliana and Goodman, 1997; Zeitlin, 1994). The type of substance, the stage of pregnancy, the way the substance is used or taken, the extent of the substance use and its duration both over time and in terms of intensity, are all significant (McElhatton, 2004).

Cocaine and heroin use during pregnancy can cause a range of problems including detached placenta, low birth weight, still birth, premature birth, microcephaly and addiction (Fitzgerald et al., 2000). Sudden infant death syndrome is between five and ten times more likely to occur in babies who have been exposed to cocaine (Dore et al., 1995). Intravenous drug use can cause HIV transmission across the placenta or the contraction of Hepatitis C. It is also worth bearing in mind that many people who use stimulants may also be involved in a range of other risky behaviours including the use of alcohol, sedatives and opiates. Polydrug use is particularly common among women with, for example, crack cocaine and alcohol frequently used together (Zuckerman, 1994). The combination of substances can therefore be a critical factor in foetal health and complicate the potential harm that can be caused. Once born, infant health can be affected by parental substance misuse at a number of levels. Babies can be born with withdrawal symptoms – high pitched crying, disturbed sleep, breathing problems, feeding problems, vomiting and diarrhoea (Coleman and Cassell, 1995). This can make them hard to care for and thus may affect bonding and attachment, as well as trying the patience of even the most forbearing and experienced parent. Problems that flow from this may also predispose children to maltreatment (Herrenkohl and Herrenkohl, 1979).

There is extensive research to confirm the damage that can be caused by in utero exposure to significant levels of alcohol use (Hepburn, 2000; Plant, 2004), particularly by 'binge drinking' where the foetus is 'shocked' by sudden exposure to high levels of alcohol followed by sudden withdrawal (Ford and Hepburn, 1997). Drinking patterns in fathers can also have an impact on birth weight and potential for heart defects (Plant, 1997). The most serious consequence of alcohol exposure is Foetal Alcohol Syndrome (FAS) causing physical, cognitive and behavioural problems (Bays, 1990; Zeitlin, 1994). A lesser condition – Foetal Alcohol Effects – still causes significant problems including feeding problems, irritability, tremors and the risk of Sudden Infant Death Syndrome (Julien, 1995). More recently this latter condition has been queried due to fears it had become a 'dustbin' term for babies with unexplained problems and current thinking favours the use of 'Foetal Alcohol Spectrum Disorder' to emphasise the continuum of effects, the range of symptoms and features and that this is not an 'all or nothing' syndrome (Plant, 2004: 76).

What seems in little doubt is the permanence of FAS/FASD. As Plant observes 'it does not go away or get better. Most children with FAS/FASD will need some form of sheltered environment for the rest of their lives' (Plant, 2004: 81). As babies they are hard to care for; as they grow up behavioural difficulties, cognitive disabilities, lack of social skills and inability to understand cause and effect, and vulnerability due to a failure to understand risk, make them demanding and nerve-wracking charges. What is helpful, argues Plant, is to ensure that they understand that they have a condition which is not their fault and that, in this instance, a label is helpful and liberating. If the child is also cared for in a stable, nurturing and non problem drinking environment, then the impact of the condition can be minimised. This has clear implications for assessing kinship placements particularly in families where there is a strong drinking culture

or where the impact of alcohol or the extent of its use is minimised or denied.

From what we know about the impact of parental substance misuse on parenting and environment, it comes as no surprise to learn that many children without additional sources of care giving and support which foster resilience develop insecure patterns of attachment. It has also been suggested by Burnell and Vaughan (2004) that different types of defensive strategies develop in children born to alcohol-misusing mothers from those born to mothers that misuse Class A drugs (opiates, cocaine, crack cocaine, heroin), although they acknowledge that this needs to be subjected to further research. According to this theory, then, alcohol exposed children develop an ambivalent attachment or *resistant/ambivalent pattern* of attachment whilst drug exposed children develop a *disorganised pattern*. They go on to argue that this in turn influences the kind of parenting they may require from substitute carers and the level of support the new family unit may require.

This typology needs to be distinguished from that which relates to children growing up with substance misusing parents, although not necessarily exposed in utero. Here the attachment pattern will be influenced by a range of factors including the emotional availability of parents and carers and all the other factors identified above in relation to the impact of the substance on parenting. The critical task here, then, is to identify the child's attachment pattern and strategies, identify the carers' patterns and try to establish a 'fit' between them, as well as ensuring that carers understand what the pattern might be about and how to respond to it.

Attachment disorder

Attachment disorder has, at its root, problematic or distorted early attachments falling within the disorganised pattern (Howe and Fearnley, 1999).The world of 'attachment disordered' children is a frightened, frightening and troubled one. They see themselves as unlovable and unworthy but capable of evoking anger, rejection and violence in others. As a consequence, they feel both powerful and evil. Other people are perceived as frightening and dangerous, but also seem frightened of them, in their turn. The confusion evoked by this conflicting range of emotions leaves them feeling out of control, helpless and vulnerable and as a result it is hard to focus or concentrate on anything around them, from social relationships to cognitive development. The absence of what Howe and Fearnley (1999: 22) call 'emotional scaffolding' finds children unable to make sense of or control their own emotions and reactions or understand anyone else's:

> The result is social confusion that results in aggression, withdrawal or both. Thus children who have experienced the greatest trauma are those least emotionally equipped to deal with them.
>
> (Howe and Fearnley, 1999: 22)

Closeness is threatening and dangerous and spells danger; the more love is offered, the more distressed, angry and controlling the child becomes. Not only is love 'not enough', it is absolute anathema to the child with attachment disorder. The only thing that matters is control; the only one you can be sure about is you. This need for control often leads to perverse and problematic behaviour, including self harm and aggression (Howe and Fearnley, 1999).

The impact of such a constellation of emotions and behaviours on a family is likely to be considerable and carers need to appreciate what attachment disorder is and be supported in managing it.

Attachment disorder and 'imported pathology': the impact on placements

The theory of 'imported pathology' appears to have originated in the work of Schore (1994, 2001). Originating in psychoanalytic thinking about projective identification and 'splitting', in which the individual seeks to get rid of 'bad' parts of the self and locate them in others, imported pathology seeks to describe or understand the way in which a 'looked after' child's unresolved grief and loss (and all the associated powerful feelings) together with the insecure, disorganised attachment pattern that has developed as a defence against this, affect the workings of the family that they join.

These feelings are of course normal, everyday and largely unconscious and most families whose members have grown up together find ways of managing them. However when a family which has developed its own systems of communication, management of pain/sorrow etc

is joined by a child with a chaotic, disorganised attachment pattern or attachment disorder, the impact can be extreme. However effective, skilled and competent the carers may have been with previous children, something about this child evokes reactions and responses that lead to ways of parenting that are unhelpful to the child although protective for the adult. The child's pain generates punitive, angry, defensive responses that are effectively reflections of the child's projections. This can lead to the continued acting out of the child's unconscious processes, resulting in the family being unable to manage the child, resulting in further upheaval and change. The consequences of this for kinship placements are obvious. Just because there is a biological link, it does not mean that this phenomenon will not occur and carers may need considerable support and skilled help in order to enable the child to re-attach in a safe way.

Loss

Cumulative losses and the impact of unresolved grief present real threats to the internal working model of children of substance misusing parents (Howe et al., 1999). Of particular significance are the invisible losses – the loss of a feeling of being loved, for example – that, because they are so hard to put into words and explain to anyone else, often remain a source of pain. 'I knew they loved me but they just didnae care that I was there . . . they were just away taking drugs and stuff' Elaine, aged 14, told researchers (Barnard and Barlow, 2003: 53).

Losses include loss of a reliable, consistent and responsive parent, loss of confidence and self esteem, loss of a 'normal' lifestyle in which it was safe to bring friends home or go off to school (Kroll, 2004). Parental substance abuse also often results in the temporary loss of parents due to imprisonment, being accommodated by the local authority or permanent separation as a result of care proceedings (Cleaver et al., 1999; Hogan, 1997). Fears about parents 'disappearing' unexpectedly – going out and never coming back – and the insecurity and uncertainty generated by these fears also abound (ChildLine, 1997). Being abandoned was a reality for many children, as was *feeling* abandoned, both by the substance misusing parent and, sometimes, by the non-substance misusing parent, whose preoccupation with the 'misusing' partner often left less time, energy and attention for the child (Brisby, 1997; Velleman and Orford, 1999). Awareness of the fact that drugs caused death was also an omnipresent source of anxiety and fear for some (Barnard and Barlow, 2003). In addition there were issues in relation to loss of normal developmental stages, loss of the kind of carefree childhood enjoyed by other, 'normal' children and the experience of being 'lost' as individuals and, as a consequence, 'invisible' to those whose role it was to care for them (Hogan and Higgins, 2001; Laybourn et al., 1996). Children and adults also felt that they had lost opportunities for fun and laughter and that this sense of losing out, on a number of levels, had had a significant impact on their sense of identity (Velleman and Orford, 1999).

Carers will need an awareness of the impact of these kinds of losses, the stages of grief that children might experience as well as the way in which they might have learned to manage and express feelings. It is often only when removed from a problematic environment that children are able to express anger or sorrow or reveal exactly what has been going on (Harbin, 2000). Both carers and workers have to be prepared for this.

Role confusion/role reversal

Both substance misusing parents and their children attest to the fact that role reversal – where children take on adult responsibilities and the parent relies on the child for emotional and practical support and advice – is a significant dynamic within the family (Bates et al., 1999; Brisby et al., 1997; Klee et al., 1998). Becoming a young carer, as research has shown in other contexts, can sometimes effectively hijack childhood, and place adult burdens on children's shoulders (Becker et al., 1998). In addition, the fact that children are 'young carers' often prevents them from being seen as 'children in need' with the attendant danger of falling through the net in relation to services (Dearden and Becker, 2001). This father was all too aware of the extent of the role reversal in his relationship with his seven year old daughter – 'She was the parent and I was the breadwinner. It was as simple as that. Being a drug addict is a 24 hour job, out robbing all the time, you're out all the time' (Hogan and Higgins, 2001: 10). For other parents, it was simply a question of expedience,

leading to children becoming 'over responsible' when parental substance use prevented them from carrying out domestic or child care duties. Some defiantly defended decisions such as keeping children at home to help with housework and child care, despite the fact that they were missing school. Others, aware of the extent to which reliance on a child was inappropriate, expressed regret and remorse:

He was doing everything for himself just like growing up at four years old ... he was having to look after his wee brother he was sort of playing mummy and daddy ... he'd get up in the morning and make his bottle because mummy and daddy are lying on the bed sparked from the night before.

(McKeganey et al., 2001: 9)

Some research indicates that role *confusion* rather than role *reversal* could occur in families where substance misuse is a feature (Laybourn et al., 1996). Here, parents' behaviour caused such embarrassment or was seen to be so stupid, childish or out of control that the child lost all respect for them. Children then felt that the parent has forfeited any right to have authority over them and the balance of power shifted as a consequence – 'you behave badly, so don't try telling me what to do'. Often such children would appear to behave just like children until the parents' problem behaviour occurred, whereupon they would become very assertive and parental. In response, parents would become sneaky in their behaviour and dread being told off. This kind of role confusion and reversal often left children unsure about who they were and what was going on. It often also led to strong feelings of disgust and, at times, hatred towards the substance misusing parent (ChildLine, 1997; Laybourn, 1996).

Parental children, used to managing alone and accustomed, perhaps, to unusual levels of freedom and lack of boundaries (as well as regular breaks from school) may pose particular challenges for carers and it may take some time to re-locate them in their appropriate stage of childhood. Rules will be challenged and authority tested; it will appear strange perhaps that an adult might query where they are going and when they will be back. Children might need to be liberated from anxieties about finance and practicalities and persuaded to relinquish their role in the monitoring of their parents' drug or alcohol use.

Is it catching? Generational transmission and a model for problem solving

Parental substance misuse can provide a potentially dangerous model for problem solving and this aspect of what might be seen as learned behaviour is something that children may well bring with them into a new family environment (Aldridge, 1999; 2000). If it is already part of the extended family system, it may also be reinforced and encouraged by example. If, as a child, you see your parent come home from work each evening, announce they have had an awful day and reach for a double scotch, this conveys a certain message about the way that grown-ups manage stress. The relationship with the substance can become the one seen as the most reliable, particularly if it also becomes associated with the belief that other aspects of functioning will also be enhanced – reduced stress, increased confidence (Sher, 1991). This is, however, a highly contentious and much debated area since the relationship between parents' behaviour, theories about intergenerational transmission, the impact of peers and the influence of the environment (particularly as it affects emotional connectedness) as well as a host of other individual variables is very complex (Archer, 2004; Lloyd, 1998; Pitcher, 2002). It is perhaps not surprising, nevertheless, that many young people who grow up with a substance misusing parent or parents often develop a substance use pattern of their own (Lloyd, 1998), and there is extensive American research which connects parental substance misuse with drug and alcohol problems in offspring (see Lloyd, 1998 for a full discussion of this). There is also UK research on Parental Modelling Theory in this context (Velleman and Orford, 1999).

Do all children of substance misusing parents develop substance misuse problems of their own? This is clearly an impossible question to answer but an important one to ask since research suggests that it is a real concern for children of parents with substance problems. Studies suggest that some children are all too aware of the power of modelling, expressing the fear that substance misuse, like measles, might be 'catching'. A sense of inevitability can take hold with children finding it hard to believe that they have choices about what and who they become (Robinson and Rhoden, 1998). As Roy, aged 16, told ChildLine 'I've been involved with drinking, drugs, fighting. I'm desperate to change. I don't want to be like dad' (ChildLine, 1997: 33).

All the young men interviewed in the study by Laybourn and colleagues had followed what they saw as the family tradition of heavy drinking. Some had also started using drugs and two had developed substance problems that had resulted in criminal activity, leading to imprisonment. One respondent observed 'It must be in the blood' whilst another felt his own drinking was 'partly learned behaviour' and that, given the high levels of alcohol consumption he had been used to seeing as a child, he saw his own as minor by comparison even though 'I know I was heavily into the drink' (Laybourn et al., 1996: 96).

As Mayer (2004) observes, however, parental substance misuse can also lead to an intensely negative, punitive and rejecting attitude to substance use rather than a deterministic stance. Whatever the reaction, carers will need to be sensitive to and aware of the impact of the parental example and the role played by the substance in the family culture.

Kinship care and parental substance misuse: issues in assessment

The fundamental dilemma in the assessment process is how to come to appropriate conclusions about families where there is substance misuse (Harbin and Murphy, 2000; Phillips, 2004). Putting the pieces together in order to answer these questions will inevitably involve a range of processes. The views of all interested parties – including a range of family members, other than the proposed carers – will need to be sought so that the situation can be viewed from a variety of perspectives. A chronology of significant events, current information, observations and other assessments will all come together. The professional judgment reached will also need to be informed by an 'evidence based' approach. This ensures that what research and theory tells us about substance misuse, parenting and child welfare is brought into the synthesis and analysis of material collected in a reflexive, dynamic process. Available evidence, its reliability and ways in which it might require further testing needs to be evaluated. Whether the assessment is being influenced by how articulate or cooperative the parents and carers are, by their attitude or factors personal to the worker, will all need to be considered, as will the impact of professionals' values and assumptions. Critical questions will also need to be asked in relation to the level of need, risk or harm to the children. Who else is worried and why? What are the family's strengths and weaknesses? What kind of support and help might work best and where might it be found both in the community and within statutory and voluntary services? Is working in partnership possible or realistic rather than tokenistic and rhetorical? How might all the professionals involved work together most effectively and who should do what? Knowledge, professional judgment, consultation, open mindedness, flexibility, humility, teamwork, sharing of ideas and a range of complex skills will all play their part, firmly grounded in a culturally sensitive approach characterised by fairness and a willingness to avoid stereotyping (see Calder and Talbot, Chapter 10).

In addition, the capacity to view a situation through a variety of different lenses and to allow oneself the luxury of not knowing and learning from someone else is critical. Communication between professionals needs to be made open and competing loyalties and demands from the child in the adult and the real child need to be addressed. Being realistic about what carers can offer; giving them the opportunity to parent but not being seduced by the fact that this is the easiest option are also important considerations. In addition, the child's perspective needs to be brought more firmly into the entire assessment process so that workers can gain a sense of what children's lives are really like (Hart 2004). This needs to involve strategies that, rather than putting children on the spot and forcing them to 'tell tales', enable them to tell a story. The use of observation and skills in communicating with children are clearly central to achieving this aim.

We will now highlight a selection of issues in assessment, illustrated by case material. All names have been changed.

The rule of optimism, natural love and cultural relativism

Some important dynamics may creep in, when it comes to assessment and the process of adaptation and change in kinship care – namely the rule of optimism, natural love and cultural relativism. Although these are identified in child care literature as relating to parenting assessments and assessing change and progress, we consider that they are equally germane to

thisdebate, where assumptions may be made in just the same way, involving similar perils and the potential for fatal mistakes to be made. The first of these is the 'rule of optimism'. Parton describes this as an approach which 'meant that the most favourable interpretation was put upon the behaviour of the parents and that anything that may question this was discounted or redefined' (Parton, 1991: 55). There is a temptation to accord the status of a giant leap forward to the slightest signs of progress or improvement, even though the evidence may be flimsy or even non existent, except in the worker's imagination. While the temptation is clear, the dangers of being over positive are obvious. Grandparents may be more willing to talk about a parent's substance use and behaviour during contact on this visit than on the last; this does not necessarily mean that they have come to terms with it, although it could mean that they have realised that this will keep the worker happy. Although it is clearly important to build on strengths and acknowledge improvement, it is also imperative that signs of change for the better do not tempt workers to avoid looking further at other factors which may counterbalance this view.

In his analysis of this tendency, Parton sees it as linked to two further 'devices' – cultural relativism and what he calls 'natural love' (Parton, 1991: 55). Cultural relativism refers to a variety of processes that come into play in relation to culture – in all senses of the term – and ethnicity. This includes applying different standards to people based on assumptions, due to lack of knowledge, awareness or understanding, that behaviour is 'cultural', rather than exploring its potential for being abusive or harmful in some way. Parton (1991) illustrated this tendency with specific reference to the Jasmine Beckford tragedy where it appeared that a white middle class social worker felt unable or was unwilling to challenge the child rearing practices or parenting behaviours of a black working class family (London Borough of Brent, 1985). There was an implicit assumption that the social worker had no right to criticise, since these behaviours could be cultural and any imposition of other standards would be perceived as racist.

Alongside cultural relativism sits what Parton (1991) terms 'natural love' – the belief that all parents love their children and that relationships between parents and children are instinctive and, well, natural. If this is your position, as Parton observes, it makes it very difficult to see anything which challenges this view, since it goes to the root of all that is natural in human behaviour. This could just as easily be applied to grandparents who may in fact associate grandchildren with the 'bad' aspects of their own child or indeed the child's other parent and find them very hard to love, particularly when behaviour militates against this. Even when they do, love may not be enough to protect them (Reder et al., 1993).

Importantly for this discussion, this constellation of devices may have particular implications in families where there is substance misuse. First, it may cause an over emphasis on the substance use and all that surrounds it, to the exclusion of what is happening to the children, particularly if assumptions about 'natural love' are also coming into play. Second, it may have implications for the way the 'drug' or 'alcohol' culture in which the family may operate is perceived. If, for example, there is a cultural assumption about lifestyle in relation to drug use (the idea, perhaps, that all drug users are a bit chaotic, come and go at irregular times and are different from 'us'), this might raise issues about whether standards are tolerated in the drug community that would not be acceptable in families where this is not an issue. Furthermore, if cultural assumptions are made in relation to race and ethnicity, in addition to assumptions about the 'drug' or 'drink' culture, this will compound the situation further. This suggests that all aspects of a family's culture needs to be explored, so that assumptions are not made at any level.

Assessing risk

Risk assessment is a complex process and can only be addressed very briefly here (for a fuller discussion see Calder and Talbot in Chapter 3). The key issues where there is substance misuse in the family are to explore the overall consequences of this and establish whether additional problems are also manifest. As we saw earlier in the chapter, violence in the family automatically increases risk to children as does co-morbidity where there is substance misuse and a mental health problem (Falkov, 1995; Forrester, 2004). Risks from both inside and outside the placement will need to be addressed. Are carers aware of the

risks posed by parents, able to anticipate them and resist the understandable urge to minimise them? How confident do carers feel about protecting their grandchildren from their children? How will they respond to parents arriving drunk or attempting to use drugs during visits? How likely are they to be able to manage the often complex dynamics of contact which include not only the visit itself but its anticipation and aftermath? How will loyalty conflicts be managed? What if rules are flouted – for example where there is an order for supervised contact and the parents breach it? How will conflicts be managed? How clear is everyone about who they are (parent? grandparent?), the extent of their power and responsibility and the centrality of the child's welfare?

What about risks from within the kinship placement? Assessing this aspect is likely to be similar to any other core assessment where the Framework for the Assessment of Children in Need and their Families (DoH, 2000) offers a range of areas for exploration (for a critical consideration see Chapter 3). What do the grandparents imagine life will be like caring for grandchildren and how will their needs be met, their questions answered, their fears and fantasies confronted? What protective factors are available in the child, the family and the environment that might militate against risk and where are the child's sources of resilience located? (Daniel et al., 1999; Kroll and Taylor, 2003).

Knowledge and understanding of the child and their needs

It is perhaps obvious to assume that grandparents and children have a history of regular contact, shared experiences and closeness. This however is not always the case and, even if it is, the degree to which children are seen as an individuals in their own right as opposed to objects/burdens/appendages may be variable. In some instances, there may have been limited contact with grandchildren as a result of the conflicts caused by parental substance misuse, with implications for the support needed to rebuild relationships and to manage potential tensions, especially if children are aware of estrangement, although not the reason for it (Pitcher, 2002).

Mrs Davy, for example, had not seen her grandchildren at all prior to a chance meeting with her daughter, Bea (from whom she had been long estranged) who asked her to assume care of her daughter Leah as an alternative to local authority fostering and with a view to her returning home. Leah had suffered considerable problems as a result of in utero exposure to heroin and had epilepsy and behavioural problems but, Mrs Davy appeared unwilling to address any of the realities associated with assuming her care, had little understanding of her need for play, attention and age appropriate activity and refused to discuss her own parenting history. Initially, in order to build a relationship, Mrs. Davy had contact with Leah but it became clear that she had no insight into Leah's needs and frequently failed to keep appointments. She ultimately withdrew her application.

The relationship between the child and the carer needs to be explored and the history of contact or lack of it and the reasons behind this need to be discussed. Do the grandparents appreciate some of the difficulties the child has experienced and their possible consequences? Are they flexible enough to integrate a new person into the household with a variety of needs and expectations? How do they talk about the child and how do they look as they do so? Do they tend to minimise any problems? Are they aware of developmental needs and the impact of loss and change? Can they manage the feelings children may have for parents whose behaviour may have been anything from less than ideal to violent, abusive and neglectful? How do they cope with rage, sorrow, withdrawal, hyperactivity? Here the use of the Strengths and Difficulties Questionnaire as well as a series of hypothetical scenarios may prove useful.

Family placements and identity

In theory, kinship placements promote continued cultural and ethnic connectedness, a sense of history, belonging and, obviously perhaps, a sense of family. However, managing differences is also a critical issue here. These may relate to differences in lifestyle, family rules and behavioural expectations. These may also relate to differing perceptions of each parent by the grandparents, apportioning of blame, and splitting – with one parent all bad and blamed and the other an innocent victim and exonerated.

Identity can also be affected by the stigma so often attached to drug users or people with serious drink problems, often exacerbated by gender expectations and assumptions about the way in which members of certain races and ethnic groups should behave (Patel, 2000). Stigma can also be compounded by social exclusion and indeed drug use dominates in areas where this is a factor (Gilman, 2000). It is important to remember, however, that substance misuse is no respecter of class or social position and although the exclusion issues may be different and resource implications might not be relevant, the impact on children's attachment, identity and belonging may be equally significant (Self in Barber, 2000).

Equally important is the way in which different ethnicities within the same family are managed – an issue highlighted by Mayer (2004) in her work with children from diverse racial and ethnic backgrounds. Here visible differences between carer and child can compound other struggles that could be taking place in a new environment. In addition, Mayer comments on the fact that children of substance misusing parents often adopt a very moralistic, anti-substance stance. Where the child is also from a mixed heritage background, the substance related behaviour may become associated with the group from which one or other parent belongs, resulting in racial stereotyping (Mayer, 2004). Children may therefore start to make assumptions about race, class, gender and use of certain substances (together with their associated lifestyles) which Mayer argues are backed up by prevailing stereotypes in British Culture – ' the white working class heroin user, the black crack user, or the thirty-something 'ladette' . . .' (Mayer, 2004: 154).

Rex's situation, although not related to ethnicity, illustrates the stereotyping, splitting, labelling process in action. Rex's grandparents wanted to assume his care but needed to see their 'child' as misunderstood and victimised, whilst the other parent carried the 'bad', 'alcoholic' label. This also became associated with class, mental health problems and lack of education. Pejorative remarks were made about Rex's mother in front of him and any bad behaviour was blamed on his mother's personality and influence. Part of the worker's task was to help the carers to understand the impact this might have on Rex's sense of identity and self worth.

Motivation: reparation, refrigeration, galvanisation or 'Canute' syndrome?

It could be argued that motivation is key in respect of any kinship care assessment but particular issues seem relevant to us in relation to family systems where there is substance misuse. A number of important questions need to be asked and rather relentlessly pursued if a clear picture is to emerge and if the children concerned are not only to be adequately protected but also enabled to adjust and develop appropriately. This includes not just examining the motivation of those grandparents who offer care but also the reasons behind a refusal to do so.

In relation to the first group, obvious areas for exploration would include the nature and quality of grandparent/parent relationships. Is there collusion about the extent of the substance problem, the family's history of substance misuse or the real reason for the application for residence? Is there likely to be collusion over continued drug or alcohol misuse in the home? Is the grandparent being threatened and coerced by a son or daughter?

Some of these themes are illustrated in this case example. Mr and Mrs Kaye, both heavy drinkers and prone to violent exchanges, separated when their daughter Lilly was four. During a contact visit when both parents became intoxicated, Lilly fell through a glass roof and was placed with foster carers. Mr. Kaye's mother, Mrs Teign, offered to care for Lilly. From the outset it became clear that Mr Kaye had coerced his mother into making the application; he insisted on being present throughout the interviews and frequently answered questions on his mother's behalf, despite being asked not to do so. He presented as controlling and dominant, emphatically describing his stable and supportive family background and close extended network. When Mrs Teign was finally seen alone, a very different picture emerged. She had had very little contact with Lilly and doubted her ability to care for her. She felt that her son would fail to comply with any order relating to contact and she would be both powerless against him and unable to protect Lilly from his drinking or his behaviour. She was only applying for residence at his insistence, adding that it was something she felt she 'should' do.

Carers may be moved by a desire for reparation/redemption or simply see themselves as 'refrigerators' – keeping children in cold storage until the parent is 'better'. In addition, a range of very different issues present themselves where care is assumed as a consequence of death caused by substance misuse and bereaved parents care for bereaved children (Hopkirk, 2002). Is the application more about guilt, reparation, compensating for the past rather than a real desire to parent? Mrs Davy had voluntarily relinquished care of her daughters Bea and Sara due to behavioural difficulties. Both had gone on to become involved in drug use and both Bea's children had been taken into care. Mrs Davy had very little contact with her daughters and only met Bea again by chance. The issue of motivation was addressed in depth during the assessment. What emerged was a confused account of a history characterised by rejection, guilt, blame and responsibility, culminating in her decision to compensate her daughter for her bad early experiences by parenting her grandchild with a view to giving her back something she had lost. It also became clear that Mrs Davy blamed social services for her daughters' problems and would not be prepared to enter into any working relationship with the department.

For some grandparents, an application is motivated by the question 'what if I don't?' Here we encounter 'Canute' syndrome – the determination to hold back the legal tide for as long as possible. The part played by the 'threat' presented by the 'looked after' system and the feelings towards those involved in it have to be considered, alongside the stigma attached to involvement with social services .

Where grandparents refuse to take on care, what is the basis for this, unless there are pressing health and financial concerns that make it genuinely impossible? Often there is a belief that the parents, relieved of care of the children, will then be free to spend their resources on drugs and alcohol and abandon themselves to the chaotic, dangerous lifestyle so often associated with such activity. Indeed in Barnard's study (2003) a number of parents reflected on the fact that their drug taking might have taken a different course had they been forced to maintain care of their children themselves and the father of one parent interviewed deliberately refused to accept care of her child since this would enable her to pursue her drug taking activities unchecked. Although it is clear that children can play a crucial role in motivating their parents to manage, reduce or stop substance misuse (Bates et al., 1999; Harbin and Murphy, 2000; Hepburn,

2000) it is still a high risk strategy to leave children in such situations unless they are thoroughly assessed, monitored and supported. Children, in our view, should not be made responsible for change in their parents.

Denial and secrecy: talking about the elephant

As we have already suggested, the denial and secrecy which often characterises and permeates family systems where there is substance misuse present further challenges to professionals attempting to assess and intervene effectively (Kroll and Taylor, 2003; Taylor and Kroll, 2004). Anecdotal evidence based on case material suggests that secrets may not necessarily be about substance misuse but that substance misuse was a response to other kinds of secrets to do with legitimacy, paternity, abuse and criminal behaviour. Often there is a family skeleton that needs to be unearthed if a real dialogue about the implications of kinship care is to be possible.

One of the challenges of working with substance misusing families relates to breaking down the wall of denial and tackling the cupboard full of secrets. Here naming the elephant, making it real and acknowledging its everyday impact is important. Disclosure brings fear and uncertainty for parents, grandparents and children; it needs to be made possible and safe and it must avoid simply focusing on how much someone has swallowed, injected or drunk. This is about the why and when of substance use and its consequences. It is also about how others in the family system react and respond and what they really think and feel about the behaviour and the reasons for it. Alongside this, the worker needs to acknowledge the range of feelings that working with substance misusing parents can generate, particularly where there are negative consequences for children.

Mr Hill and Ms Jay were both very involved in heroin use, accruing considerable debts and becoming involved in theft to fund their habit. Although Ms Jay reduced her use during her pregnancy with Robbie and he was born without any withdrawal symptoms, she resumed her habit immediately afterwards. Problems escalated, Robbie was often neglected and unsupervised and there was domestic violence. Finally Mr Hill's parents applied for an interim residence order. From the outset, they were in denial that their son bore any responsibility for the life he had led thus far or that he had a drug problem; Ms Jay was the problem and their son was an innocent victim. Over time they were able to admit that they had had their suspicions but had not been able to face the truth and the role they might have played in their son's behaviour. They also felt unable to confront the fact that he could have contributed to their grandson's neglect. Their devastation, in the face of the impact of the elephant, was ultimately tackled and they were able to prioritise the welfare of their grandson over their son and supervise contact appropriately.

In contrast, the elephant in the Teign family was a longstanding member and had grown enormously over the years. As we saw above, Mrs Teign could only find a voice when separated from her son and she revealed three significant family secrets – that alcohol was a theme that ran through three generations, that she herself had a history of alcohol misuse and was a 'binge' drinker, and that her son had regularly assaulted her. She was hugely relieved when the decision was made not to support her application as she clearly felt unable to go against her son's wishes or disobey his orders.

Discovery, blame and guilt: complex families, complex feelings

Family breakdown involving substitute kinship care raises a number of complex dilemmas where substance misuse by parents who are also relatives is an issue. Children, parents and grandparents or other family members will bring a range of emotions to this situation and may have very different ways of managing them. Children's relief at leaving what might have been a chaotic, violent, impoverished and unpredictable environment may be tempered and tangled by guilt, anxiety about the parent(s) left behind and resentment that the degree of freedom they may have enjoyed, as well as their adult status, may be curtailed. Parents may feel relief, guilt, shame and anger with themselves which may get projected onto both carers and children. Carers in turn may feel resentment at having to parent once again, triumphant that 'they were right all along', guilty for the part they may have played in the substance misuse itself, and prone to blaming the parent in front of the child. Alternatively they may be shocked at the discovery of drug or alcohol related behaviour and inclined to blame the other partner, the social worker or any other convenient repository for difficult feelings. Many of these complex emotions may be played out in the contact arena, and are much harder to manage within kinship care arrangements which may be voluntary and informal. As we have seen, parental substance misuse can have a significant impact on child development, attachment patterns, self esteem and behaviour and the children may bring with them a range of challenges for which the carers may be unprepared and which may make them harder to care for and to love.

How much do carers really know? The extent of the substance problem may come as a surprise to relatives or may have been a long standing source of friction, possibly leading to rejection (Hart, 2004). Although there are no specific data about the level to which carers were aware of substance problems, general research into grandparent placements indicate that, although most had either an inkling that all was not well or knew everything about the situation, about 25 per cent were genuinely shocked to discover there were problems (Pitcher, 2002). In their study of pregnant drug users, Klee and colleagues (2002) found that 40 per cent of the mothers in their admittedly small sample knew nothing about their daughters' drug use, creating both physical and emotional barriers, fears of causing harm or hurt and the need for deception and subterfuge. Significantly, perhaps, 52 per cent of the women in the sample came from what the authors describe as 'dysfunctional' families where divorce or separation were commonplace, leading to feelings of rejection and blame for subsequent problems. In Barnard's study which looked at parents' perceptions of the part played by their parents or relatives in the care of their children (Barnard, 2003: 296), it was interesting to note that 'a high proportion reported dysfunctional family backgrounds' which included alcohol problems, some drug misuse and some continuing problems with drink at the time of placement. This generational connection has been the subject of much debate as we have already seen. Mothers were also sometimes seen as a source of additional threat by their daughters, where concern about a child could lead to official intervention.

What this highlights are the feelings of guilt, responsibility and blame that circulate throughout the family system (Barnard, 2003), particularly when the substance misuse itself may be a reflection of wider family problems which are unresolved between the adult 'child' and their parent (Velleman and Orford, 1999). Equally striking were the mixed feelings expressed by parents about the support they were receiving because of the impact it had on their role as primary carer 'I couldn't be that mother and I wanted to blame everybody around me who were taking care of Anne . . .' (Barnard, 2003: 296). Here, then, are a range of complex matters that need to be explored at the assessment stage.

What we should be looking for in kinship carers where there is parental substance misuse

Apart from the obvious characteristics and skills associated with 'good enough' parenting, Mayer (2004) draws attention to three additional qualities that kinship carers should possess. An understanding of the impact of parental substance misuse on children's behaviour and development is perhaps almost too obvious to state but its importance cannot be underestimated. It is essential to be able to distinguish such behaviour for what it is, as distinct from malicious, wilful behaviour which can be controlled. Much problematic behaviour, as we have already seen, is often about loss, anger, rejection as well as related to in utero damage and its consequences. It will also be affected by the child's age and developmental stage (Kroll and Taylor, 2003). Mayer also stresses the importance of what might be called a grievance-free environment, so that past conflicts and disputes do not contaminate the present and children are able to retain a positive sense of who they are. Her final point relates to carers' willingness to 'talk openly about substance misuse within the family setting while maintaining respect for the child's parents or previous carers' (Mayer, 2004: 157). This is particularly crucial as a means to crack open the carapace of secrecy and denial so prevalent in substance misusing systems.

Summary

Far from being a fairy tale ending for children, kinship placements where there is substance misuse may require considerable support as family members struggle with a range of emotions, tensions and behaviours. As Mayer observes, 'Family members can feel desperately sad and perhaps even guilty that their kin have experienced neglect or abuse at the hands of a parent' (Mayer, 2004: 156) and require a considerable range of qualities to manage what may be a difficult situation. Practitioners therefore need to be aware of both the dynamics and the impact of substance misuse on the wider family system and the way in which attachment patterns and behaviour can be affected. Equally importantly, professionals need to move from a policing or monitoring role towards a facilitating relationship with carers, parents and children, where there is real potential for disclosure, honesty and engagement with the struggles that may be taking place within the system. It is only through a robust understanding of the processes of denial that a real engagement with 'elephants' and their impact can take place; by the same token, it is only through connecting with the raw pain, sorrow and anger within the system that healing and resolution are possible. Finally, it is important to remember the children concerned – often lost, invisible and forgotten – as we grapple with the levels of substance use in parents, the secrecy and avoidance in carers and the injunctions placed upon us by local authorities. They have their own stories to tell, their own view of the situation and have seen, understood and experienced more than we probably ever want to acknowledge. Just because they appear to be safe does not mean that the elephant and what it leaves in its wake have disappeared.

References

Advisory Council on the Misuse of Drugs (2003) *Hidden Harm: Responding to the Needs of Problem Drug Users.* London: Home Office.

Aldridge, T. (1999) Family Values: Rethinking Children's Needs Living With Drug Abusing Parents. *Druglink.* March/April, 8–11.

Aldridge, T. (2000) *Family Values: Rethinking Children's Needs Living With Drug Abusing Parents.* Paper presented at the 'Substance Misuse and Child Protection' Conference, June.

Alison, L. (2000) What are the Risks to Children of Parental Substance Misuse? in Harbin, F. and Murphy, M. (Eds.) *Substance Misuse and Child Care: How to Understand, Assist and Intervene when Drugs Affect Parenting.* Lyme Regis: Russell House Publishing.

Ammerman, R.T. et al. (1999) Child Abuse Potential in Parents With Histories of Substance Misuse Disorder. *Child Abuse and Neglect.* 23: 12, 1225–38.

Archer, C. (2004) Substance Misuse, Attachment Organisation and Adoptive Families. In Phillips, R. (Ed.) *Children Exposed to Parental Substance Misuse: Implications for Family Placement.* London: BAAF.

Awiah, J. et al. (1992) *Race ,Gender and Drug Services.* London: ISDD Research Monographs 6.

Barber, L. (2000) Self Control. *The Observer Magazine.* 11th June.

Barnard, M. (1999) Forbidden Questions: Drug Dependent Parents and the Welfare of Their Children. *Addiction.* 94: 8, 1109–11.

Barnard, M. (2003) Between a Rock and a Hard Place: The Role of Relatives in Protecting Children From the Effects of Parental Drug Problems. *Child and Family Social Work.* 8, 291–9.

Barnard, M. and Barlow, J. (2003) Discovering Parental Drug Dependence: Silence and Disclosure. *Children and Society.* 17, 45–56.

Barth, R.P. (1999) After Safety, What is the Goal of Child Welfare Services: Permanency, Family Continuity or Social Benefit? *International Journal of Social Welfare.* 8, 244–52.

Bates, T. et al. (1999) *Drug Use, Parenting and Child Protection: Towards an Effective Interagency Response.* Liverpool: University of Central Lancashire.

Barrio, C. and Hughes, M.J. (2000) Kinship Care: A Cultural Resource of African-American and Latino Families Coping With Parental Substance Abuse. In Delva, J. (Ed.) *Substance Abuse Issues among Families in Diverse Populations.*

Bays, J. (1990) Substance Abuse and Child Abuse: Impact of Addiction on the Child. *Paediatric Clinics of North America.* 37: 4, 881–904.

Becker, S., Aldridge, J. and Dearden, C. (1998) *Young Carers and their Families.* Oxford: Blackwell.

Beeman, S. and Boisen, L. (1999) Child Welfare Professionals' Attitudes Towards Kinship Foster Care. *Child Welfare.* 78: 3, 315–57.

Bell, J. and Sim, M. (2004) Meeting Placement Challenges: One Local Authority's Response. In Phillips, R. (Ed.) *Children Exposed to Parental Substance Misuse: Implications for Family Placement.* London: BAAF.

Bettelheim, B. (1987) *A Good Enough Parent.* London: Thames and Hudson.

Brisby, T., Baker, S. and Hedderwick, T. (1997) *Under the Influence: Coping With Parents Who Drink Too Much A Report on the Needs of Children of Problem Drinking Parents.* London: Alcohol Concern.

Broad, B. (2001) Kinship Care: Supporting Children in Placement With Extended Family and Friends. *Adoption and Fostering.* 25: 2, 33–41.

Brookoff, D. et al. (1997) Characteristics of Participants in Domestic Violence Assessment at the Scene of Domestic Assault. *Journal of the American Medical Association.* 277: 17, 1369–73.

Brooks, D. and Barth, R. (1998) Characteristics and Outcomes of Drug-Exposed and Non-Drug-Exposed Children in Kinship and Non-Relative Foster Care. *Children and Youth Services Review.* 20: 6, 475–501.

Brooks, C.S. and Rice, K.F. (1997) *Families in Recovery: Coming Full Circle.* Baltimore: Paul Brookes.

Brown, S. (1988) *Treating Adult Children of Alcoholics: A Developmental Perspective.* New York: John Wiley.

Buckley, H. (2000) Child Protection: An Unreflective Practice. *Social Work Education.* 19: 3, 253–63.

Burnell, A. and Vaughan, J. (2004) Therapeutic Interventions. In Phillips, R. (Ed.) *Children Exposed to Parental Substance Misuse: Implications for Family Placement.* London: BAAF.

Chaffin, M., Kelleher, K. and Hollenberg, J. (1996) Onset of Physical Abuse and Neglect: Psychiatric, Substance Abuse and Social Factors From Prospective Community Data. *Child Abuse and Neglect.* 20: 3, 191–203.

ChildLine (1997) *Beyond The Limit: Children who Live with Parental Alcohol Misuse.* London: ChildLine.

Cleaver, H., Unell, I. and Aldgate. J. (1999) *Children's Needs Parenting Capacity: The Impact of Parental Mental Illness, Problem Alcohol and Drug Use and Domestic Violence on Children's Development.* London: The Stationery Office.

Coleman, R. and Cassell, D. (1998) Parents Who Misuse Drugs And Alcohol. In Reder, P. and Lucey, C. (Eds.) *Assessment of Parenting: Psychiatric and Psychological Contributions.* London: Routledge.

Daniel, B. Wassell, S. and Gilligan, R. (1999) *Child Development for Child Care and Protection Workers.* London: Jessica Kingsley.

Dearden, C. and Becker, S. (2001) Young Carers: Needs, Rights And Assessments. In Horwath, J.

(Ed.) *The Child's World: Assessing Children in Need.* London: Jessica Kingsley.

Department of Health (2000) *Framework for the Assessment of Children in Need and Their Families.* London: The Stationery Office.

Dore, M.M. Doris, J.M. and Wright, P. (1995) Identifying Substance Misuse in Maltreating Families: A Child Welfare Challenge. *Child Abuse and Neglect.* 19: 5, 531–43.

Elliott, E. and Watson, A. (1998) *Fit to be a Parent: The Needs of Drug Using Parents in Salford and Trafford.* Manchester: Public Health Research and Resource Centre, University of Salford.

Elliott, E. and Watson, A. (2000) Responsible Carers, Problem Drug Takers or Both? In Harbin, F. and Murphy, M. (Eds.) *Substance Misuse and Child Care: How to Understand, Assist and Intervene when Drugs Affect Parenting.* Lyme Regis: Russell House Publishing.

Falkov, A. (1996) *A Study of Working Together Part 8 Reports: Fatal Child Abuse and Parental Psychiatric Disorder.* London: The Stationery Office.

Famularo, R., Kinscherff, R. and Fenton, T. (1992) Parental Substance Abuse and the Nature of Child Maltreatment. *Child Abuse and Neglect.* 16: 475–83.

Feig, L. (1998) Understanding the Problem: The Gap Between Substance Abuse Programmes and Child Welfare Services. In Hampton, R.L., Senatore, V. and Gullotta, T.P. (Eds.) *Substance Abuse, Family Violence and Child Welfare: Bridging Perspectives.* Thousand Oaks: Sage.

Fitzgerald, H.E. Lester, B.M. and Zuckerman, B.S. (2000) *Children of Addiction: Research ,Health and Public Policy Issues.* New York: Routledge Falmer.

Flores, P.J. (2001) Addiction as an Attachment Disorder: Implications for Group Therapy. *International Journal of Group Psychotherapy.* 51: 1, 63–81.

Flynn, R. (2002) Research Review: Kinship Foster Care. *Child and Family Social Work.* 7, 311–21.

Fonagy, P. et al. (1994) The Theory and Practice of Resilience. *Journal of Child Psychology and Psychiatry.* 35: 2, 231–57.

Ford, C. and Hepburn, M. (1997) Caring for the Pregnant Drug User. In Beaumont, B. (Ed.) *Care of Drug Users in General Practice.* Abingdon: Radcliffe Medical Press.

Forrester, D. (2000) Parental Substance Misuse and Child Protection in a British Sample: A Survey of Children on the Child Protection Register in an Inner London District Office. *Child Abuse Review.* 9, 235–46.

Forrester, D. (2002) Picking up the Pieces. *Community Care*. 12–18 December, 36–7.

Forrester, D. (2004) Social Work Assessments With Parents Who Misuse Drugs or Alcohol. In Phillips, R. (Ed.) *Children Exposed to Parental Substance Misuse: Implications for Family Placement*. London: BAAF.

Forrester, D. and Harwin, J. (2004) Social Work and Parental Substance Misuse. In Phillips, R. (Ed.) *Children Exposed to Parental Substance Misuse: Implications for Family Placement*. London: BAAF.

Gleeson, J.P. and Hairston, C.F. (Eds.) (1999) *Kinship Care : Improving Practice through Research*. Washington DC: CWLA Press.

Harbin, F. (2000) Therapeutic Work With Children of Substance Misusing Parents. In Harbin, F, and Murphy, M. (Eds.) *Substance Misuse and Child Care: How to Understand, Assist and Intervene when Drugs Affect Parenting*. Lyme Regis: Russell House Publishing.

Harbin, F. and Murphy, M. (Eds.) (2000) *Substance Misuse and Child Care: How to Understand, Assist and Intervene when Drugs Affect Parenting*. Lyme Regis: Russell House Publishing.

Hart, D. (2004) Care Planning for Children Looked After as a Result of Parental Substance Misuse. In Phillips, R. (Ed.) *Children Exposed to Parental Substance Misuse: Implications for Family Placement*. London: BAAF.

Harwin, J. and Forrester, D. (2002) *Parental Substance Misuse and Child Welfare: A Study of Social Work with Families in which Parents Misuse Drugs or Alcohol*. Report to the Nuffield Foundation.

Harwin, J., Owen, M. and Forrester, D. (2003) *Making Care Orders Work*. London: HMSO.

Hastings, J. and Typpo, M. (1984) *An Elephant in the Living Room*. Minneapolis, MN: Comp. Care.

Hayden, C., Jerrim, S. and Pike, S. (2002) *Parental Substance Misuse The Impact on Child Care Social Work Caseloads*. Portsmouth: Social Services, University of Portsmouth.

Hepburn, M. (2000) *Gender Issues: Women's Perspectives in Substance Misuse*. Keynote Speech at the Substance Misuse and Child Protection Conference, London, June.

Herrenkohl, E.C. and Herrenkohl, R.C. (1979) A Comparison of Abused Children With Their Non Abused Siblings. *Journal of the American Academy of Child Psychiatry*. 18, 260–6.

HMSO (1989) *The Children Act, 1989*. London: HMSO.

Hogan, D.M. (1997) *The Social and Psychological Needs of Children of Drug Users: Report on Exploratory Study*. Dublin: The Children's Research Centre, University of Dublin.

Hogan, D.M. (1998) Annotation: The Psychological Development and Welfare of Children of Opiate and Cocaine Users: Review And Research Needs. *Journal of Child Psychology and Psychiatry*. 39: 609–19.

Hogan, D. and Higgins, L. (2001) *When Parents Use Drugs: Key Findings from a Study of Children in the Care of Drug-Using Parents*. Dublin: The Children's Research Centre, Trinity College, Dublin.

Hopkirk, E. (2002) Adoption after Bereavement. Adoption and Fostering. 26: 1, 15–24.

Howe, D. et al. (1999) *Attachment Theory, Child Maltreatment and Family Support*. London: Macmillan.

Howe, D. and Fearnley, S. (1999) Disorders of Attachment and Attachment Therapy. *Adoption and Fostering*. 23: 2, 19–30.

Hunt, J. (2003) *Family and Friends Carers*. Scoping Paper DoH www.doh.gov.uk/carers/familyandfriends/htm

Jaudes, P.K., Ekwo, E. and Van Voorhis, J. (1995) Association of Drug Abuse and Child Abuse. *Child Abuse and Neglect*. 19: 9, 1065–75.

Juliana, P. and Goodman, C. (1997) Children of Substance Abusing Parents. In Lowinson, J.H. (Ed.) *Substance Abuse: A Comprehensive Textbook*. Baltimore: Williams and Wilkins.

Kearney, P., Levin, E. and Rosen, G. (2000) *Working with Families: Alcohol, Drug and Mental Health Problems*. London: NISW.

Kelley, S.J. and Damato, E.G. (1995) Grandparents as Primary Carers. *Maternal Child Nursing*, 20, 326–32.

Klee, H. Jackson, M. and Lewis, S. (2001) *Drug Misuse and Motherhood*. London: Routledge.

Klee, H., Wright, S. and Rothwell, J. (1998) *Drug Using Parents and their Children: Risk and Protective Factors*. Report to the Department of Health. Manchester Metropolitan University.

Kolar, A.F. et al. (1994) Children of Substance Abusers: The Life Experiences of Children of Opiate Addicts and Methadone Maintenance. *American Journal of Drug and Alcohol Abuse*. 20, 159–71.

Kroll, B. (2004) Living with an Elephant: Growing up With Parental Substance Misuse. *Child and Family Social Work*. 9, 129–40.

Kroll, B. and Taylor, A. (2000) Invisible Children? Parental Substance Abuse and Child Protection: Dilemmas for Practice. *Probation Journal*. 47: 2, 91–100.

Kroll, B. and Taylor, A. (2003) *Parental Substance Misuse and Child Welfare.* London: Jessica Kingsley.

Laybourn, A. Brown, J. and Hill, M. (1996) *Hurting on the Inside.* Aldershot: Avebury.

Lloyd, C. (1998) Risk Factors for Problem Drug Use: Identifying Vulnerable Groups. *Drugs:Education, Prevention and Policy.* 5: 3, 217–32.

London Borough of Brent (1985) *A Child in Trust.* London: London Borough Borough of Brent.

Marcenko, M. Kemp, S.P. and Larson, N.C. (2000) Childhood Experiences of Abuse, Later Substance Use and Parenting Outcomes Among Low Income Families. *American Journal of Orthopsychiatry.* 70, 316–26.

Mather, M. (2004) Finding Out About the Past to Understand the Present: Working With the Medical Advisor in Adoption and Foster Care. In Phillips, R. (Ed.) *Children Exposed to Parental Substance Misuse: Implications for Family Placement.* London: BAAF.

Mayer, S. (2004) The Needs of Black and Dual Heritage Affected by Parental Substance Misuse. In Phillips, R. (Ed.) *Children Exposed to Parental Substance Misuse: Implications for Family Placement.* London: BAAF.

McElhatton, P. (2004) The Effects of Drug Misuse in Pregnancy. In Phillips, R. (Ed.) *Children Exposed to Parental Substance Misuse: Implications for Family Placement.* London: BAAF.

McKeganey, N. Barnard, M. and McIntosh, J. (2001) *Paying the Price for their Parents' Addiction: Meeting the Needs of the Children of Drug Using Parents.* Glasgow: University of Glasgow Centre for Drug Misuse Research.

Minkler, M., Roe, K.M. and Price, M. (1992) The Physical and Emotional Health of Grandmothers Raising Grandchildren in the Crack Cocaine Epidemic. *Gerontological Society of America.* 32, 752–61.

Mulvey, E.P. (1994) Assessing the Evidence of a Link Between Mental Illness and Violence. *Hospital and Community Psychiatry.* 45: 7, 663–8.

Murphy, M. and Oulds, G. (2000) Establishing and Developing Co-Operative Links Between Substance Misuse and Child Protection Systems. In Harbin, F. and Murphy, M. (Eds.) *Substance Misuse and Child Care: How to Understand, Assist and Intervene when Drugs Affect Parenting.* Lyme Regis: Russell House Publishing.

Orford, J. (2001) *Excessive Appetites: A Psychological View of Addictions.* 2nd edn, Chichester: John Wiley.

Owusu-Bempah, J. and Howitt. D. (1997) Socio-genealogical Connectedness, Attachment Theory and Child Care Practice. *Child & Family Social Work.* 2, 199–207.

Parton, N. (1991) *Governing the Family: Child Care, Child Protection and The State.* London: Macmillan.

Patel, K. (2000) The Missing Drug Users :Minority Ethnic Drug Users and Their Children. In Harbin, F. and Murphy, M. (Eds.) *Substance Misuse and Child Care: How to Understand, Assist and Intervene when Drugs Affect Parenting.* Lyme Regis: Russell House Publishing.

Phillips, R. (Ed.) (2004) *Children Exposed to Parental Substance Misuse: Implications for Family Placement.* London: BAAF.

Pitcher, D. (2002) Placement With Grandparents: The Issues for Grandparents Who Care for Their Grandchildren. *Adoption and Fostering.* 26: 1, 6–14.

Plant, M. (1997) *Women and Alcohol: Contemporary and Historical Perspectives.* London: Free Association Books.

Plant, M. (2004) Parental Alcohol Misuse: Implications for Child Placement. In Phillips, R. (Ed.) *Children Exposed to Parental Substance Misuse: Implications for Family Placement.* London: BAAF.

Reder, P., Duncan, S. and Gray, M. (1993) *Beyond Blame.* London: Routledge.

Reder, P. and Duncan, S. (1999) *Lost Innocents: A Follow-up Study of Fatal Child Abuse.* London: Routledge.

Sher, K.J. (1991) Psychological Characteristics of Children of Alcoholics; Overview of Research Methods and Findings. *Recent Developments in Alcohol.* 9, 301–26.

Schore, A. (1994) *Affect Regulation and the Origin of the Self.* Hillside NJ: Laurence Erlbaum Ass.

Schore, A. (2001) The Effects of Early Relational Trauma on Right Brain Development, Affect Regulation and Infant Mental Health. *Infant Mental Health Journal.* 22, 201–69.

Standing Conference on Drug Abuse (1997) *Drug Using parents: Policy Guidelines for Inter-Agency Working.* London: Local Government Association Publications.

Tunnard, J. (2002a) *Parental Problem Drinking and its Impact on Children.* Dartington: Research in Practice.

Tunnard, J. (2002b) *Parental Drug Misuse a Review of Impact and Intervention Studies.* Dartington: Research in Practice.

Velleman, R. (1993) *Alcohol and The Family.* Occasional Paper, London: Institute of Alcohol Studies.

Velleman, R. (1996) Alcohol and Drug Problems in Parents: An Overview of the Impact on Children and The Implications for Practice. In Gopfert, M., Webster, J. and Seeman, M.V. (Eds.) *Parental Psychiatric Disorder: Distressed Parents and Their Families*. Cambridge: Cambridge University Press.

Velleman, R. and Orford, J. (1999) *Risk and Resilience:Adults who were the Children of Problem Drinkers*. Amsterdam: Harwood Academic Publishers.

Weir, A. and Douglas, A. (Eds.) (1999) *Child Protection and Adult Mental Health: Conflict of Interests?* Oxford: Butterworth Heineman.

Winnicott, D. (1964) *The Child, The Family and The Outside World*. Harmondsworth: Penguin.

Woodcock, J. and Sheppard, M. (2002) Double Trouble: Maternal Depression and Alcohol Dependence as Combined Factors in Child and Family Social Work. *Children and Society*. 16: 232–45.

Zeitlin, H. (1994) Children With Alcohol Misusing Parents. *British Medical Bulletin*. 50: 139–51.

Zuckerman, B. (1994) Effects on Parents and Children. In Besharov, D.J. (Ed.) *When Drug Addicts have Children*. Washington DC: Child Welfare League of America/American Enterprise Institute.

Promoting Contact between Family and Friends: Research Findings, Cautionary Notes and a Structure for Assessment

Cath Talbot

Social work practice is rife with inconsistency, hesitation, presumption and stereotypes, in respect of matters of contact between family and friends. Half of all siblings in long-term placements are separated, yet siblings represent the past, the present and the future (Ellison, 1999). Sibling relationships have the potential to last longer than marriages, or the relationship between parent and child (Tomlinson, 1999). Adults, separated from siblings, through adoption often report feelings of sadness and loss and this is the case even when they never knew the adoptee (Pavlovic and Mullender, 1999). In a study with a similar research question, Prynn found that the loss of a sibling in childhood is a traumatic event. These emotions continue to be felt in adulthood (Prynn, 1999).

In practice, the separation of siblings is common, yet research and legislation argue against it (Elgar and Head, 1999). One study, published in 2002, found a range of practice on a continuum of very poor to brilliant. Of concern is the finding that children are left to grieve quietly as the wishes of new carers take precedence over the child's wishes and needs and birth parents' wishes having little impact on contact decisions (Thoburn, 2004). Practice can be particularly poor in respect of consultation with the children themselves (Macaskill, 2002). Yet siblings are custodians of family members and meanings: they are closely connected to senses of identity and belonging and have the capacity to offer life-long support (Elgar and Head, 1999). As Rushton, et al. (2001) have recognised, there is a need to identify practice assumptions, and test them out. Our observations of practice are endorsed by research evidence that contact between siblings, in particular, is an underestimated feature of permanency planning (Mullender, 1999). These decisions about contact have life long consequences for the children concerned and contemporary research, which has directly sought the views and experiences of the

children concerned, presents important evidence of their ongoing sense of loss when separated from birth families, (see for example, Macaskill, 2002; Rushton, et al., 2001).

Sadly, there is no provision, in the Children Act, for children to have a right to contact with siblings, though Section 34(2) provides for contact between the child and 'any other named person'. There is a strong argument that children's perspectives will be different to adults and children's views must be pursued (Eiser, Molay and Morse, 2000). We must understand children's own views about who they regard as siblings, and this may well be more extensive in black families (Mullender, 1999). The placement of siblings together and the ongoing contact between siblings needs to be clearly understood as a protective feature across placement options. One recent finding, for example, has been that rejection by birth parents was associated with later problems in interaction with adults, for children placed separately from siblings but not for siblings together. Also, there was considerable improvement to be made in arrangements to promote ongoing contact between separated children (Rushton, et al., 2001). These matters need to be understood in the context of many decades of concern in respect of the stability of long-term stranger foster placements and the general consensus that the disruption rate for long-term foster care is about 50 per cent (McCauley, 1996). This chapter is a plea for professionals to make child focused decisions that prioritise the maintenance of safe significant family relationships unless there are clear risks and consequences associated with such a decision that outweighs the benefits.

It is suggested here that there is no objective 'truth' in respect of the value of ongoing contact arrangements. Responses to this question are guided as much by implicit professional and personal values than by irrefutable evidence. The longitudinal study of Wilson and Sinclair (2004) concluded that the arguments for contact are not conclusive, but they are persuasive and the birth parents cited by children in the study remained very important throughout the placement. This study also found that ending contact may be associated with placement stability where there is strong evidence of prior familial abuse. Macaskill has considered the concept of 'safe contact', concluding with the following contraindications:

- There are multiple attachments and a risk of confusing the child.
- There is a threat of harm to the child.
- The birth parents cannot be sufficiently emotionally reconciled, to be able to manage ongoing contact.
- The demands on the carers is too great.
- There is such risk to the child that long-term, skilled facilitation or supervision is required.

Macaskill's (2002) study found difficulties associated with:

- Risks of encountering an abuser.
- Sexual innuendo.
- Further emotional abuse.
- Poor quality interaction.
- Passing of drugs.
- Parental inappropriate demands for physical contact.
- Inappropriate references.
- Recreating distorted relationships.
- Mobile phones.

Conversely, the arguments for the continuation of contact are where:

- This is needed to promote the child's identity.
- It can manage the tendency for children to develop fantasies about their family relationships and their experiences.
- It provides an opportunity to deal with the development of a sense of rejection and self-blaming.
- It enhances the carer's own feelings of 'entitlement' and to be open and honest about relationships and about the placement, (Macaskill, 2002).

Promoting children's identity in substitute care is a complex process indeed. Neil and Howe (2004) refer to the 'paradox of adoption': adoptive families both integrate the child, but differentiate the child, through their openness and honesty about the child's birth family and subsequent adoption. Adopted children have to manage additional psychological tasks, over and above the minefield of the usual developmental hurdles. Whilst forming new and secure attachments, often in the context of previous attachment complexities, children are dealing with feelings of loss and rejection, on a long term basis. One key resource lies in the characteristics of the adopters. Whilst carers' anxieties about contact with the birth family may be common, anxious carers promote insecurity in children. Carers who are able to connect to their own sense of loss in their life history have a greater potential to understand the contact and identity needs of the children in their care. Those who are flexible, empathetic and communicate openly are the most likely to promote contact in the long term (Neil and Howe, 2004).

Neil and Howe (2004) proposed a transactional approach which joins the psychological profiles of the triad of the child, the birth parents and the carers. Each member of this triad will have characteristics which may be associated with either a positive or negative prognosis for contact. If these are assessed, and made explicit, clarity may be introduced into the plan for contact. This assessment will also suggest areas for work towards change so that a long term, flexible, child focussed arrangement can best be achieved. It will also advise on the frequency and quality of contact and the support that will be needed over time. Fundamentally, the quality of contact flows from the quality of the relationships that may be achieved (Beck and Schofield, 2004, Neil and Howe, 2004; Thoburn, 2004; Wilson and Sinclair, 2004). When assessing the capacity of substitute carers, the position on contact can be a very good test of values and Thoburn contends that those carers who have the skills to manage contact are likely to have those other characteristics that achieve successful placements (Thoburn, 2004). Writing about the characteristics of substitute carers, Neil and Howe (2004: 232) observe that the:

Actual experience of contact with an accepting birth relative increases empathy, understanding, confidence and feelings of entitlement for permanent carers who initially felt anxious, uncertain, and reluctant about contact. Reality dispels fear and fantasies.

Of interest is that black carers are particularly good at understanding the contact needs of children. Thoburn (2004: 201) calls attention to her finding that 'family placement workers have much to understand from black families about how to facilitate comfortable contact arrangements'.

Although there has been relatively little social research on the quality of sibling relationships, there is evidence that sibling placements have better outcomes than single child placements (Rushton, et al., 2001). In her review of pertinent research, Mullender (1999) presents a persuasive account of the link between placement stability and the placement of siblings together, including the finding that as many as 50 per cent of the sample of children placed alone had disrupted placements, and that being placed alone was a risk factor, even when other potential variables were kept constant. Single placements are particularly vulnerable to disruption when the single sibling is joining an established family. One important finding has been that professionals do not consider the long-term significance of sibling relationships: decisions are often restricted to a consideration of adults' views in respect of the importance of the current relationship (Rushton, et al., 2001). One study, which directly sought the views of children from middle childhood in long-term fostering arrangements, found that children who had contact with birth relatives were positive and described the sadness amongst those children whose links had been severed. The study also found the children to be preoccupied and strongly identified with their birth families and these significant feelings were not dependent on the existence of current contact, nor upon its level. In all of the three stages of this longitudinal study, birth family members featured predominantly in the investigation of the children's identity, and there was worrying evidence of a lack of emotional involvement between the children and their foster families (McCauley, 1996). Macaskill's (2002) study of contact arrangements found that restricting of contact to an annual arrangement left children to fantasise, and was associated with high anxiety and expectations. Most of the children had mixed feelings, but half wanted to see more relatives and there was a range of expectations, from wanting to check on the welfare of family members, to large emotional investments in ongoing contact. The children in this sample were resolute in their wish to see their birth relatives and the study concludes with a message that must be heard: 'please tell social workers to let us see our birth relatives for the simple reason that

they are our real relatives'. Yet, another British study found that 50 per cent of placements had no plan for sibling contact, and when there was a plan, this rarely included all siblings (Dance and Rushton, 1999).

Powerfully, Mullender uses 'Paddington Bear' in her argument that practice must change, and carefully promote sibling contact. Children are not Paddington bears, who arrive in placement with their suitcase and sandwich, ready to leave past attachments and simply start again (Mullender, 1999). As Elgar and Head (1999) note, siblings help retain family memories and meanings and have the potential to give life-long support and support a sense of self-identity and belonging. Mullender sets a powerful challenge for professionals assessing the merits of contact, by questioning the professional capacity for adults to accurately measure the quality of sibling relationships anyway:

> . . . the more siblings share and the closer they are, the harder it is for anyone else to know what is going on in their interactions because they adapt their behaviour and their interactions to one another.
>
> (Mullender, 1999: 5)

The point here is the absolute importance of child focused assessment, and avoidance of over-confident and even arrogant adult intervention. Jones (1999) contributes an important argument that children's apparent reactions often cover up their true feelings, but children who lose contact with siblings experience further emotional loss, to add to, and complicate the grief already suffered through the loss of parents and extended family. These powerful feelings may not be acknowledged or allowed to heal. Kosonen's (1999) study of siblings in foster care found that mothers and siblings were most frequently cited on the children's eco-maps, and consistently more than the foster carers. Whilst some social workers had tried hard to maintain links between siblings, the study concluded that sibling contact was not properly taken into account and that placements were based on 'conventional wisdom' rather than the views of the children and an assessment of sibling relationships. The sample of fostered children defined family as being associated with love, care, mutual support and respect and it is significant that these associations were not just restricted to biological relationships. Elgar and Head (1999) challenge some common professional assumptions about sibling relationships, in the discussion about the 'normality' of sibling contact, if it is not overly competitive, or produced by a real or perceived preference of a parent. Of interest, is their argument that there is no real evidence that sibling caretaking is harmful, and in some cultures, it is the norm. This is endorsed by Jones, in her argument that sibling rivalry does not imply a problematic relationship (Jones, 1999). Prevatt-Goldstein (1999) and in her discussion of black siblings, describes a normal feature of sibling relationships as the presence of the older sibling's natural sense of responsibility for younger siblings. This is not 'substitute parenting'. It represents the early stages of a life-long relationship of significance. This has become 'pathologised' in Western concepts of child development, and there is a similar process applied to many working class families. Again, Head and Elgar (1999) conclude that there is no evidence for separating siblings because one has taken a caretaking role towards the other. In their study of adult birth siblings, some participants had taken some parental role, but regarded it as a bonding process (Pavlovic and Mullender, 1999). Mullender concludes that even when sibling relationships are troubled and even hostile, this does not mean that they can improve and become important. The relationship will improve if the children's needs are being met (Mullender, 1999).

In Neil's (1999) study of patterns of contact in post-adoption placements, as many as 42 per cent of children were having contact with all siblings, 23 per cent were having contact with some siblings, and 35 per cent were having no contact with siblings or birth parents. As many as 58 per cent of children had one or more siblings elsewhere, with whom there was no contact. Paternal siblings were more likely to become 'lost' and siblings were more likely to retain contact when the separated child is living in a kinship placement. This represents much loss. In the study of Head and Elgar, 72 per cent of children who had been sexually abused had been separated from their siblings, (Head and Elgar, 1999). This practice has continued, despite the National Adoption Standards, which state that children must be placed together and that when children are separated, there should be direct work with the children, with a clear explanation of the decision (Department of Health, 2001). A review of American research into kinship care estimated that 78 per cent of children had

maintained a contact arrangement that involved at least weekly contact, and which continued to dominate children's experiences, despite the potential for disruption (Waterhouse and Brocklesby, 1999). A review of the New Zealand experience suggested lesser contact, but supported the premise that kinship placements maintain sibling contact, and concluded that siblings are more likely to be placed together in kinship placements than they are in unrelated placements (Worrall, 2001). The value of contact is further elevated when we understand that UK research, in the post Children Act period gives a picture of children moving in and out of care, rather than the previous tendency for children to have a single and longer period in the care system (Farmer, 2001). Contact is crucial to reunification and whilst kinship placements encourage contact with parents they make return to parents less likely (Farmer, 2001). The current knowledge base in respect of kinship care cannot yet explain this phenomenon.

In their study of local authority planning and decision making for children, Beckett (1997) found little evidence of references to policy and procedure in this area and concluded that the need for competent assessment structures is urgent. Ellison proposes that local authorities adopt an 'inclusive approach', based on 'tangible policy', with a 'recognition of needs, attachment and vulnerability' (Ellison, 1999). This should include a commitment to work on damaged sibling relationships (Tomlinson, 1999). Destructive elements of sibling relationships may have been nurtured within birth families, but a failure to address these will only mean that they will continue into the future (Head and Elgar, 1999). Siblings need professional input.

On a practical level, Mullender (1999) is very helpful. We should start with the children's understandings of significant relationships. Genograms should be completed and *updated*, as relationships are never static. These should consider child-adult relationships and child-child relationships (we would add, child-pet relationships). Carers should be required to network. Local resources should be developed and supported. The case holding team should be working closely with the family placement team, operating with the same philosophy and goal. Finally, it is essential that research messages are understood and taken on board. The gap between evidence and current practice is of real concern. Indeed, it can be emotionally abusive to the most vulnerable of children. Instead, placement and contact decisions should properly consider the importance of sibling relationships over a lifetime. Children should be consulted as experts in their own lives (Mullender and Pavlovic, 1999).

Conclusions

Whilst kinship placements offer greater prospects for continued contact, this is not without complexity. Nobody is neutral in kinship placements (Galloway and Wallace, 2002), though it is important to recognise that ongoing contact in kinship placements is not associated with instability (Broad, Hayes and Rushforth, 2004). The transactional model of Neil and Howe is of great assistance here. The triad of child, birth parent and carer have characteristics which can be assessed to inform a prognosis for contact and the changes that might be needed to produce the best possible outcome for the child, (Argent, 2002; Macaskill, 2002; Neil and Howe, 2004). We produce Table 1 to set out some ideas for workers approaching the issue of contact to help them risk assess the situation in the context of prognosis indicators.

Table 9.1   Checklist of indicators for contact prognosis

Part A: Children

Positive indicators	*Evidence*
Infant placement No established pre-placement relationship with birth parent Secure attachment Secure placement Healthy psychosocial development Emotional intelligence Absence of severe behavioural/positive or neutral relationship with contact birth parent	
Indicators of difficulty	*Evidence*
Insecure attachment Insecure placement Major behavioural/ mental health problems Troubled relationship with birth parent Contact re-traumatises Child does not want contact Multiple attachments: risk of confusing the child	

Part B: Birth relatives

Positive indicators	*Evidence*
Never been primary carer Accepts carers as new psychological parents Affirms new carers Can work constructively with new carers Relinquishes parenting role Relates positively to the child Contact validates placement Decreases anger, guilt, anxiety	

Table 9.1　*(continued)*

Part B: Birth relatives *(continued)*

Indicators of difficulty	Evidence
Does not accept placement Child is discouraged from new attachments Serious abuse/trauma of the child Rejecting of the child Serious personal difficulties, e.g. drugs/alcohol Any threat of harm	

Part C: The carers

Positive indicators	Evidence
Good level of sensitivity, openness Empathy, reflective capacity Recognition of benefits for child Accepting of child's curiosity Conveys positively regarding birth parent Resolved feelings of 'ownership'/attachment Collaborative capacity Early involvement in contact Direct involvement in contact	

Indicators of difficulty	Evidence
Fixed anxiety about contact Low levels of sensitivity child openness, empathy, reflective capacity Unresolved feelings of 'ownership'/attachment Lacks collaborative capacity No direct involvement	
Summary of changes needing to be made	
Timescale:	
Action by whom?	

References

Argent, H. (Ed.) (2002) *Staying Connected: Managing Contact Arrangements in Adoption.* London: BAAF.

Beckett, S. (1999) Local Authority Planning and Decision-Making for Looked-After Siblings. In Mullender, A. *We are Family: Sibling Relationships in Placement and Beyond.* London: BAAF.

Beck, M. and Schofield, G. (2004) Promoting Security and Managing Risk: Contact in Long-term Foster Care. In Neil, E. and Howe, D. *Contact in Adoption and Permanent Foster Care.* London: BAAF.

Dance, C. and Rushton, A. (1999) Sibling Separation and Contact in Permanent Placement. In Mullender, A. op. cit.

Eiser, C., Mohay. H. and Morse, R. (2000) The Measurement of Quality of Life in Young Children. *Child Care, Health and Development.* 26: 4.

Elgar, M. and Head, A. (1999) An Overview of Siblings. In Mullender, A. op. cit.

Ellison. M. (1999) Planning for Sibling Continuity within Permanency: Needs Led or Needs Unmet? In Mullender, A. op. cit.

Farmer, E. and Pollock, S. (1999) Sexually Abused and Abusing Children: Their Impact on Foster Siblings and other Looked-After Children. In Mullender, A. op. cit.

Galloway, H. and Wallace, F. (2002) Managing Contact Arrangements in Black Kinship Care. In Argent, H. op. cit.

Jones, A. (1999) The Achievement and Sustainability of Sibling Contact. In Mullender, A. op. cit.

Kosonen, M. (1999) Core and Kith Siblings: Foster Children's Changing Families. In Mullender, A. op. cit.

Macaskill, C. (2002). *Safe Contact: Children in Permanent Placement and Contact with their Birth Relatives.* Lyme Regis: Russell House Publishing.

Maddocks, P. (2002) *Fostering for the Future. Inspection of Foster Care Services.* London: DoH.

McCauley, C. (1996) *Children in Long-Term Foster Care: Emotional and Social Development.* Aldershot: Avebury.

Mullender, A. (Ed.) (1999) *We are Family: Sibling Relationships in Placement and Beyond.* London: BAAF.

Mullender, A. and Pavlovik, A. (1999) Sibling Research and Practice Implications for Placement Decisions. In BAAF, *Assessment, Preparation and Support: Implications from Research.* London: BAAF.

Neil, E. (1999) The Sibling Relationships of Adopted Children and Patterns of Contact after Adoption. In Mullender, A. op. cit.

Neil, E. (2002) Contact after Adoption: The Role of Agencies in Making and Supporting Plans. *Adoption and Fostering.* 26: 1.

Neil, E. and Howe, D. (Eds.) (2004) *Contact in Adoption and Permanent Foster Care: Research, Theory and Practice.* London: BAAF.

Prevatt-Goldstein, B. (1999) Black Siblings: A Relationship for Life. In Mullender, A. op. cit.

Rushton, A. et al. (2001) *Siblings in Late Permanent Placements.* London: BAAF.

Thoburn, J. (2004) Post Placement Contact between Birth Parents and Older Children: The Evidence form a Longitudinal Study of Ethnic Minority Children. In Neil and Howe, op. cit.

Tomlinson, J. (1999) Siblings Together: Myth or Reality. In Mullender, A. op. cit.

Waterhouse, S. and Brocklesby, E. (1999) Placement Choices for Children-Giving more priority to Kinship Placements. In Greeff, R. (Ed.) *Fostering Kinship: An International Perspective on Kinship Foster Care.* Aldershot: Arena.

Wilson, K. and Sinclair, I. (2004) Contact in Foster Care: Some Dilemmas and Opportunities. In Neil and Howe, op. cit.

Chapter Ten

Assessment in Kinship Placements: Towards a Sensitive, Evidence-based Framework

Martin C. Calder and Cath Talbot

Introduction

In Chapter 3 we articulated many limitations with the tools currently used to assess kinship placements. Drawing upon the available materials we identified the need for a sensitive, evidence-based assessment framework for kinship placements that would:

- Recognise that in most cases placements have already taken effect when the assessment is undertaken.
- Operate with a presumption that a placement within the family is the optimally desirable option other than where there is clear irrefutable evidence of risks that cannot be permitted or managed.
- Accept that kinship care is fundamentally different than stranger foster care and the primary goal must be the maintenance of the child within the (extended) family or friendship network – whether this is an informal family or formal service-driven placement.
- Understand that kinship carers have different profiles to those of 'mainstream' carers and integrate a consideration of this.
- Consider the multiple roles that a kinship carer may play for the child: caregiver, grandparent and parent.
- Acknowledge that the application of a higher threshold for accepting kinship placements as acceptable is discriminatory and unjust and represents risk enhancement for the child since it deprives them of better outcomes via kinship placements. *This requires an understanding of research evidence.*
- Acknowledge that the application of a lower threshold for accepting kinship placements is dangerous for children unless the risks have been clearly defined, assessed as manageable and resources committed to help support the risk management and planning process.
- Address kinship placement-specific issues such as contact that may require some structure and

prohibitions if the child is to be effectively safeguarded.
- Introduce a risk component into the assessment process in an enabling (self-reported) way that balances assets with weaknesses and which prioritises the support required to sustain the placement.
- Consider the best legal route for the child and the carers and build the implications into the assessment.
- Shift towards the paradigm of empowerment recognised by Broad (2004).

Although there are acute limitations associated with the assessment framework it is unlikely to be replaced by central government for some considerable time. In order not to deskill workers or unnecessarily confuse them, our remedial framework starts with a re-conceptualisation of the assessment framework triangle to reflect the specific issues within kinship placement assessment. In doing so we will then extend it to embrace two further dimensions: the professional issues associated with the placement; and the need to conduct a risk assessment to safeguard the child.

Broad et al. (2001) called for comprehensive assessments of need to assess suitability and reduce the risk of placement breakdown. In so doing we needed to recognise that assessment is best undertaken between a social worker and a kinship caregiver in partnership, although we have some way to go on this.

As a starting point we are advocating an adaptation to the assessment framework triangle that reflects the need to assess the child, the birth parents and the kinship carers (see Figure 10.1). These dimensions reflect the complexity and uniqueness of the kinship placement: we are no longer restricting our assessment to one family situation (where we examine the parent's capacity to meet the child's developmental needs) but to the birth family, the kinship placement family, the impact of this for the child, as well as

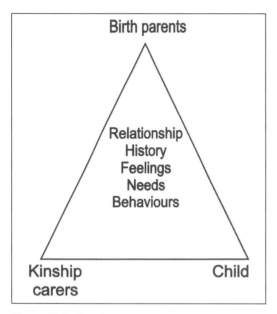

Figure 10.1   A preliminary structure to assess kinship placements

the unique tensions between different strands of the family over the new arrangements. Whilst this offers a structural solution, it also needs to be accompanied by an attitudinal change in workers to one that views kinship as the primary placement option rather than a secondary one when local authority resources are limited; and one that is enabling rather than approving.

Using this structure as our starting point, we will add in the necessary components that require assessment in all kinship placements. Before so doing, we feel it is important to re-name the different circumstances that may trigger a kinship care arrangement, as each signals the need for a modification of a generic model, with different areas requiring different emphasis and exploration. Kinship care arrangements may arise as:

- The first option for social services once the family situation has broken down.
- A final resort for social services after other care options have failed.
- A continuation of birth parent support already provided by the carer.
- An option selected by the young person themselves after a crisis at home (Broad et al., 2001).

The origins of the problems may lie in child protection issues, an inability of the previous

carer to cope, or the young person's difficult behaviour or problems. In situations where the child is being placed following abuse then the additional dimension of risk needs to be included and where it is an informal arrangement a strengths-loaded, mutually agreed assessment process should be the starting point. The context of the current increase of kinship care is relevant in that we have increasing numbers within the care system, a reducing level of choice especially for 13–16 year olds, and concerns regarding the quality of care provided.

Birth parents

Some birth parents may experience the removal of their child as bad, but this may be compounded if the child is placed with their parents or others; this information is public knowledge, and thus leads to multiple consequences for them in their home community; and the loss of their parent as they remember them in favour of someone who is prioritising the care of their child over their relationship and needs.

Child

The history that exists between the child and the carer often means that they have some understanding of the child's specific needs, how they may or may not have been met when living with their parents, and how they may be met or compromised in the future. This is important to build into any assessment as we are able to assess the needs of a specific child in contrast to stranger placements which are assessed to embrace a wide range of children, limited only by an age banding and/or ability level and gender. As such, any assessment of kinship carers should explore:

- The child's experiences of living in their birth family and the quality of previous care provided (positive and negative). The implications of the specific poor experiences such as domestic violence, intergenerational sexual abuse, drug and alcohol abuse and parental learning difficulties require additional consideration as they will continue to impact on the child, the wider family and the prognosis for outcomes.

- Their response to such experiences (resilient or vulnerable?).
- The impact of such experiences on their development to date and signposts for future behavioural or emotional responses and the carer's capacity to manage these or feel comfortable seeking assistance if they can't.

We need to assess whether the child is aware of and caught up in any conflict and how they make sense of this without assuming responsibility.

Workers also have a responsibility to consider the issues raised for any other children living in the household or who has significant contact with the kinship carer's family. Workers need to consider whether the number of children in the household will determine the level of care afforded to the subject child and whether there is likely to be any jealous responses which may create additional problems of child management for the carers. The wishes, feelings and needs of the carer's own resident and dependent children will impact on the stability of the placement and need to be explored.

It is useful to examine the nature of the impact of any harm within the family of origin necessitating the kinship care arrangement. Children may be resilient to harm or they may be adept at concealing impact via internalising behaviours such as depression or self-harm.

Resilience comprises a set of qualities that helps a person to:

- Withstand many of the negative effects of adversity.
- A resilient child has more positive outcomes than might be expected given the level of adversity threatening their development.
- Bearing in mind what has happened to them, a resilient child does better than they ought to do.

Rutter (1985) identifies three key factors associated with resilience:

- A sense of self esteem and confidence.
- A belief in own self-efficacy and ability to deal with change and adaptation.
- A repertoire of social problem-solving approaches.

It is therefore essential that workers examine the child's self-esteem and confidence, self-efficacy and social problem-solving approaches. We also need to consider how the caregivers encouraged resilience in their own children and how they can encourage this in the subject child. For a detailed description of the resilience literature the reader is referred to Calder, Peake and Rose (2001) and the resilience-vulnerability matrix within the Assessment Framework.

Kinship carers

Kinship care differs in a number of significant ways from stranger foster care, primarily due to prior knowledge and often experience of caring for the child.

Any assessment needs to address the specific supports that are needed to sustain such an arrangement so as to ensure continuity of care and maximising the child's needs being met. Indeed, the issue of support to kinship carers is one that features at the top of any list produced to reflect kinship carer's views and needs. Words such as collaboration and partnership appear regularly as a reflection that ideally any such placement enables a child to sustain meaningful connections and continuity that ensure permanence. However, partnership is not a panacea and is certainly not reflective of a common approach from workers. Calder (1995) identified four distinct partnership models that reflect the diversity of practice and which can explain why some approaches to partnership are experienced as alienating, controlling and unsupportive by some kinship carers. The four models of partnership as related to kinship placements appear below:

- **The expert model:** where the professional takes control and makes all the decisions, giving a low priority to the family's view, wishes or feelings, the sharing of information, or the need for negotiation. This might be understandable in the conduct of removing children from their birth family in situations of high-risk, but it serves no useful purpose when applied to kinship carers unless the objective is to undermine the placement.
- **The transplant (of expertise) model:** where the professional sees the carers as a resource and hands over some skills, but retains control of the decision-making. This is understandable in circumstances where little is known about the carers at the point of placement, especially if there are some objections from the birth

parents; but it should be a starting point rather than an end point.

- **The consumer model:** where it is assumed that the carers have the right to decide and select what they believe to be appropriate and the decision-making is ultimately in their control. This is clearly appropriate when they have care of the child and the placement has not been affected by the professionals; and it should represent a progression of the relationship with carers once relationships are established.
- **The social network/systems model:** where parents, kinship carers, children and professionals are part of a network of formal and informal development, and social support for the family and the child. They are capable of supplementing existing resources via the facilitation of the social worker who should draw more on the extended family while complying with statutory requirements. This is often where kinship carers would like to locate professional agencies: they are there to support them in their task rather than directing operations.

The challenge for workers is to find ways of moving through the various models as they can be seen as a continuum that evolves as relationships develop. The costs of starting and maintaining an expert partnership is that it is always going to preclude permanency, as the locus of decision-making rests in the professional rather than the family domain. Any assessment of partnership potential may not always be greeted with enthusiasm from carers who have cared for a child for some significant period of time and who may have a detailed understanding of their experiences and needs while the professionals are both playing catch-up as well as making judgements about what they learn (see Laws and Broad, 2001).

Assessing prospective carers

A sensible starting point for workers is to get prospective carers to talk without prompts about the child, and their relationship with the child. This should give workers a good indication about their potential suitability as carers. Where there are a number of children involved in the placement we need to consider each child's needs alongside the need for placement together with the additional responsibility and stresses (as well as joys) this brings. Workers need to consider a number of factors with the carers that include:

- The carer's expectations of the child: bearing in mind the history of the child and the anticipated or known behavioural challenges this may bring.
- The carer's expectations of the care giving role: will they have sufficient resolve and energy to derive pleasure from the arrangement or are they simply motivated by a sense of duty to avoid professional solutions.
- Their understanding of loss and grief. There are a great many losses that carers may experience through accepting the placement and these include:
  - Interruptions in their life cycle: swapping retirement for raising a child.
  - Loss of time for friends and interests.
  - Loss of financial security.
  - Loss of role, such as swapping the grandparent role for one of parent.
  - Loss of their own children if they are concerned about the situation or circumstances that led to the placement, as well as their attitude about a continuing relationship on a significantly different footing, where the protection of the child has to be prioritised but often in a way that does not divorce them from supporting and helping them resolve their problems.

It should be remembered that carers who have experienced multiple losses may not be well placed to help the child in their care deal with this issue. We also need to ensure that the assessment of loss addresses three specific areas:

  - The degree of pain, hurt, and stress that results from the loss.
  - Capabilities and experiences in dealing with loss.
  - Projected limits and tolerance for future losses and stressors.

                                    (Crumbley and Little, 1997)

- Their understanding of the potential 'impact factors' of abuse for the children (see Calder, Peake and Rose, 2001 for a detailed review of this issue in relation to sexual abuse and Bell (Chapter 6) this volume).
- Their capacity for behaviour management in a range of presenting circumstances, such as anger, acting out, etc. Are they flexible in their approach to discipline?
- Their capacity to work with parents and professionals and often to walk the tightrope between the two.

Workers need to explore the capacity of the carers to support relationships between the child and their parents, siblings or significant others. This is essential in the medium to long term as it relates to the child's developing sense of identity. This should include both maternal and paternal relatives as kinship placements often exclude one side of the birth family. This can be explored with well considered genograms and eco-maps in which both children and adults participate. We need to explore support needs in detail and develop a sense of acceptance that such requests will not be received and processed as admissions of failure.

The nature of the formal and informal support that carers can call in is an integral component of any assessment. There is a need to look at how best to sustain a kinship placement over time when the need for support may incrementally increase over time, linked to factors such as age and health.

Workers need to identify all the significant adults living in the home and involve them in an assessment even if there are no plans for them to be the primary carer for the subject child. This is essential if we are to examine not only the individual and what they can offer the child directly or indirectly but also whether there are any family dynamics that cause concern and require further assessment. This must be able to tolerate multi-causal explanations within families.

There is also a very clear need to assess both the kinship carers in some detail. Experience across social care assessments informs us that the primary focus of assessment is the female carer and the male carer is often an afterthought. This is inappropriate as we again need to examine their individual strengths and weaknesses, the respective roles and responsibilities assumed within the household, and areas of consistency and inconsistency or approach around areas such as discipline and involvement in day-to-day caring tasks with the child. For a detailed discussion around the engagement of men in assessment work the reader is referred to Hackett (forthcoming).

Workers need to assess the carer's motivation for caring for the child as there is a correlation between motivation and capacity to attain particular outcomes. Crumbley and Little (1997) identified a range of motivating factors for relatives:

- A sense of loyalty to the family, the partner or the child. They may express the conviction that families should take care of their own.
- A strong attachment to the child. Some caregivers have already assumed the role of primary or secondary caretaker at points in the child's life.
- Duty or obligation. These caregivers may feel trapped and even resentful.
- Guilt about the way they raised their own children or their role in the situation that led to the child needing placement.
- A desire to rescue the child from abuse, neglect, or being raised in the foster care system.
- Anger with the parent or the agency.

Social history

Taking a social history is a critically important part of the assessment and one which the Form F guides us more than the Assessment Framework. This might include:

- Developing a genogram with the family to identify who is who and also their significance, level of involvement and whether there is any relevant child protection or criminal background.
- Their childhood experiences: including patterns of care, roles and responsibilities, positive and negative memories, family boundaries, rules, identity, discipline, support towards independence, values and attitudes toward a range of issues, such as continuity of care, work-life balance, etc.
- Any prior evidence of abuse or neglect?
- Any prior experiences of social services involvement? If so, for what reasons? What is their recollection of the intervention? How does this relate to their current attitude towards professionals, especially social workers?
- How the couple met: what their roles and responsibilities are; their attitude towards their own children and the current presenting situation? What causes conflict and how is this resolved?
- How did they raise their children? Can they identify areas with hindsight that they did well and what they could have done better or differently (often with the benefit of hindsight)? Do they accept any responsibility for contributing to their children's problems? Have

they attempted to intervene and offset the risks to the child previously?

- What tensions exist currently within the immediate and extended family and what proposed management options can they identify/enact?
- How able are they to provide the necessary care and protection to the subject child? How willing and able are they for getting involved in interests, hobbies and activities? How will they adapt from their previous role with the child to one which has clear boundaries and structure? For example, how willing and able are grandparents in making the transition from indulgence to a more managerial role?

As CWLA (2003: 22) articulates well, 'Kinship carers are likely to understand the child's need for protection because they are aware of the situation that led to the child needing placement away from the family. On the other hand, the kinship family has come to the attention of the child welfare agency because of abuse, neglect, or substance abuse and the family dynamics that may have contributed to these problems need to be carefully assessed to determine if they are present in the kinship family as well'. Clearly issues remain if the carers cannot see that harm has occurred or accept it has happened but may struggle to manage the contact between the parents and the child. In such circumstances workers have to assess the capacity of the carers to protect the child from any future harm and this will be informed by their understanding of the areas of concern as well as their history of and capacity to enforce appropriate and safe boundaries. An indicator of this may lie in their prior ability to resolve or work with conflicts in a way that has not involved the child.

There is a need to assess the capacity of the caregivers to provide safe care for the child and in doing so have one eye on reducing the likelihood of any allegation being made against them (see Calder, 2005 for detailed guidance on how to achieve this). When the child moves into the care of the caregiver they will often have experienced harm of some description and they may be exhibiting challenging behaviour for which the carers require some support and guidance. The caregivers may have difficulty in understanding and tolerating such behavioural problems that result from harm histories and they need information to help them understand as a preface to managing and hopefully tolerating it. In some cases, they may have been shielded from any such knowledge by the parents in the first instance and then by the child latterly: either out of a sense of loyalty or protectiveness. Regan and Butterworth (2005) have articulated this pictorially in Figure 10.2 where they separate out

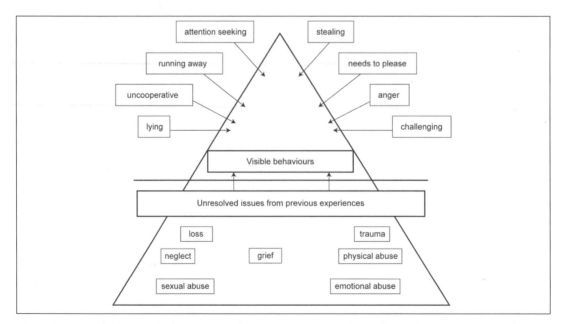

Figure 10.2   A child who has had negative experiences (Regan and Butterworth, 2005)

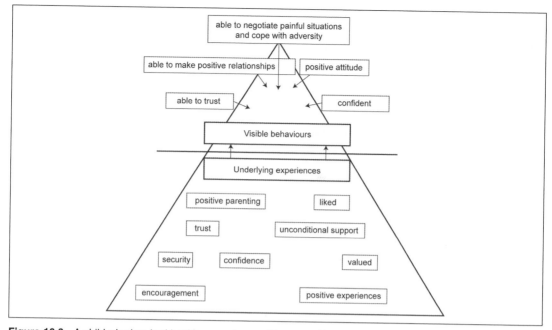

Figure 10.3 A child who has had healthy experiences (Regan and Butterworth, 2005)

- Routines: including bathing, transporting, meals, bedtimes etc.
- Physical contact: between adults and children; how we comfort children; boundaries during play.
- Privacy: general boundaries and guidelines, e.g. toileting.
- Sexualised behaviour: boundaries that exist within the home.
- Discipline: the range of sanctions that are used within the household.
- Health and safety: for activities about the home, coping with emergencies, i.e. fire drill.
- Visitors to the house: understanding and commitment to the household's safe care practice.
- The fundamental messages that underpin everything that happens in the house (mission statement).

Figure 10.4 Reflecting safe care practices within the house (Rose and Savage, 1999)

the visible behaviours that are in the carers' faces from the invisible origins of such behaviours. It is the invisible dimensions that need to be addressed if we are to meaningfully effect change. We can contain behaviours in the absence of cause but we can only effect change when we understand and locate the cause. The latter is also correlated with sustained as opposed to short-term change and for children this has to be our aspiration.

We are trying to work with the caregivers to provide a nurturing and safe environment that achieves some reparation from previous harm (see Figure 10.3) and which sees a reduction in the visible challenging behaviours to more developmentally positive behaviours, reflective of consistent parenting. In order to introduce such a discussion with the caregivers we can ask them what needs the child is likely to have based upon their past experiences; what behavioural responses have they witnessed or been aware of from the child thus far, and what care will the child require (over and above what has previously been offered) to try and help the child attain their appropriate developmental potential. We should also explore with them what previous experiences for the child will make them feel unsafe and how this might be addressed.

Rose and Savage (1999) have produced safe care plan issues to consider (see Figure 10.4) for such situations that can usefully bring the subject alive for the caregivers and the child and encourage the formulation of specific agreed rules of safe care for each child in the placement.

This might include broad issues of respect, judgements, morality, language, culture and religion. There also needs to be more specific messages for children who are looked after; i.e. being in care is not their fault; not the only one; not replacing/in competition with birth parents; it is right that plans are made with them about the future.

Rose and Savage (1999) have also produced a useful structure for the analysis and understanding of a child's behaviour (see Figure 10.5).

Impact issues

Workers need to consider how they can formally build impact issues for the caregivers into the assessment triangle recommended in Figure 10.1. The following issues are reported as the impact issues of being a carer:

- Shortage of money.
- Loss of freedom and independence.
- Overcrowding.

Date/Day: Time:

Name of young person:

Was anyone else involved?   Yes/No

If yes, who?

In what capacity were they involved?

If another child was involved, was this voluntarily?

Had force/violence/coercion/threats/bribes been used?

How did the other child react?

What emotional state were they in?

Brief description of circumstances

Do you know what happened directly before the incident?

Was there anything that triggered the behaviour?

If you had to intervene, what happened?

What was your response to the situation and young person?

How did the young person react?

What happened afterwards?

What was the young person's response?

Was the child's social worker/Family Placement Worker informed?

If so, who?

What was their response?

Anything else you feel relevant?

Figure 10.5   Record of Behaviour or Incident (Rose and Savage, 1999)

- Age and ill-health.
- Managing difficult behaviour.
- Managing birth parents and other relatives.
- Managing contact.
- Support issues (see Laws and Broad, 2001).

In many cases of grandparent caregiver assessment, issues of age and health feature heavily, and this is consistent with exploring the longer-term plans for the child. We know from research with grandparents (Pitcher, 2001) that there are consequences of assuming the caring responsibility for their grandchild and these include exhaustion, as well as loss of friends and a social life and disappointment. These need to be factored into an assessment of this nature. We also need to explore with the kinship carers the plans they have for the future, the plans they see as appropriate for the child, and the synchronicity between the two. We also need to examine in some detail their current life and then insert the child's timetable within this and look at what conflicts and clashes there may be as a basis of helping them determine whether they can defer their own needs to those of the child.

This is often coupled with generational differences: how they may describe the care that they offered their own children and that which they anticipate giving the subject child may not be consistent with contemporary parenting. For example, they may describe physical chastisement in their upbringing that did not harm them and as such they see objections to smacking as being overly tolerant. Some describe the administration of whisky as a means of calming a child and facilitating sleep, whilst this would not normally be accepted practice currently.

Issues of finances are relevant here also as many caregivers report severe financial constraints that may affect if not prohibit the caregiving offered.

Within any social history the workers need to consider both the factual information as it was provided and then move on to explore what reflections the caregivers have on previous patterns and past behaviour. It may be prudent to talk to the children and young adults who have been raised within the caregiver's family to benchmark information provided. Previous records from all the key agencies need to be examined and in some circumstances ex-partners need to be traced and interviewed. Formal references also need to be secured and

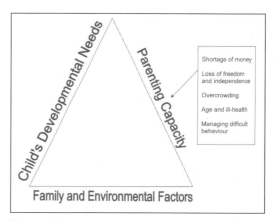

Figure 10.6 Adapting the assessment framework to embrace kinship caregiving

contextualised specifically to the subject child. Workers need to elicit the views of other children living in the household both to uncover their views about the placement as well as how and what they have been told about it. They may have anxieties about how to communicate this to their friends, they may feel marginalised or jealous or resent the fact that the carers' time has been further divided.

Figure 10.6 represents an adaptation of the original triangle where unless these issues are addressed then the potential is for them to compromise the carers from being able to deliver the appropriate parenting for the subject child.

A further variation of this might come in the shape of a diamond where we insert the carer issue into the original assessment framework triangle in acknowledgement that unless carers' needs are met then their parenting capacity for the subject child is likely to be reduced or more inconsistent (see Figure 10.7) (Calder, 2003b).

The following materials derive from DoH (2001) in relation to carers of disabled children but the considerations are exportable to kinship carers as follows:

1. **Carer's role**
   - Carer's choice – does the carer feel they have a choice?
   - How willing and able are they to provide care?
   - How much time is taken up with caring?
   - Which parts of the role does the carer actively want to do (if any)?
   - Which parts of the role can the carer manage without help?

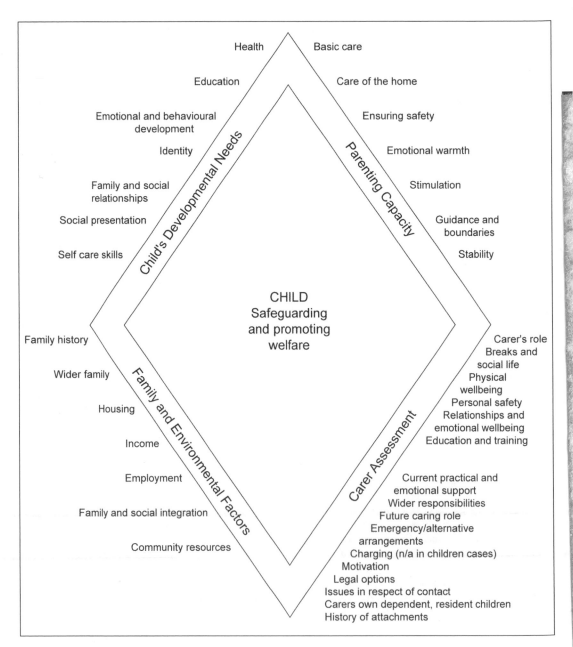

Figure 10.7   Kinship carer diamond (developed from Calder, 2004)

- Which parts of the role does the carer find particularly difficult?
- Which parts of the role does the carer actively not want to do?
- Does the carer understand the condition of the cared person?
- Does the carer feel they would like training in how to manage any part of their role?

(Moving and handling, stress, understanding the condition.)
- Does the caring role conflict with or undermine other family roles such as parent or breadwinner?
- What is the carer's perception of their situation?

- What is/are the outcomes the carer would like to see to help them in their role?
- What is the carer's view of the most important outcomes to achieve for the person they care for? Are these in conflict with the cared for person's view?
- Is the carer also a service-user or eligible for support, as a community care service-user?
- Where appropriate a weekly time sheet may help demonstrate the extent of the role/lack of sleep etc.

2. **Breaks and social life**
   - Can the carer regularly get a break (at the appropriate time of day/week) to enable them to have time for themselves/leisure/time with friends?
   - When did the carer last have a break i.e. time off for themselves, rather than time to go shopping or time to go to the dentist or doctor?
   - Might the carer need a degree of active encouragement to take breaks and maintain their social life, to avoid social isolation becoming a problem at a later stage?
   - Can the carer get a break to deal with wider responsibilities e.g. attending a child's sports day?

3. **Physical well being and personal safety**
   - Is the carer well?
   - Is the carer undertaking any tasks that put them at risk?
   - Is there any aspect of risk in caring for the cared person?
   - Is the carer stressed, anxious or depressed?
   - Is sleep affected, if so how badly?
   - Is the carer receiving any treatment?

4. **Relationships and mental well being**
   - Is caring having an impact on relationships, either with the cared for person or other members of the family, friends etc?
   - If the carer is a parent, is caring making this role harder?
   - Are stress, depression, anxiety present or likely without support?
   - Is spirituality significant to the carer? Are they able to maintain any spiritual practices or faith-related activities which are important to them?

5. **Care of the home**
   - Are there any issues about care of the home?
   - Does it all fall to the carer?

6 .**Accommodation**
   - Are there any problems with where the cared for person lives? (long distance caring/lack of time to look after property)
   - Can equipment/adaptations help?
   - Is carer's own accommodation (if different) a problem?
   - Should housing authorities be involved in the assessment?

7 .**Finances**
   - Are finances a problem?
   - Can the carer get the advice they need on benefits, managing debt, charges etc?

8. **Work**
   - There should be no assumption that carers will give up work to care – how can they be supported?
   - Does the carer want to stay in work or return to work – what are the options?
   - Is advice available on these issues, including advice for returners on benefits, charging etc so that the carer can make informed decisions on what is best for them in all the circumstances.

9. **Education and training**
   - Does the carer want to develop their skills either work-related or otherwise?
   - Are they at risk of having to give up education or training because of their caring role?

10. **Current practical and emotional support**
    - Who/what helps the carer at the moment?
    - Is there enough of this support and is the carer happy with receiving such support from these sources?
    - Is the carer aware of carer's support groups/counselling services etc in the area?

11. **Wider responsibilities**
    - What other wider responsibilities does the carer have – parent, child carer, other caring roles, work, volunteering etc?
    - Should other workers be involved to help advise on parenting and childcare issues or about services that might help?
    - Is balancing these responsibilities causing the carer stress?
    - Are other roles suffering or perceived to be suffering?

12. **Future caring role**
    - How does the carer see the future?
    - What factors are likely to affect the willingness or ability to care long term?

13. **Emergencies/alternative arrangements**
    - If the carer suddenly became ill what would happen?
    - What networks are there to support in an emergency?
    - Can a contingency plan be made?
    - Does the carer know who to contact in an emergency?

14. **Access to Information and Advocacy**
    - Are carers aware of how to get more information and who from?
    - Do they know about what to do if things go wrong or if they want to complain?
    - Are there sources of carers' advocacy locally they should be aware of?
    - If they have internet access, are they aware of *www.carers.gov.uk*?
    - Are they aware of *www.ukonline.gov.uk* which is developing a portal for carers' information during 2001?

15. **Agreed outcomes**
    - What are the agreed outcomes for the carer in relation to their health and well-being, quality of life, as well as the sustainability of their caring role?
    - Is there conflict between the carer and cared for person's desired outcomes?
    - Are Direct Payments appropriate in lieu of a service to give the carer flexibility?
    - Where is there disagreement?
    - Where may there be problems in delivering the outcomes?
    - Where particularly services are identified as the best way to deliver certain outcomes, what are the carer's preferences about the way such services might be delivered (e.g. timing, fitting in with routine, are Direct Payments appropriate in lieu of a service to give the carer flexibility?)

16. **Complaints and challenges**
    - It is important to ensure that carers and cared for people are aware of the local council's complaints procedure.

17. **Review**
    - When will the assessment be reviewed?
    - In considering timing of review – are needs likely to increase or fluctuate; is there risk to carer or user or frequent crises?
    - Who will be responsible for setting up review?

18. **Charging**
    - It is important that information on charges and financial assessment are clearly explained to both the carer and the parents as part of the assessment process.

Inter-relationships between these domains

The triangular structure (Figure 10.1) at the beginning is a relatively static one and this does not reflect two key considerations. Firstly the role of the professional and their agency in influencing the kinship care arrangement; and secondly recognising that unlike stranger foster care, the continued involvement of the parent with the kinship carer and the placement is much more likely. As a reflection of this latter set of unique circumstances, any assessment has to examine the ongoing relationships to try and predict the capacity of the parent and carer to work collaboratively to identify and then meet the child's needs. Conflict is common but not associated with placement breakdown (Broad, 2001).

The issue of loss spans all the domains and it is important not only to assess them in relation to the child, the carers and the parents but also to explore how they interact and the degree of impact. One of the key issues for assessment relates to the redefinition of roles and responsibilities, that arise from the kinship care arrangement. As previously indicated, carers assume a parenting role from the parents, and this may either be welcomed or frowned upon by the child, as well as leaving many children confused by the changes. Great care is needed to examine how children experience these changes and what the adults need to do to ensure this is not aggravating the harm they may have experienced.

It is important to assess the nature of the relationship between the parents and the kinship carers. This should include a historical as well as a current dimension as past capacity to work together is a useful indicator of how the future relationship may be managed; as well as how well they have concealed any conflict from the child.

In all these areas workers have to remember to link this to an assessment of the impact on the child of the new arrangement (as well as any prior harm) and also to link this to levels of risk, prognosis for all the parties to work together to achieve a mutually agreed outcome or goal and the potential to deal with and sustain change.

The issue of contact is a critical consideration in arrangements of this nature. Workers need to be clear about the nature of the relationship between the child and the parents and then move on to examine whether the caregivers have any concerns about the contact, and how comfortable they would be in managing these concerns: prior to and after with the child as well as during if they are deemed the appropriate supervising officers. Considerations need to include a safety plan if things go wrong, for example if the parents present under the influence of drink or drugs or threaten or use violence (verbal as well as physical).

Family group conferences

One mechanism for bringing family members together for both assessment and planning purposes is the Family Group Conference or meeting. Originated in New Zealand, Maori (New Zealand's indigenous people) had hotly contested the widespread removal of children from their homes that had characterised the past. In response, they advanced the view that decisions must involve the families, including *whanau* (all those descended from common grandparents), *hapu* (clan) and *iwi* (tribe) and should not be usurped by professionals. The outcome of the debate was agreement that issues around children and young people should be resolved in partnership between the state and families. The underlying intention was to involve families, to give families responsibility to deal constructively with the presenting concerns and to restrict the power of professionals, in particular the power of social welfare professionals. At the same time, it was seen to be the state's responsibility to provide services that can support families and provide for the needs of children and young people in ways that are culturally appropriate and accessible.

A family group conference (FGC) is a formal meeting *in care and protection cases*, for members of the family group to discuss with social workers what needs to be done to make sure a child or young person is safe and well cared for. They are a mechanism that enables the formal state systems to work in partnership with informal family and community systems, recognising the knowledge and expertise of family and informal systems and recognising the knowledge and expertise of professional systems. Family group conferences put families in charge of the decision making; the process strengthens families and respects and affirms each family's unique cultural experience. They operate very differently from

existing decision making mechanisms that are dominated by professionals and tend to take away the responsibility for decision making from families and the community and often discourage the participation of the family. Family group conferences make sure that power and responsibility is more evenly shared between the family/community (informal) and professional/agency (formal) networks. Family group conferences harness and build on the knowledge, strengths and resources in families and communities. They provide a framework for families, the community and agencies to work collaboratively to safeguard and promote children's welfare. The FGC is a means of balancing children's need and right to be safe, with their need and right to be in a family. Professionals are expected to play a low key role in the family group conference. Overall, conferencing offers a participatory option that empowers families and allows them, without increasing the stigma or blame, to play a pivotal role in arriving at decisions about their children. It provides a clear mechanism for ensuring that the voice of the child is heard within the decision-making process. It offers increased clarity about professional roles and responsibilities, and accountability for practice to family members. Where there are concerns about risks to the child the model leads to improved risk assessments, targeted protection plans, and plans which the family are committed to implement; and it tackles social exclusion and strengthens communities (Calder, 2004).

A professional dimension

Professional practice is often dictated by procedures and protocols that can be experienced by all involved as constraining if they are applied in a blanket inflexible way. Clear processes and systems operate for the assessment and approval of stranger foster carers that are not easily replicated in kinship care. For example, the latter often emerges in an informal, unstructured or occasionally in an emergency way.

As we have identified earlier, the attitude of the worker and/or the agency to kinship care placements is significant, and may be contingent upon whether it emerged as an informal family arrangement or was created by professional request. Whilst this is an important indicator of attitude toward the placement, workers need to build relationships, assess need and mobilise any required support simultaneously. Since placements may have already taken place or need to be made imminently (precluding the need for short-term foster or residential care), workers should have this embedded in their work as it is a central pivot of the assessment framework (DoH, 2000). Experience tells us that delayed service provision following need identification can be an aggravating risk factor that requires professional management. Any intervention must be designed to enable the family to care for the child and provide the needed connections and continuity that ensure permanence. Kinship carers invite professionals to premise their assessment and decision-making with a belief that they are uniquely qualified to care for the child given the family context and pre-existing relationship, and are more likely to work actively and with a problem-solving outcome in mind. Workers who approach their task from a different starting point are unlikely to forge a meaningful relationship with the kinship carers and worse still are likely to induce or compound fear, distrust and anxiety that are disabling and may potentially deflect their attention and energies from the child.

We know from the experiences of families within the child protection arena that:

- Doing to families does not create an environment conducive to engagement or change.
- Excluding families from the decision-making process heightens resistance, lowers motivation and creates a 'them and us scenario'.
- Families will not sign up to or implement plans they have not been party to constructing or with which they fundamentally disagree.
- Involving families in plans enhances ownership and this is correlated with greater and more sustained change.
- Working together successfully requires the integration of formal and informal systems.
- The roles and responsibilities of professionals are often unclear and this impedes the construction and implementation of the child protection plans.
- Task allocation is idealistic rather than realistic.
- The focus on registration deflects us from planning and risk assessment (Calder, 2004).

There is a considerable body of research in relation to partnership that is relevant here. We know that parents value certain characteristics of professionals in the execution of their jobs, and these include:

- Communication which is open, honest, timely and informative.
- Social work time with someone who listens, gives feedback, information, reassurance and advice, and is reliable.
- Services: which are practical, tailored to particular needs and are accessible.
- An approach which reinforces and does not undermine their parenting capacity.

One example of poor practice is where we attempt to communicate honestly what the process will involve and maybe what some of the concerns are that need to be explored yet this is wrapped up in professional jargon and acronyms which alienate and dis-empower the kinship carers. We need to think carefully about what we want to communicate and then examine the options available to achieve this end. Workers should be alert to the fact that just because something has been communicated it has not necessarily been either received or understood by the other party.

The breadth of the assessment considerations should inform the choice of the worker assessing the suitability of the placement, and should ideally be conducted by co-workers with family placement and community-based social worker practice assessment. The requisite minimum knowledge base for staff includes an understanding of child abuse and neglect, child development, the impact of separation, loss and harm on children, family systems and structures, negotiation and conciliation, and building and maintaining formal and informal networks of support.

It is essential that workers retain their basic assessment skills and maintenance of the process when conducting kinship assessments. It is not a case of throwing the baby out with the bathwater but about building on established foundations. Adaptation and flexibility are essential ingredients of practice. In this sense, the following represents a summary of essential assessment considerations.

The stepwise assessment

One exemplary model for workers is the stepwise assessment (Samra-Tibbets and Raynes, 1999), which invites workers to attend to tasks in a sequential order in detail to maximise the information available. In the first block, *planning* is essential. This is often left out by professionals, as they feel pressured to get on with the task. There needs to be a careful look at what information they already have, and what still needs to be gathered. There needs to be some agreement on channels of communication, as it is unrealistic for the worker to expect to know everything at every stage of the process, as in a responsibility chart.

The second block attends to issues of *hypotheses*. This is defined in the dictionary as 'a starting point for an investigation'. There is evidence to show that workers sometimes begin the assessment with one particular hypothesis and gather evidence to support this. This can be dangerous as it actually forms a conclusion before the assessment has begun. The workers should consider all possible hypotheses, be open minded in gathering evidence, and prioritise hypotheses only where there is clear evidence to do so. They need to take a step back from the early intervention in order to generate the maximum number of possibilities, so as not to shut down any avenue prematurely. The initial hypothesis is necessarily speculative and is used as the basis for gathering more information that will either confirm or refute it.

In the third block, there is a need to *gather information*. Nothing is more sterile than information collecting for the purpose of information collecting, as would be likely using the existing Assessment Framework recording forms or the BAAF Form F. The kind and amount of information collected will be dictated by the defined problem for work and the preliminary goals that are established. It is difficult to deal with areas of data collection concretely because the specific areas to be explored depend on the situation. There are, however, some principles that should be considered:

- It is a joint process and the client should be involved in helping to determine the areas to be explored.
- The client should be aware of the sources being used for data collection (e.g. they may not always be asked for their permission).
- There should be a connection between the problems identified and the data collected, and the client should be aware of any connection.
- It is critical to explore all areas the clients see as connected as well as helping them to understand the areas the worker seeks to explore.
- Data collection goes on all the time, but it is critical to the problem identification, goal setting, and assessment stages of work.
- It is crucial that the worker understand the client's view of all areas of data collection – their thinking, feelings and actions.

There is a tendency to gather too much information, and we need to guard against too much information as well as irrelevant information. The information must be analysed and analysis can only be properly achieved through evidenced-based practice. We may modify our original hypothesis many times as the new information is gathered from the family. Since the major purpose of a hypothesis is to make connections, how information is gathered is extremely important. The worker must take a neutral position and try not to imply any moral judgements or to align themselves with any one faction of the family. Change often comes about through the worker's ability to stand outside the family and gain a holistic view. The intervention is then geared at the most relevant of the presenting problems. In gathering information, it is helpful to keep the following questions in mind:

- What function does the symptom serve in stabilising the family?
- How does the family function in stabilising the symptom?
- What is the central theme around which the problem is organised?
- What will be the consequences of change?

Cleaver et al. (1998) identified a useful list of the blocks to identifying risk and include:

- The unknown – that is knowledge of signs and symptoms and knowledge of the law that was not adequate.
- The known but not fully appreciated – the need to identify what is important from a 'flood of relevant data'.
- Interpretation – being able to correctly interpret information in the context of assessing risk.
- Objective and subjective information – failure to distinguish fact from opinion, being too trusting and uncritical.
- Unappreciated data – information may not be appreciated if it has come from a source which is distrusted.

of dual pathology – information
issed if the receiver is decoyed by a
different problem.
- Certainty – investigators may have a false sense
  of security about a particular interpretation
  (e.g. medical assessments of sexual abuse in
  Cleveland).
- Competing tasks within the same visiting
  schedule, e.g. fostering and child protection.
- The known and not assembled – individuals
  may hold information which they can
  withhold or which is not pieced together with
  the rest.
- Not fitting the current mode of understanding
  – this has also been described as a loss of
  objectivity, and the importance of supervision
  is highlighted.
- Long standing blocks – assumptions made at
  an early stage which influenced later
  interpretation of information (p9).

The fourth block requires the information
collected be *tested* out. Professionals will bring
information gathered, as well as the concerns
that they have had, in order to assess the level
of risk to the children, and the potential for
change in the family. Strategies for doing this
and for involving the family will need to be
agreed.

In the *decision* block, the professionals are being
asked to make recommendations for the
longer-term plan, and this is a recommendation
to the fostering panel and court. In the *evaluation
block*, we should consider the future risk to the
children, the potential for change within the
family, recommendations for future action and
the resources required to achieve them. The
assessment needs to move beyond the changes
required, to identifying whether change is
possible, and what motivations exist for change.
Accompanying this must be some hope of
reaching the goal, an ability to consider what has
gone wrong and some opportunity for change in
the situation. The assessment should differentiate
between factual information and unsubstantiated
information, and opinions. It should aim to
enhance the potential within the kinship carers
and the parents at all times, rather than
undermining it, and a failure to achieve this can
result in a refusal to engage in the assessment
process. We shouldn't forget that the assessment
is where the protective intervention meets the
therapeutic one.

Strengths-based approach

We have already made great play of the need to
work in a partnership way with caregivers and in
order to facilitate this best then we need to
employ a strengths-based approach. This is
apparent within the Assessment Framework in an
unbalanced way as it ignores risk by eliminating
it from the professional vocabulary. However
there are some merits to the strengths-approach
(see Calder, 1999).

The strengths' perspective clearly demands
that we adopt a different way of looking at
individuals, families and communities. All must
be seen in the light of their capacity, talents,
competencies, possibilities, visions, values and
hopes, however dashed and distorted these may
have become through circumstance, oppression
and trauma. Personal qualities and strengths are
often forged in the face of abuse and oppression
(Saleebey, 1996).

The strengths' perspective is rooted in the
belief that people can continue to grow and
change; that many of the barriers people, labelled
as belonging to 'disadvantaged groups', face in
meeting basic needs for shelter, food and positive
community participation, tend to come from
educational, political and economic exclusion
based on demographic rather than individual
characteristics.

For social workers to shift towards the
strength's approach they need to have some
understanding of its underlying beliefs. They
must also not lose sight of the need to take
appropriate action to protect children whenever
necessary. The following summary is offered to
workers in this context, as the strengths'
approach cannot be adopted on a blanket basis
without reference to individual circumstances.
The social worker doesn't change people, but
aims to act as a catalyst for clients' discovering
and using their resources, to accomplish their
goals (Saleebey, 1992). This makes it less likely
that workers will 'rescue' clients and more likely
to reinforce their strengths, even in a crisis.

Any proactive approach to child protection
focuses on family strengths and capability in a
way that supports and strengthens family
functioning. All families have strengths and
capabilities. If we take the time to identify these
qualities and build on them rather than focusing
on correcting deficits or weaknesses, families are
not only more likely to respond favourably to

interventions, but the chances of making a significant impact on the family unit will be enhanced considerably. A major consideration as part of strengthening families is promoting their abilities to use existing strengths for meeting needs in a way that produces positive changes in family functioning. This can be achieved by using empathy or attempting to promote some mutual agreement between each other.

Using the principles of the strengths' perspective with abusing families may be the only chance to empower families to change their behaviour. Yet uncovering strengths cannot be accomplished in a simplistic manner, as they 'are not isolated variables, but form clusters and constellations which are dynamic, fluid inter-related and inter-acting' (Otto, 1963). Developing a strengths-based practice involves a paradigm shift from a deficit approach to a positive partnership with the family, and will involve:

- The relationship between a worker and a family must be reframed from an adversarial one to a helping alliance and partnership with the family. This suggests a major emphasis on the engagement phase.
- Empowering individuals and families to discover and use the resources and tools within and around them.
- Integrating knowledge of resilience in workers as it may be crucial to families in overcoming future risks (DePanfalis and Wilson, 1996).

Although the child abuse field has just begun to apply the strengths' perspective to its repertoire, there is a catalogue of documented benefits to date:

- An emphasis on strengths as well as on risks increases the opportunity for developing a helping alliance – a crucial element in achieving positive treatment outcome and risk reduction.
- Positive reinforcement for positive conditions and behaviours is more effective than trying to convince or coerce individuals to alter negative conditions or behaviours.
- Cultivating strengths offers the opportunity for more permanent change.
- Emphasising strengths helps family members build in successes in their lives, which in turn should help them more effectively manage crises and stress.

- Helping families through short-term positive steps empowers families to take control of their lives.
- Celebrating successes changes the tone of treatment, for both client and helper.
- Communicating a true belief that a family can change destructive patterns helps to promote more long-lasting change (DePanfalis and Wilson, 1996).

Whilst we should shift towards a strengths-led approach to children's services, we cannot overlook or shirk our statutory responsibilities to continually assess risks and dangerousness to those children we are seeking to protect (Clark et al., 1990).

DeJong and Miller (1995) have described several interviewing questions that a worker can use to uncover client strengths related to the goals of clients:

Exception-finding questions
These are used to discover a client's present and past successes in relation to the client's goals. Eventually these successes are used to build solutions, e.g. an alcoholic who has tried of their own volition in the past to stop drinking but has lapsed. Most families can offer one exception and the worker can then explore how this happened, particularly how the client contributed to this.

Scaling questions
These are a clever way to make complex features of a client's life more concrete and accessible for both client and worker. They usually take the form of asking the client to give a number from 0 to 10 that best represents where the client is at some specified point, e.g. Do you accept the need for social work help to resolve the problem? This scale can be used repeatedly at different points of the process. The responses form the basis of the follow-up questions from the worker that should aim to uncover, affirm and amplify the client's strengths.

Coping questions
These questions accept the client's perceptions of their situation (however desperate) and then move on to ask how the client is able to cope with such overwhelming circumstances and feelings. As the worker helps the client to uncover coping strengths, their mood and confidence usually rise. Sometimes new ideas for coping emerge that the client has never thought of before. Where clients

return to the problem descriptions and associated feelings of discouragement, the worker should listen/empathise, before returning to a focus on strength's exploration and affirmation.

'What's better?' questions
These are useful in continuing the work of building solutions and uncovering client strengths. It increases the chances of uncovering exceptions and associated strengths that are the most meaningful and useful to the client at the present time. By asking what is better since the last time focuses on the process of work and change.

Risk dimension

Calder (2003c) has produced a generic risk assessment, analysis and management model designed to resurrect risk into all our assessments in a way that acknowledges strengths and risks and looks at ways in which we can balance them and come to informed and evidence-based decision-making. The significant questions for any risk assessment should include:

- What is the time frame for which the risk assessment is being carried out?
- What is the nature of the abuse or neglect that we fear might occur or continue?
- Assess all areas of potential risk.
- Define the behaviour to be predicted.
- Current incident of concern
- Take into account both internal and external factors.
- Locate the risk.
- Identify any risk heightening factors.
- Be aware of risk factors that may interact in a dangerous manner.
- Examine the nature of the risk factors.
- How serious are the consequence of it occurring for the child, for the child's family and for the agencies involved?
- What are the strengths in the situation being analysed?
- Do any risk reducing factors exist?
- What are the prospects for change in the situation and for growth?
- What can be offered to build on strengths and combat weaknesses?
- What is the risk associated with intervention?
- What is the family's motivation, and capacity, for change?

This can be represented once again in a diamond package that inserts risk back in to the assessment (see Figure 10.8) (Calder, 2004b).

Desired outcomes

Outcomes are an essential driving force for all involved in trying to intervene effectively to safeguard a child. CWLA (2003) identified five desirable outcomes of kinship care:

- The child will be protected and nurtured.
- The child's developmental needs will be met and any delays will be addressed.
- The child will maintain connections to important people from his or her birth family.
- The child will have lifelong connections to a family.
- The child's caregivers will be able to work with the agency and with community resources so that the services and supports he or she needs are provided (p18).

Outcome measurement and prognosis

Pitcher (2001) identified a useful structure for balancing the risks and benefits for a child of a grandparent placement that is worth mention here (see Figure 10.9).

An early decision to discount carers is appropriate following a viability assessment, and any continuing concerns about their understanding of, and ability to meet, the child's needs is the critical consideration. In reaching such a conclusion, however, we do need to be alert to the time element involved in processing the information and moving through shock and denial to acceptance. Discounting a kinship placement does not prohibit an exploration of continued involvement of some kind in the child's life, or accepting that a future placement may be a viable option, and emergency action is rarely justified to remove a child from a placement unless what can be offered is similar or better. It is this critical threshold which many social services are struggling to cross, and we cannot ignore the emerging literature and research basis supporting the efficacy of kinship care placements. Conversely, workers do need to guard against continuing a placement simply because there is no better alternative. There is

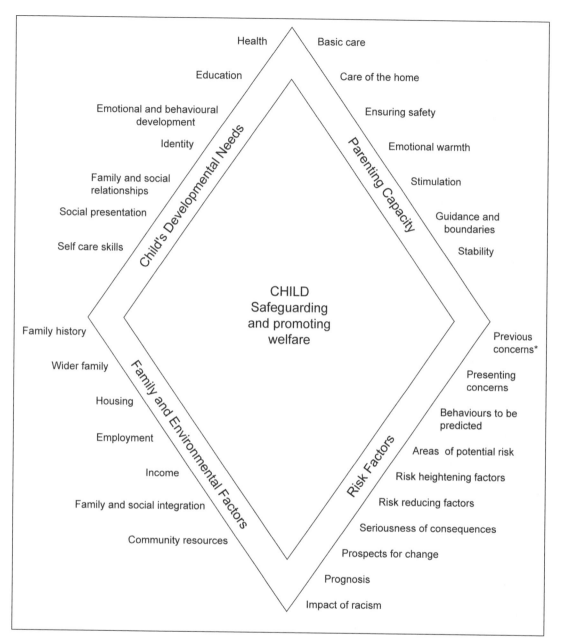

Figure 10.8   The risk diamond (Calder, 2004)

pressure to sustain the placement for this reason alone and it has nothing to do with the child's needs and safety.

Kinship care must be properly explored for all children and young people. The new Special Guardianship Orders will heighten this requirement (Talbot and Kidd, 2004). Black children, facing the destructive impact of racism, are particularly vulnerable and this must be

recognised. Institutional racism was again confirmed by the MacPherson report (1999). International evidence suggests that kinship care has acted as a buffer against racism, yet Ince finds that we still have to ask.

To what extent can local authorities continue to apply an ethnocentric approach to child care practice when there is a growing need to make a critical appraisal of outcomes for

Potential benefits	Issues for assessment	Potential risks
1. Family is likely to see the child as less problematic than would a non-relative carer	Child's need for care	1. There may be concerns about age, health, housing etc.
2. A less drastic change for the child, especially if there is already a strong bond	Child's need for stability and continuity	2. It cannot be assumed that the child knows, or likes the relative
3. It is usually what the child wants	Child's need for identity	3. Other values may be more important. Best interests.?
4. Greater likelihood of lifelong contact with all family members	See Chapter 9 this volume	4. The child may remain in a dysfunctional family system
5. Child can see that some members of their family have succeeded	Family's relationship towards birth parent	5. The carer may be very negative toward the birth parent, or conversely be collusive
6. If a parent feels less threatened good quality contact is more likely		6. The family is less likely to receive money, training and ongoing professional support
7. The child is less likely to worry about their parent		7. Social services' involvement or control may seem intrusive or unnatural
8. Placement less likely to break down, or need professional support	Family's need for professional support	

Figure 10.9   Analysing assessment information (Pitcher, 2001)

black children and young people who are looked after and being prepared for leaving the care system?

(Ince, 2001)

Kinship care, however, must not be seen as an easy or simplistic option, and as Broad (2001) concludes 'Kinship care is not simply another placement choice with a single function. It is multi-functional, carrying important child protection, family support, and placement functions' (p159).

Assessments must balance strengths, difficulties and attend to risk. They must address the capacity to change and empower families to do so. These are complex and skilled tasks and professionals deserve support and resources to develop practice in kinship care. If professionals are unsupported then children and young people are unsupported. Children and families deserve skilled intervention. Children and young people should live within their families, whenever this is possible: this is a strong legal principle and should be the fundamental value base of all professional intervention with children and families.

Consider the views of this 15 year old young woman, living a four hour drive away from her birth family with a female adult kinship carer:

I have no space and no bedroom, sometimes I get to sleep in the bed but mostly I sleep on the pull out bed in the lounge. There's no space for friends to visit, no room for my brother to stay, no room to study, no privacy but I am the lucky one. My brother lives with a stranger, (a foster carer). I feel happy where I live.

References

Broad, B., Hayes, R. and Rushworth, C. (2001) *Kith and Kin: Kinship Care for Vulnerable Young People.* London: NCB.

Broad, B. (2004) Kinship Care for Children in the UK: Messages from Research, Lessons from Policy and Practice. *European Journal of Social Work,* 7: 2, 211–27.

Broad, B. (Ed.) (2001) *Kinship Care: the Placement Choice for Children and Young People.* Lyme Regis: Russell House Publishing.

Calder, M.C. (1995) Child Protection: Balancing Paternalism and Partnership. *British Journal of Social Work.* 25: 6, 749–66.

Calder, M.C. (1999) Towards Anti-oppressive Practice with Ethnic Minority Groups. In Calder, M.C. and Horwath, J. (Eds.) *Working for Children on the Child Protection Register: An Inter-agency Practice Guide.* Aldershot: Ashgate.

Calder, M.C. (2003) *A Prognosis Framework for Cases Involving Sexual Abuse Within the Family: Practice Guidance Series Paper 2.* Leigh: Calder Training and Consultancy.

Calder, M.C. (2003b) *Carer's Assessments for Parents of Disabled Children.* Salford City Council: Child Protection Unit.

Calder, M.C. (2003c) *RASSAMM: Risk Assessment, Analysis and Management Model.* Leigh: Calder Consultancy.

Calder, M.C. (2004) *Origins and Location of the Family Group Conferences in the Structures and Systems.* Presentation to Flintshire Family Group Conference Chairs, June 2004.

Calder, M.C. (2004b) Child Protection: Current Context, Central Contradictions and Collective Challenges. *Representing Children,* 17: 1, 59–73.

Calder, M.C. (2005) Allegations of Abuse against Foster Carers: Prevention, Protection and Procedural Considerations. In Wheal, A. (Ed.) *The RHP Companion to Foster Care.* 2nd edn. Lyme Regis: Russell House Publishing.

Calder, M.C. with Peake, A. and Rose, K. (2001) *Mothers of Sexually Abused Children: A Framework for Assessment, Understanding and Support.* Lyme Regis: Russell House Publishing.

Child Welfare League of America (2003) *A Tradition of Caring: A Guide for Assessing Families for Kinship Care.* Washington, DC: CWLA.

Clark, B., Parkin, W. and Richards, M. (1990) Dangerousness: A Complex Practice Issue. In Violence against Children Study Group's, *Taking Child Abuse Seriously.* London: Unwin Hyman.

Cleaver, H., Wattam, C. and Cawson, P. (1998) *Assessing Risk in Child Protection.* London: NSPCC.

Crumbley, J. and Little, R. (1997) *Relatives Raising Children.* Washington, DC: CWLA.

DeJong, P. and Miller, S.D. (1995) How to Interview for Client Strengths. *Social Work.* 40: 6, 729–36.

epanfilis, D. and Wilson, C. (1996) Applying the Strengths Perspective with Maltreating Families. *The APSAC Advisor.* 9: 3, 15–20.

DoH (2000) *Framework for the Assessment of Children in Need and Their Families.* London: HMSO.

Hackett, S. (forthcoming) Engaging Men. In Calder, M.C. (Ed.) *Encouraging More Effective Practice with Involuntary Clients.* Lyme Regis: Russell House Publishing.

Ince, L. Promoting Kinship Foster Care: Preserving Family Networks for Black Children of African Origins. In Broad, B. (Ed.) op. cit.

Laws, S. and Broad, B. *Looking after Children within the Extended Family: Carer's Views.* Leicester: De Montfort University.

Otto, H.A. (1963) Criteria for Assessing Family Strengths. *Family Process.* 2, 329–37.

Pitcher, D. (2001) Assessing Grandparent Carers: A Framework. In Broad, B. (Ed.) *Kinship Care: The Placement Choice for Children and Young People.* Lyme Regis: Russell House Publishing.

Regan, L. and Butterworth, J. (2004) Safe Care. In Wheal, A. (Ed.) *The RHP Companion to Foster Care* 2nd edn. Lyme Regis: Russell House Publishing.

Rose, K. and Savage, A. (1999) Safe Caring. In Wheal, A. (Ed.) *The RHP Companion to Foster Care.* Lyme Regis: Russell House Publishing.

Rutter, M. (1985) Resilience in the Face of Adversity. *British Journal of Psychiatry.* 147: 598–611.

Saleebey, D. (Ed.) (1992) *The Strengths Perspective in Social Work Practice.* New York: Longman.

Saleeby, D. (1996) The Strengths Perspective in Social Work Perspective: Extensions and Cautions. *Social Work.* 41: 3, 296–305.

Samra-Tibbets, C. and Raynes, B. (1999) Assessment and Planning. In Calder, M.C. and Horwath, J. (Eds.) *Working for Children on the Child Protection Register: An Inter-agency Practice Guide.* Aldershot: Arena.

Talbot, C. and Kidd, P. (2004) Special Guardianship Orders-Issues in Respect of Family Assessment. *Journal of Family Law.* 34, 273–80.